MAX POHLENZ
*Late Professor of Ancient History, University
of Göttingen, Germany*

FREEDOM IN GREEK LIFE
AND THOUGHT
The History of an Ideal

Translated from the German by C. Lofmark

It was not the French Revolution that made the idea
of freedom a basic factor in Western Civilisation: it
had already played a major part in the philosophy
and the political life of Ancient Greece, where the basic
thoughts and ideals of our culture were first given
shape. In clearer and simpler form the Greeks faced
the problems inherent in Western Civilisation which
beset us so much more bewilderingly and elusively today; from that confrontation, from their formulation
of the questions and their particular way of seeking the
answers, we have derived not only the patterns of our
conceptual thinking, but often the concepts themselves.
This is certainly the case with the idea of freedom. In
this book Max Pohlenz, the distinguished Professor of
Greek at Göttingen, traces the idea of freedom from
the time when men first became conscious of it – giving
a brief semantic account of the words they used to
express the new concept – and its development through
the whole of Greek life and thought.

At the present time, when the word "freedom" has
acquired so many associations and emotional overtones that the concept can no longer be grasped with
clarity and objectivity, it will be rewarding for the non-
Hellenist, no less than for the Classical scholar, to be
conducted by an experienced guide through the thought
and history of Greece in pursuit of its origin. There he
will see how the idea arose and grew, how it was introduced into politics and translated into historical and
social fact, the real and the theoretical problems it
created and the response of philosophers and politicians to them.

MAX POHLENZ

FREEDOM IN GREEK LIFE
AND THOUGHT

THE HISTORY OF AN IDEAL

D. REIDEL PUBLISHING COMPANY / DORDRECHT-HOLLAND

THE HUMANITIES PRESS / NEW YORK

GRIECHISCHE FREIHEIT / WESEN UND WERDEN EINES LEBENSIDEALS
First published by Quelle und Meyer, Heidelberg
Translated from the German by Carl Lofmark

SOLE DISTRIBUTORS FOR U.S.A. AND CANADA
THE HUMANITIES PRESS / NEW YORK

Library of Congress Catalog Card Number 66–18684

Printed in The Netherlands by D. Reidel, Dordrecht

CONTENTS

PREFACE   IX

CHAPTER I.   THE GREEK URGE TOWARDS INDEPENDENCE   1

CHAPTER II.   THE DEVELOPMENT OF THE IDEA OF FREEDOM
      IN THE ARCHAIC PERIOD   3

CHAPTER III. THE CLASSICAL AGE   10

The War of Liberation and Its Consequences   10

Political Freedom   17
   Freedom in the City-State   17
   Freedom in Internal Affairs   21
   Freedom as a Formative Factor in Cultural Life   34

Inner Freedom   45
   Introspection   45
   The Self   50
   Freedom of the Person and Its Religious-Ethical
   Limitations   55
   The Self and the Good   59
   The Soul and the Problem of Freedom   63
   Freedom as Independence of the Outside World   71
   Self-Control and Freedom of the Intellect   81
   "Education for Freedom" as a Community's Cultural   102
   Ideal

CHAPTER IV. THE HELLENISTIC AGE   106

Political and Legal Freedom   106

The Intellectual Situation in the New Age   115
   Human Perspectives   115

Human Freedom 120
   Free Decision as the Characteristic of the Reasoning Being 120
   The Problem of Free Will 124
   The Freedom of the Moral Personality 133
   The Further Development of the Idea of Freedom Within
   the Stoa 139
   The Concept of Freedom as Common Intellectual Property 143
   Freedom as a Principle to Live by 151

CHAPTER V.   RETROSPECT AND PROSPECT 161

   Greek and Christian Freedom 161

NOTES 180

INDEX OF PROPER NAMES 201

TRANSLATOR'S NOTE

I am most grateful to Mr. A. J. Brothers of the Classics Department, Saint David's College, Lampeter, for many helpful criticisms and for his valuable advice on innumerable details in connection with the Greek.

C.L.

PREFACE

There is no slogan so much in vogue today or used in so many different senses as the word "freedom". No sooner have we read it in a newspaper of the free world in the West than we hear the echo from the East: "Freedom? Only we have it, freedom from capitalism and exploitation". Every political party has freedom in its programme, and for each of them it means something different. Slavery is considered incompatible with man's right to personal freedom, but modern civilisation offers free men the forced labour camp. The use of the word has extended far beyond the realms of politics and law. Quite apart from scientific, academic and other kinds of freedom, Luther praises the precious freedom of the Christian, and for modern philosophy freedom has even become the essence of human life.

What do all these conceptions have in common, and in what spiritual soil do they have their roots?

This question merits fuller consideration by philosophers than it has received so far. The archaeologist, too, might do well to give it his attention. It was not on the streets of Paris that the spirit of man was first stirred by the cry "liberty and equality", but in the Athens of Pericles long before. The idea that freedom is man's birthright was first proclaimed on Greek soil, and the inner freedom that was taught there is the forerunner of modern existentialism. In this field too the Greeks anticipated problems we still confront today.

It may therefore be worth while to reflect upon the nature of the freedom of the ancient Greeks and trace its development. This may perhaps, also help us to clear up much of the haziness attaching to the modern use of the term. But for that reason it must be emphasised that the purpose of this book is purely historical. It is intended as a contribution to the fuller understanding of Greek man.

To Dr Walter John and Dr Heinrich Dörrie, who has returned to freedom, I wish to express my sincere thanks for reading the proofs and for many valuable suggestions.

Göttingen, Autumn 1954

M. P.

CHAPTER I

THE GREEK URGE TOWARDS INDEPENDENCE[1]

The fundamental characteristic of the ancient Greek is his strong urge to be master of his fate, which makes him form his own opinion about things around him and shape his life accordingly. He does not underestimate the obstacles he meets and is deeply aware of the human limitations to which he is subject. He recognises that he lives within a community, to which he must conform, even if it means the sacrifice of personal wishes, if he is to survive at all. Only too often it is his experience that unforeseen events thwart his will, that even the most powerful hero in his advance to victory is menaced by death. He then recognises the power of an inexorable fate that determines all events and assigns to him too the part he will play in them. He is conscious that there exist everywhere about him higher beings, who are none the less real for being unseen. They are bearers of the life that fills the whole world. They are the beings who bring growth or blight to the fruits of the field, health or sickness to his cattle and himself; and, when something extraordinary happens to him, he also feels that some invisible power is intervening in his personal life, whether it is some undefined daemon, an agent of fate, or one of the great gods, who have their dwellings either in the depths or up on Olympus but who are continually intervening in what takes place on earth. They are "the more powerful ones", and men are well advised to strive for their favour and avoid their wrath.

But even Zeus himself, the highest of the heavenly host, is not the almighty lord of heaven and earth. For he, too, like the other gods, remains within the world and its order. That is why the Greek feels towards the gods a relationship, of subordination, it is true, but not of absolute dependence. He also does not know that anxiety neurosis which, of a result of terrible experience, can weigh upon man today and is sometimes passed on unwittingly to a quite different generation.[2] The Greek has a sense of reality which fully recognises and experiences not only what is beautiful in life but also its hardships. He sees the dangers that threaten him. But his essential feeling is not a fear that puts him on the defensive, but a positive

1

will to live, an urge to shape his life within the limits imposed upon him by the order of the universe, according to his own nature and his own will. Aeschylus makes Eteocles sternly rebuke the Theban maidens for their senseless fear. Eteocles himself devotes all his strength to the defence of his native town and engages without fear or faltering in the fatal civil war, because this is what his own nature and his sense of duty dictate. Already in Homer, it is at the very moment Hector is looking certain death in the face and recognising that he has been cheated and betrayed by all the gods that he rises to his full human stature. It is not fear that overpowers him; his one thought is:

> Let me not end my life unstriving, unrenowned,
> But mighty deeds bequeath to generations unborn.

To mortal man, the gods are able to decree physical death; but even then there is one thing of which they cannot deprive him, the right and the power to act as he himself freely decides. He has no power to modify the outward march of events. But within himself he remains master of his decisions.

That is the spiritual soil on which the Greek idea of freedom was able to grow. But it needed a long time to develop clearly, and it has been realised in history in many different ways.

CHAPTER II

THE DEVELOPMENT OF THE IDEA OF FREEDOM IN THE ARCHAIC PERIOD

The conception of freedom implies its antithesis. Free men only exist where there are unfree men. The awareness of freedom could only arise in a place where men lived together with others who were not independent but had a master over them whom they served and who controlled their lives. We speak nowadays of free and unfree men, and so did the ancient Greeks. But historically it was the existence of the unfree, the slaves, that first gave the others the feeling that they themselves were free.

Already in the age of Homer, slavery was for the Greeks a social institution and a necessary part of the divinely ordained world order even when they realised that it ultimately depended on human power.[1] Slavery originated in the general practice of kidnapping of human beings by pirates and in the right of war which permitted the victor, after capturing a town, to kill or sell the men, and to carry off the women and children as booty, to use them as servants at home or to trade them as living chattels. That had not been forgotten at the time when most slaves were either purchased or born in the master's house.

As Aristotle put it (*Pol.*, I. 3, p. 1253b, 32), slaves were even then in the eyes of the law "living property" which the master could arbitrarily dispose of as freely as of his cattle or other possessions. Nobody had anything to say to Odysseus when he had the wanton maid-servants hanged in his own courtyard. But if there is mention now and then of the fear the slave feels for his master, the relationship obtaining between them is more generally of the patriarchal kind. For the number of slaves was not yet very great, and even those who tilled the fields or tended the cattle remained members of the household (οἰκῆες)[2] in close personal contact with their master. Agamemnon was delighted at the prospect of the warm welcome he would receive not only from his wife and children but also from the servants (*Od.*, XI, 431). Similarly, the genuine devotion linking servant to master is nowhere more beautifully shown than in the case of the swineherd Eumaeus.

At the beginning of the *Politics* Aristotle had declared that the original

3

cell of society was the household to which, in addition to the master with his wife and children, the servants belonged. It is therefore in the home that social distinction first appears. The people are not called free and unfree, but master and servant. In the household there were free persons in positions of service[3], and it was first of all a matter of relationship between the individual master and his subordinates, not of a distinction between two classes in the community. Linguistic usage in the epic shows this very clearly. Again and again we find the word δμώς to signify man-servant. This word is related to verbs like δάμνημι and δαμάω, and expresses, like them, the compulsory nature of the servitude. It embraces, however, not only the slaves but also the free men who are forced by economic necessity to serve a master, and it is by no means always clear which of the two categories is meant. This contrasts strikingly with later usage which, by employing for the unfree the legal term δοῦλος quite definitely indicates that they are slaves and distinguishes between them and the free labourers. It is significant that in Homer's epics the term occurs very rarely. The masculine form δοῦλος is not found at all, while the feminine δούλη occurs only twice, and then refers to a woman captured in war who shares her master's bed.[4] Derivatives from the same stem are certainly found, which show that the idea was not entirely unknown, but on the whole there can be no doubt that the old word δμώς was gradually squeezed out by the new one, which distinguished the slave more clearly from the free man and that in the later period the word δμώς survived only in poetic language.

It can thus be no mere coincidence that the word ἐλεύθερος, 'free', which later the Greeks always had on their lips, is still found very seldom in the epic. As a designation for free men, it is not used at all, any more than the word "freedom". Even the adjective "free" we find in only two forms. The sixth book of the *Iliad* ends with Hector's ardent prayer to Zeus to grant the Trojans[5] one more opportunity to make a free drink offering to the everlasting gods for their having driven the Achaeans from their soil. A little earlier, when taking leave of his wife, the same Hector sorrowfully imagines her having to do the menial work of a maid-servant in Argos, because a Greek had carried her off, depriving her of the free light of day (ἐλεύθερον ἦμαρ ἀπούρας): this moving image makes such a deep impression that the half-line recurs in two other passages of the *Iliad*. There thus emerges for the first time a conception of freedom which presupposes

4

as its counterpart the slavery of the individual, while at the same time showing a consciousness that the freedom of the individual is bound up with the freedom of the community.

The changing linguistic usage reflects a changed evaluation of social conditions. It was first of all in the household that the distinction between master and servant became noticeable, and only gradually did men realise that the unfree servants as a group constituted a different class in the community, a group whose members were deprived of the right of directing their own affairs. Only thus could it happen that those who did enjoy that right, who had no master over them and could therefore play their part in the life of the community, were no longer merely called 'men' (λαοί) but came to feel themselves free men. The chaos caused by war also made them aware how closely their own freedom was linked with that of the father-land.

With the idea of limited rights was easily associated that of inferiority. It was still far from the time, certainly, when a proud aristocracy claimed to recognise the slave from his appearance as a shuffling, bent man who never held his head erect (Theognis, 535). But Homer's Odysseus already tells his father, who meets him in the guise of an ill-treated servant:"Your build and size are not those of a slave. You look more like a king".[6] A man's inner life is, of course, more important than his appearance. Eumaeus, himself a king's son, stolen and sold when a child, says in sorrow: "All-seeing Zeus takes half the good out of a man the day he becomes a slave" (Od., XVII, 322). He then thinks to himself how much more he might have achieved as a free man. But the cause of his lament is the behaviour of the maid-servants in the courtyard: "When servants no longer feel their master's firm hand they are no longer ready to work as they should". The loss of independence also takes away the sense of responsibility.

That the poet was not here passing a contemptuous judgment on slaves can be seen from the character-drawing of Eumaeus. Rather do his words show compassion for men who had met with such a fate, and a humane conviction that slaves are not mere beasts of burden but human beings. True manhood can thrive only in freedom.

In the first half of the seventh century Hesiod considers as absolute necessities on a farm a house, a wife, and draught animals. He does not mention slaves, but takes for granted that the farmer should have, over and above the labourers that he engages for the harvest, other servants in regular employment with him – these are presumably slaves. But they are members of his household, with whom he feels a close bond, whereas he is in bitter conflict with the aristocratic lords who deny him his rights. He does not think of a community of free men as distinct from slaves. He never uses the words ἐλεύθερος and δοῦλος and their derivatives.[7]

But the time was at hand that brought about a complete change in the social structure of Greece. From having been a dividing line between peoples, the sea became the bridge which made contact possible with the most distant lands. Colonies were founded, more and more territories were opened to commerce, and in the homeland itself large concerns were started which produced goods for the new markets. This led to a demand for cheap labour, a demand which, with the help of the traffic in slaves from neighbouring barbarian lands, could easily be met. There was a sharp rise in the number of slaves and by the end of the seventh century they already constituted a separate social class, which had to be incorporated by legal measures within the social organism. It was also soon recognised that this was not a purely legal problem. Even so humane a lawgiver as Solon issued decrees which in effect excluded slaves from the gymnasia. Although slaves were for the most part not of Greek origin, he was guided not so much by national interest as by the civic notion that these institutions which fostered public spirit must remain uncontaminated.

The number of slaves was also increased by the fact that the accelerated economic development was threatening the existence of the free citizen. Easier circulation of currency rendered possible by the development of minting money, favoured the accumulation of great fortunes, but seriously endangered the economically weak, especially the small peasants who up to that time had been the backbone of the free population. When they had been obliged to borrow money in the lean years and were unable to pay the high rates of interest, they were threatened not merely with loss of their mortgaged land but with becoming servants and slaves of their creditors. Solon gives a horrifying account of the conditions under which they consequently suffered. In Athens in 594 he had been invested with extraordinary powers to steer the ship of state through the crisis. After carrying out reforms he gives account of his actions in a poem:

6

> To their god-given fatherland I brought
> Many a man who, justly or unjustly,
> Was sold to foreign slavery, and many
> Who flew from creditors from land to land
> And in their exile lost their Attic tongue.
> Those who at home bore shameful slavery
> Cringing in fear before a cruel master,
> These I set free. Laws gave me power, and I,
> Combining power with justice, used it wisely.[8]

But for Solon the statesman and patriot there was something more important than what he had done for the individual citizens. Behind the picture of the land-owners from whose fields he had removed the mortgage menace, he had the vision of the divinity to whom belonged all the attic soil, and he called upon mother earth herself to witness the crowning of his achievements:

> You were enslaved, but now, now you are free!

The freedom he had given his fellow citizens was enjoyed also by the deity of the native soil. Patriotic and religious feeling combine to endow the word freedom with the deepest significance and the most solemn tones.

It is also relevant that he himself, like his Athenians, had learned just at that time to appreciate the importance of freedom in the purely political sphere. In profoundly serious poems he had earned that trust which had led his fellow citizens to call upon him to reform the state. These poems had counselled the citizens to unite and especially warned the leaders against selfishness and *hybris*, which must necessarily bring about civil war and thus the enslavement of the whole city. Towards the end of his life he was to remind his fellow-citizens bitterly of that prophecy, since Peisistratus had in fact risen to power as a dictator: "Through your own blindness, you have brought about your enslavement." Tyranny could no more become a permanent institution in Athens than elsewhere in Greece, for Greek sensibility could not stand one man being master of the whole community. The private citizen suffered intensely from that inequality before the law that is inseparable from monarchy. That is why the regicide was glorified in Athens as "the bringer of equality before the law". As early as 521, after the death of Polycrates, the people of Samos

– according to Herodotus – had erected an altar in gratitude to "Zeus the Liberator", and that undoubtedly was how the Athenians also felt.

In those struggles the real slaves as such had hardly any part. They had now become a clearly separate social class. But, just as in Hesiod, the contrast between them and the free men was unimportant compared with the distinction between the aristocratic master class, who considered that they alone were good and capable, and the rising classes, who claimed to be of equal human worth. Small wonder, therefore, that in the literature of the time, which is produced mainly by the master class, there is little mention of free men and slaves. It is a deliberate insult when Alcaeus, in Solon's time, patronisingly reproaches his opponent Pittacus, whom he usually describes as "the son of bad parents" [9], that he, too, has a reputation to lose "like the free men of good families".

Influenced already by the tremendous experience of the Persian Wars, Pindar (to be considered more fully later) did not fail to praise Hiero for having endowed the newly founded city of Aetna with "divinely ordained freedom" in its Dorian constitution. But apart from that, he hardly ever uses the words "free" or "slave".

The same is true of the *Mirror of Aristocracy* of Theognis, which is full of the contrast between the "worthy" and the "unworthy". There is an occasion when an emigrant is driven through personal vexation to tell a cheeky maid-servant that he is at any rate better than a slave – but that is all. The aristocrat was sensitive about only one aspect of slavery. It is seen in the *Odyssey* (IV, 12) where the bastard son of a slave mother holds a position of equal rank to a free man in Menelaus' court. When a nobleman now declares that a slave can be recognised from his outward bearing, he does so so that he may add as a warning the line "From the womb of a maid-servant a free line cannot be born". For the aristocrat purity of blood is now a matter of life and death. But much more dangerous than a liaison with a slave-woman is the temptation to marry one of the "unworthy" for the sake of money.

Taking a look backward, we can draw certain conclusions. The awareness of freedom has its origin in the sphere of private relationships, in the difference felt by the "master" and his family between themselves and the servant, who was part of the master's property and had no right to conduct his own affairs. The next step was to lump together as a separate class in society all those who were without that freedom. Opposed to this group were the men who were free in their own right, who thus first became aware of the full significance of the fact that as such they enjoyed the prerogative of taking part in running the affairs of the community. The continual danger that they might themselves become enslaved if the fatherland were subjugated, inevitably led to the recognition of the freedom of the community as the highest good. The concept was transferred from the private sphere when in the class struggles the victory of the other party was described as slavery, so that freedom came to be appreciated from the point of view of home politics as well. The social cleavage between free men and slaves remained, quite naturally, notwithstanding party quarrels within the citizen body, and it called for a high degree of self-confidence when Archilochus, in a poem as early as the seventh century, openly defied all prejudice about rank by saying that he lived in poverty and that his mother was a slave.[10] In that early age the fundamental claim was thus put forward for the first time that a man and his work are to be judged not by the extrinsic accidents of birth but by his intrinsic quality. Archilochus himself was bold enough to assert himself as a free person.

Our records of this early period are meagre.[11] Even so one thing does stand out. Hector already knows only too well what the freedom of the fatherland means for the individual's fate. Yet it finds expression only in that one passage of the *Iliad*, where feeling for the city is most powerfully evident. Nowhere else in the *Iliad* are we told – as we might expect judging by Herodotus – that the Trojans are fighting for the freedom of the fatherland. In the martial elegiacs of the period the fighting men are certainly called upon to sacrifice their lives for the fatherland, but the word "freedom" is not used, although the Greeks of Asia Minor must have known what was at stake for them in fighting the Great Powers of Asia. A really major experience was still necessary, it would appear, before the concept of freedom and enslavement could become central in the thoughts and feelings of the national community.

CHAPTER III

THE CLASSICAL AGE

THE WAR OF LIBERATION AND ITS CONSEQUENCES

At the end of the sixth century the Greeks of Asia Minor belonged to the Persian Empire. Its rule was not oppressive. For these Greeks, of course, military service and payment of tribute were compulsory but the Great King seldom interfered with internal matters. He was content with appointing as governors submissive Greeks who admittedly were called tyrants but who maintained as far as possible the old administrative forms and took care not to hurt unnecessarily the feelings of their fellow citizens. Intervention in economic and cultural life was completely avoided. But uppermost in the minds of the Greeks was the thought that they were subjects of a barbarian in a foreign land, and comparison with the homeland made them resent this status as servitude. The vivacious temperament of the Ionians made it easy for the tyrant Aristagoras of Miletus when in the year 500 for purely personal motives – he was under threat of punishment by the Great King – he called on his fellow citizens to revolt and went so far as to hold out a prospect of the restoration of popular self-government. In the motherland his prayer that they should "save their Ionian blood-relations from slavery" fell in Sparta upon deaf ears, but the Athenians decided to send twenty ships to their aid.[1] That could not of course keep the insurrection from collapsing, but it gave Darius a welcome pretext to pursue energetically the expansion of his empire over Europe, which had been planned long since, and had begun with his attack on the Scythians. As early as 491 his herald appeared in Greece to claim "water and earth" in token of subjection. In Sparta and Athens the fury at this arrogance was such that, without the least regard for the sacred laws of hospitality, the envoys were brutally murdered. In the following year there was an attempted Persian landing on the coast of Attica, and the Athenians later claimed the glory of having at Marathon "repelled from their city, indeed, from all Hellas, the day of servitude".[2] In reality this battle was simply a curtain-raiser, as was discovered only too soon after the year 490. More and more often came news of the mighty war preparations Xerxes was making to achieve success where his father had failed. Once more the heralds came to claim earth and water, and the danger this time came so near that not a few Greeks more or less willingly gave in. All the more firmly did the "more right-minded" who were "resolved to remain free" close their ranks (Herodotus, VII, 178, 157) and so came into being a League which could for the first time claim to be truly pan-Hellenic in character. Suddenly and with amazing clear-sightedness the Greeks realised what was at stake. It was no mere skirmish with neighbours, nor was it really a life-and-death struggle: it was the defence of something higher that gave to life its significance and value. "When the fate of all Hellas was in the balance, we sacrificed our lives to rescue her" – the Corinthians inscribed on the monument to the men who fell at Salamis (Simonides, 95b). "The decision is now in the balance: shall we be free men or slaves?", an officer calls to his men in the Ionian uprising according to Herodotus (VI, 11), and in his work we regularly hear similar expressions on the lips of the fighting men. That was really the feeling that inspired them. The Greeks understood their struggle with the Persians as a fight for freedom in the deepest sense, and it was that which gave them the power to conquer. The same spirit informs Aeschylus' the *Persians:*

> Forward, sons of Hellas, free the fatherland!
> Free your children, wives, the high seat of your gods,
> The graves of your fathers – for all of these we fight!

That is what the fighting men at Salamis shout in this play to spur themselves on (402). "Well we know how gigantic is the superior strength of the Persians. We shall nevertheless defend ourselves as well as we can, because it is for freedom we fight" – this is the answer given by the Athenians to the tempting offer of the Persian Supreme Commander Mardonius (Herodotus, VIII, 143). After the victory of Plataea, Pausanias erected on the city market square an altar to "Zeus the Liberator"[3], expressing the common gratitude of the whole of "liberated" Hellas; to commemorate it the Eleutherian festival was instituted, to be held every four years. In Athens too there is a statue and a temple to Zeus Eleutherios, and this title came so much from the heart of the people that it almost replaced the usual name *Soter*, "the Saviour". It spread as far as Sicily where it was also realised that the struggle against the Etruscans and Carthaginians was a fight for freedom. In the year 470, when Pindar opened his twelfth Olympian Ode to Himera with a prayer to Tyche, the daughter of Zeus Eleutherios, he certainly was not thinking mainly of the fall of the tyrant Thrasydaeus[4], but of the victory of Himera which in the Festival Song on Hiero (*Pyth.*, 175ff) he puts on a level with the Battle of Salamis because in both cases Hellenic land was saved from servitude.

Similarly, in the epigrams inscribed on the monuments[5], which at first confined themselves to the plain facts, it became more and more usual to extol the liberation of the fatherland as the essential service rendered by the fallen and often all Hellas is named as the fatherland. For it intensified the impression of a great experience to regard a battle as a glorious deed and nothing less than the liberation of Hellas. A blind eye was turned to the not inconsiderable number of sympathisers with the Medes, and in picture and festival oration a parallel was drawn with that great pan-Hellenic undertaking of ancient times, the Trojan War.

Even Pindar, who, as a Theban aristocrat had in the Spring of 480 counselled peace and neutrality, and who after the Battle of Plataea had been deeply concerned that his town might be punished by the Greeks, fully recognised that the Greeks of the fatherland, like those of the West, had to fight the barbarians in defence of their independence; and in a dithyramb[6] he extolled renowned Athens for having at Artemisium laid the glorious foundation-stone of Hellenic liberty.

Gratitude to Zeus the Liberator was deeply genuine. But the Greeks were not inclined to be satisfied with a "now thanked be all the gods" and simply to accept freedom as a gift from the deity. There was an old saying that God helps those that help themselves. In the *Persians* of Aeschylus (742, cf. 395), Darius applies it sorrowfully to his deluded son, but it holds for the victors too, and the play expresses as well as gratitude to the gods, pride in one's own achievement. But there is more to it than this. Whatever the Greek experiences he wants to understand thoroughly, and so he always inquires into the causes of things and the course they take. The tragedian found the ultimate significance of Xerxes' downfall in his *hybris*, which led him to disregard his human limitations. But the divine order which this revealed also makes the victory intelligible from the human point of view. In the Aeschylus play, the Queen Mother tells how in a dream she saw Xerxes trying to yoke to his chariot two women, one in Persian and the other in Dorian dress, one proudly and willingly bending to the yoke while the other broke it and flung Xerxes to the ground. It is part of the nature of things that the Greek is unfit to bear the yoke of servitude, and that it is which gives him the will to defend himself and the strength to win.

The other Athenians felt as Aeschylus did. Fate now sent them a man who helped them to recognise as a precious national asset what had formerly been only a part of their unconscious make-up.

Herodotus, in his historical work, deliberately portrayed the Greek war as one of liberation.[7] Time and again he uses the words "freedom" and "servitude", whereas the traditional notions of fame and *arete*, much more applicable to individuals, appear less and less. But he does not let himself be drawn into any sort of vague sentimentality or wave of naturalist enthusiasm. He uses precisely the concept of freedom to put the war into historical perspective. The unity of his work, which is so colourful and seems to proceed on so many different levels, resides in the thought, which as its *Leitmotif* determines the structure of the whole work: the great war was the last phase of a long development whereby the Persians had brought under their yoke the whole of Asia[8], and were finally encroaching on Europe with a view to enslaving it also. That was the true cause of the war, and that is why it was essentially a war of liberation.

Herodotus came from Asia Minor, where East and West were in direct contact, and there were lively exchanges, material and spiritual, between Greeks and non-Greeks. This led naturally to comparison, and with a view to studying the characteristics of the Eastern peoples, he undertook long journeys of exploration. He was also interested from the outset in the history of these peoples. He was never exclusively a geographer. We cannot tell when he drew up the plan for his great historical work. Early in his travels, however, there were two things that particularly engaged his attention, things that were to become significant in his later exposition. One was something utterly foreign to the Greek, the imperialism of the East which in its drive towards expansion knew neither measure nor bounds. The other was the fact that, although the Persians had in a short time, and without very great difficulty, overrun the age-old realms of Lydia, Egypt and Babylon, they had failed when confronted with the resistance of a small people.

The historian was thus confronted with the crucial problem – how to account for the fact that the Greeks had been able to achieve victory over the barbarians' superior power in men and in material resources. For him the reason could only lie in the will to freedom of a people prepared for self-sacrifice, which drove them all to exert themselves to the utmost. But he only saw this will to freedom clearly when he compared it with the attitude of other peoples. It is because "they love freedom", he tells us, that they rejected out of hand the proposal of Mardonius that he exercise authority in Greece under the aegis of the Great King (VIII, 143). A little earlier an anecdote is told which, as so often with Herodotus, is of great symbolic significance. To atone for the murder of Xerxes' envoys, two Spartan volunteers offer to be handed over to the Persian king. On the way they are asked by a Persian why the Spartans are unwilling to put up with Xerxes, who knows how to reward friends generously. They answer: "That you cannot understand, for you only know the life of slaves: you have never learned whether liberty is sweet or not. If you had, you would be advising us to fight for it not with the spear alone but with the axe as well" (VII, 135). That shows the deep gulf which separates Greek from Oriental sensibility. All through Herodotus it can be seen right down to the smallest detail. The Greeks knew perfectly well that the Great King in his official correspondence referred to his satraps as his servants. So even for a man like Xerxes' cousin Mardonius, Herodotus uses as a matter of course the term δοῦλος and the latter therefore unhesitatingly addresses the Great King as ὦ δέσποτα, Master, whereas with the Greeks, whether those visiting the court or those residing there as emigrants, the word never crosses their lips; they only call him King (ὦ βασιλεῦ). Both the Spartans gladly offer their lives to make amends to the Great King, but they refuse as unworthy of free men the salutation that consists of flinging themselves on the ground before him, the *proskynesis*. Yet that was the custom in the Orient, and Aeschylus certainly intends no disparagement of the Persians when in his tragedy he makes the noblemen of the kingdom pay homage to the Queen Mother in accordance with the ceremonial of the court. We sense the difference, however, when in the *Agamemnon* the noblemen of the chorus greet their victorious home-coming King as free men, and dare to express frank criticism (783ff.). The Greeks are by no means overbearingly chauvinistic, but they do feel themselves different from other peoples. That certitude became part of their flesh and blood as a result of the Persian War. It had also made them realise where the true freedom lies that had become the source of their strength.

14

The Greeks waged the war of their own free will as confederates enjoying equal rights, whereas their opponents were compelled by the will of a single individual. They were not unaware of the military advantages inherent in the enemy's organisation but they also knew what it cost. In the tragedy of Aeschylus the Persian Queen Mother cannot grasp why the Greeks were able to defeat the army of Darius, although not forced to keep on fighting through fear of a master, whose slaves or subjects they were. The historian, taking up the tragic poet's idea, makes it the subject of a conversation between Xerxes and the exiled Spartan king Demaratus (VII, 101–104). The Great King is convinced that the Greeks will not join battle because there will be no masters to force them into action, with the lash if need be. But he is told that in any case numerical superiority will not make the Spartans yield. "For though they are free, they are not wholly free. They still have over them the law as their ruler, the *nomos*, which they fear much more than your people fear you, and that is what obliges them not to flee the most powerful host but to remain at their posts and conquer or die." This *nomos* is compatible with freedom, for it is the rule of conduct which these men have given themselves. True freedom does not exclude obligation but rather finds in it the firmness to defend itself against attack from any quarter.

For the Spartans the "law" consisted in their *kosmos*, their old way of life derived from Lycurgus. Herodotus is also thinking, however, of the other Greek peoples, and so uses deliberately the commoner word *nomos*, which embodies for every Greek the idea of the constitutional state. This found its complete distinctive expression in the city-state, which in principle conferred on every citizen equality before the law, but required as its counterpart their readiness to give up their lives and property for the community. It was the spirit of this city-state which had so brilliantly proved its worth in the war. No wonder that for the Greeks from then on that city-state was inseparably bound up with the idea of freedom. It was part of the people's essential character and distinguished them from the barbarians. Aristotle indeed recognised the Greek *polis* as the true state. The barbarian groupings of peoples, the *ethne*, did not really deserve to be called 'states'.

Following the war of liberation, the Greeks distinguished themselves as a nation ever more sharply from the barbarians. At the same time, however, the idea underwent a slight change.

15

Herodotus in his introduction announces that he is going to tell the story of the war between the Greeks and the barbarians. His barbarians are in fact the Persians. But it is as clear to the historian as to Aeschylus that behind the Persians was ranged the whole might of Asia which Persia had massed together under its leadership.[9] He is likewise convinced that Persian imperialism is directed not against little Hellas alone but has as its goal the whole inhabited world "as far as the sun shines", and thus the whole of Europe. Parallel with the antithesis of Greek and barbarian appears that of Europe and Asia.

As early as the seventh century Anaximander of Miletus had, with the wide vision of genius, divided the inhabited world into two geographical areas of Europe and Asia and this division remained valid even when the exceptional situation of African Libya was gradually recognised. But it was not until after the Persian War that this scientific observation became part of the mental outlook of the whole people. Athens had been warned at Delphi as early as 480 about "Ares approaching on the Persian war chariot".[10] The Athenian epigram about the warriors at Artemesium celebrated this victory over "the manifold peoples of Asia", and in 449 the Athenians rejoiced that the hard won victory at Cyprus was the greatest "since the sea separated Asia from Europe and the Great War flared up". Herodotus occasionally poked fun at the airy fabrications of the Ionian geographers with their dividing-up of the earth, but for him, too, the great antithesis is between Asia and Europe and that is how he arrived at the notion of the different types of character separating the two groups of mankind. For himself, naturally, it is the Greeks who always command his attention, and he loses no opportunity to illustrate with little anecdotes the difference between the Greek constitutional state and Asiatic despotism and servitude. But soon more general conclusions were drawn.

When somewhere around the year 430 the young physician Hippocrates[11] made a great research voyage to the Black Sea to study the influence of climate on a people's body and soul, and published his findings in his work on neighbouring countries ($Περὶ ἀέρων ὑδάτων τόπων$), he mentioned the Greeks only once, and then only incidentally: otherwise he simply contrasts the Europeans and the Asiatics. The main difference he found is that the Asiatics lack the courage and energy of the European, and he puts the blame for this not exclusively on the enervating climate but also on the despotic forms of government which paralysed the strength of

16

will of the subjects. For him the exception only proved the rule: those Asiatic barbarians who remained autonomous were remarkable precisely for their valour. Here scientific theory is obviously influenced by the nation's experience of the Persian Wars.

Thus the picture of the Europeans which Hippocrates sketched was unintentionally given Greek features. As the geographical horizon gradually widened, men grew aware of course of the differences between the peoples of Europe, and with this the old contrast between the Greeks and the barbarians could return. But one thing remained: the contrast between East and West which Herodotus as historian had first proclaimed. And we can well imagine that for him the old antithesis was not only geographical or racial but ideological as well. The picture of the West took form in accordance with the Greek will to freedom and the East became the homeland of the slave mentality.

POLITICAL FREEDOM

Freedom in the City-state

The war of liberation was for the Greek people the supreme experience and of decisive significance in their political and spiritual development.

The fierce blaze of pan-Hellenic sentiment was admittedly not strong enough to enable the League which the "right-minded" had formed, to grow up into a political unification of the nation. For that same will to freedom, which had endowed the Greeks with the strength to ward off foreign domination, induced every single city-state to try and maintain its own freedom at all costs and to resent any interference with its self-government, its autonomy. This precluded their merging into a great single state.

It was indeed an inevitable consequence of the victory that the Greeks of the colonies, who had either fought on the side of their blood relations or had at least dissociated themselves from the Persians at the battle of Mycale, had to be shielded from the vengeance of the Great King and the threat of renewed subjugation. That was only possible if they entered into a close political relationship with the mother country. The Spartans maintained of course their old aversion to overseas commitments, but for that very reason they were not at all displeased when in 478 the Athenians made a separate alliance with the Ionians, at their request, for the pro-

17

secution of the war. They had no idea that in so doing they were affording grounds for a dualism that might split the nation and become a danger to themselves.

The immediate objective of the alliance was to liberate the Greeks who were still subject to the Persians, and this objective was gained after long fighting. An agreement with the Persians was reached in the year 449 whereby, for practical purposes at least, the exercise of sovereign rights over the Greek coastal cities was waived, and the spheres of influence at sea were also clearly defined.

Meanwhile the Delian Confederation had long outgrown its original purposes and, "in the stresses and strains of internal growth", as Thucydides put it, it had taken on quite a different character. From being a relatively loose alliance of equal states, it had become a rigid organisation which included nearly half of the Greek world of the East, an ἀρχή, an empire in which the military and economic predominance of Athens, its administrative seat, made itself felt so strongly that the other confederates could officially be designated as subjects. It was only too natural for Athens to pursue its own power politics and let its decisions be directed by the selfish interests of its citizens. Even coercion, combined with interference in the autonomy of member states became unavoidable. Athens naturally took good care that within each city-state a party bound to itself by common interests should be at the helm. The general feeling of discontent increased to a dangerous extent and was due, less to specific points of difference, than to a deep seated aversion to the oppression they now suffered: "They had no desire to exchange servitude under the barbarians for the same thing under the Greeks." (Thucydides, III, 10, 3). Even the statesmanship of Pericles was unable to stem the tide. Modern scholars have levelled against him the charge that by not laying a firm foundation by introducing common citizenship throughout the confederation he failed to stifle the discontent at its source. But this sort of thing was quite foreign to the political thinking of the Greeks. For it was in the nature of the *polis* that as free men the citizens could exercise in person their right to vote and that was only possible in a small area. Much as he tried to spare the feelings of the confederates Pericles could not be blind to the fact that the hegemony of Athens was regarded as tyranny and that it could be kept going only through force. The Spartans were of course well aware of the feelings of the federated states and, as opposition to the ascendency of

Athens became so keen that it could be resolved only by warfare, then for the first time the slogan: "independence for the small states", proved the most effective form of propaganda. The Spartans went into battle with the cry: "Freedom for the Greeks". At first, indeed, Athens managed to stifle every urge to secession and, even after the Sicilian catastrophe, her resistance was still so strong that Sparta did not shrink from resorting to methods most deeply resented by the best men in her own ranks – making a secret agreement to hand over to the Great King in exchange for subsidies the Greeks inhabiting Asia Minor.

By the year 404 things had reached the point that the walls of Athens were destroyed as triumphant music was played and men rejoiced that this day meant for Hellas "the dawn of freedom".[12]

The Greeks had soon to acknowledge that the liberation meant only a change of masters and that the victor was pursuing power politics quite as egotistically as had the hated Athenians. For the Spartans it was in the long run impossible to abandon the Greeks of Asia Minor. It led to conflict with the Persians and in 396 King Agesilaus of Sparta, like a new Agamemnon, called upon the Hellenes to make common cause in a campaign that was to restore freedom to their brothers in Asia (Xenophon, *Hell.*, III, 4). But Sparta's old friends refused to join the armies. Persian gold brought about a coalition against Sparta. Sparta was ultimately obliged to ask Persia for reserves, and in 386 the Great King was able to dictate a peace whereby all the city-states of the motherland should have self-government but those in Asia should be subject to him. The exhaustion and the need for peace was so great that even the Athenians acquiesced, although they had rejected peace on the same terms only a few years before. Plato was then prompted of course to a most bitter satire on Athenian policy[13] which in its "passion for liberty" had liberated even the Great King of Persia and so helped him on to new power.

Similarly, the self-government of the small states which the "King's Peace" brought about, had the effect in practice of restoring Spartan ascendency. The unscrupulous use she made of that power soon brought repercussions, and already in 378 a new naval league arose under the leadership of Athens, which was directed this time not against Persia but explicitly against Sparta. In order to prevent a recurrence of Athenian "tyranny" each member of the league was guaranteed not only self-determination in respect of its internal affairs but also complete independence externally.[14] Thenceforth αὐτονομία and ἐλευθερία became the solid two-fold formula for complete 'sovereignty' and 'freedom' which were always guaranteed in treaties concluded between equal partners.

Yet even these guarantees did not suffice to overcome the opposition to any league; and however urgently men with so pan-Hellenic an outlook as Isocrates pleaded for unity and a common defensive front against the hereditary Persian foe, the sterile civil war for hegemony went on. Yet once again the word "freedom" worked its magic spell as Demosthenes called on men to defend it against Philip, but at Chaeronea in the year 338 the Greek militia nevertheless surrendered to the trained army and the strategy of the Macedonian king. In Greece the effective master henceforth was the representative of a people who though admitted to be of kindred stock were not felt to belong to the Greek nation. Philip knew the Greeks well enough not to think of incorporating them in his kingdom or forcing them into any unified state which would go against their nature. All he wanted was that they should be linked together in a pact which, while respecting their desire for self-government, demanded the internal peace of the nation and bound Greece and Macedonia together in a defensive and offensive alliance, giving him personally the supreme military power.

With propaganda and clever exploitation of pan-Hellenic sentiment he managed to get adopted as the league's first resolution "that the age-old crimes of Persia shall at last be fully avenged". He himself, to be sure, was murdered in 336 at the very height of the preparations, but his son, Alexander, soon came forward as the leader of Hellas against the Persians. The Greeks of Asia Minor were thereby also set free but only of course to be incorporated into the new empire.

Thus what the best of the Hellenes had so long been yearning for became a reality. In the League of Corinth all Hellas was for the first time knit together in a single political organisation – only Sparta grumbling on the side lines. But it was only too clear that this unity had come about only because of the pressure of external events, and Macedonian supremacy was always resented as a foreign overlordship. With the battle of Chaeronea the political independence of the Hellenes had in practice come to an end.

The historical course of events shows with painful clarity that for the Hellenes political freedom had two different aspects. The very urge to freedom which had forged the Greek city-state and successfully defended it against external enemies, developed in internal affairs, into a narrow-minded particularism which could not suffer any kind of allegiance and so prevented the nation achieving any unity by its own efforts.

We can, however, only understand its role in foreign policy if we trace the influence which the idea of freedom exerted on the inner life of the city state, the *polis*, and on the relations of the individual to the state.

Freedom in Internal Affairs

The Sparta-Athens dualism[15] which developed after the War of Liberation and split all Greece into two camps was no accidental opposition of two rivals for power, but was most deeply rooted in the different characteristics of their stock. Thucydides had already come to that conclusion, and considered it necessary in order to understand the events, to explain through the mouth of the Corinthians and of the Spartan King Archidamus the essential difference between their ways of life (I, 70–84). The Spartan is conservative, clumsy, prudent, slow in decision, of great courage, but calculating carefully before engaging in war.[16] His strong point is *sophrosyne*, tenaciously clinging to traditional ways of life and hereditary ownership of property but never engaging in unreflective action, being averse to all adventure. The Athenian, on the other hand, is forever thinking of something new, is progressive, changeable, quick in decision as in action, living hopefully in the future, never standing still, reckless, full of high-flown plans and fully prepared for any effort or sacrifice. The historian leaves it in no doubt that it was the dread of imperialism, to which their way of life was leading the Athenians, that was the decisive factor that drove the Peloponnesian people to war.

No wonder that this opposition operated in domestic politics too and became immediately apparent after the war of liberation.

With a people for whom valour and manliness were the supreme values, alike in the individual and the community, the Spartan *kosmos* was the natural way of life. The concrete form it had taken even before the sixth century, was the outcome of a specific historical situation, where a small ruling class was opposed to a numerically far greater mass of people, and saw them not as compatriots but as subjugated enemies, with the result that even in the fourth century the ephors formally declared war on them every year (Plutarch, *Lycurgus*, 28). The Spartans thus became a caste of warriors who might be called to arms at any moment, and since this situation became permanent like a lava stream solidified, when the danger

21

was no longer so great, it was possible for the political structure to develop which the Greeks themselves called the "armed camp state".[17]

In such a situation only the welfare of the community mattered and the life of the individual was consequently adjusted to this aim with iron logic. This explains all those characteristics which already seemed so remarkable in antiquity – exposing children, state education with the sole object of turning boys into good soldiers, but also including girls so as to ensure a strong progeny, and finally the way of life of the men, who were fully occupied, in peace as well as in war, with military training, substituting comradeship for family life and threatening the emigrant with death as a deserter. The right to a private life did not exist.

As a result of that military discipline and bias Sparta held at the outbreak of the war of liberation undisputed leadership in Greece, and it was therefore natural that leadership in war also fell to her. After the victory at Plataea she could legitimately feel that her *kosmos* had proved its worth in face of the gravest dangers. The state had also overcome without great difficulty the internal political troubles brought about by the lust for power of the tyrant Pausanias. The Spartans therefore felt not the slightest reason for modifying anything whatever in their state structure.

In Athens it was quite another matter. Here too, certainly, the citizens could be proud of their achievements and feel convinced that these were partly due to their state constitution. But there was no age-old tradition behind that conviction. It was only in the year 507 that Kleisthenes had completed the reorganisation of the state, and it caused grave misgivings, not only among "the friends of the tyrants". But there was something far more important. Within a single generation Athens had completed a transformation that went much deeper than any violent revolution could have effected. As a result of Themistocles' naval policy Athens had changed from being a second-rate agrarian state on the "Dorian Sea", as Pindar called the Saronic Gulf that stretched out before it, into becoming the strongest Greek sea power; and though the labourers out in the country were still the backbone of the population, life was shifting more and more toward the mighty growing city, which soon became the commercial centre as well as the strongest coastal citadel of all Greece. But among the citizens in the town itself a new class suddenly rose in importance. These were the people without landed property, the *thetes*, who had had during the war at sea plenty of opportunity of rendering service to the fatherland as seamen or artisans, and who therefore in Greek eyes might also claim rights in the body politic. In order to bind these people more closely to the state, Solon had already guaranteed them at least participation in the People's Assembly and in the popular juries. But so far as we can see it is only after the Battle of Salamis that any practical results were achieved.

The *thetes* themselves, however, were not yet interested in being appointed to offices which were not remunerated. It was felt sufficient therefore to throw them open at least to the middle classes and the small farmers. A *thes*, too, can hardly have dared to speak to any motion before the Assembly. But now he too could feel a certain pride at being a citizen enjoying equal rights with others and at his vote carrying its weight in the major decisions taken. What must it have meant to every Athenian when he heard the herald call out in the *ekklesia* "Who wishes to address the assembly? Who has good counsel for the people?" As early as 421 Euripides says in the *Suppliant Women*: "Is not that perfect equality for the citizens?" (438ff).

Immediately before that the poet makes Theseus, the mythical representative of the Athenian ideal, extol his city on the grounds that what counts there is not the caprice of an individual who recognises no law other than his own will, but a "common law binding all citizens and affording equal rights for rich and poor". Euripides then calls to mind the old name of the Kleisthenian constitution, the *isonomia*[18], which was still for Herodotus, the name of the "fairest" form of life in a state (III, 80). And precisely the language of Herodotus shows that this expression was only gradually being replaced by another which corresponded better to the new feeling for the state. It is "democracy". The term was probably coined originally by its aristocratic adversaries and meant that form of the state in which not the "best" but the common people, the *demos* wield the power. But *demos* was also used in another sense, i.e. for the whole 'people', and so the adherents of the new regime could take up with self-conscious pride what had been meant as a term of derision, because it signified for them that democracy is not the dictatorship of a class but is that constitutional form in which the whole nation governs and only the well-being of the community prevails (Thucydides, II, 37, 1). And that first democracy was a popular state in a much more valid sense than its modern successors. For in Athens "not only did all power issue from the people", but it was directly exercised by them. In consequence all officials as well as the council were deliberately subordinated to the People's Assembly which held the power to decide all important issues, just as the administration of justice was entrusted to the juries elected by the people. In that way even the simplest "common man"[19] could have the uplifting consciousness of being a bearer of the state's sovereign power.

The equality of all the citizens is one of the fundamental pillars of Athenian democracy, but along with it goes another. Equality and liberty are slogans which exercised their magic power for the first time in the Athens of Pericles before they became, via the French Revolution, the dominant elements in modern political thinking. This pairing of terms seems so self-evident that people hardly even wonder how it came about historically.

Nevertheless, there is a problem here. We have seen that in the early days of Greece the term "freedom" was not employed as a political slogan, and was used only by way of contrast to tyranny. And when during the Persian Wars it became an ideal for which it was worthwhile to risk property and life, the main consideration was protection against foreign domination. What was it, we may ask, that suddenly invested the idea of freedom with such significance in the internal political life of the state that, alongside equality, it became the second underlying principle of democracy?

For an answer we may again be guided by Thucydides who makes Pericles develop the political ideal in the famous passage of the funeral speech (II, 35).[20] There can be no doubt that this discourse is in form and content the work of a historian but renders faithfully thoughts which the statesman himself expressed in the official service commemorating the fallen. We may also take it that in his oration Pericles mentioned the ultimate motives that were active in forming his people's ideals of democracy and freedom.

What is significant is that he gives an image of public life in Athens which is quite deliberately shown as the antithesis to the Spartan way of life. And since the Greeks had an innate love of comparison, we can well believe that their dislike of the way of life, which the leading Greek state had established for itself, tempted the ambitious Athenians, even when expressing their own natural feelings for freedom, to adopt the opposite position.

For Sparta too freedom was of course the highest good. But all that the individual citizen here wanted was that his fatherland be free and independent. To his soldierly mind it was obvious that political life must be governed by the most rigorous order and discipline, and that compulsion of the individual could not be dispensed with. Other Greek states however had different attitudes. When during the Ionian revolt [21], for example, the decisive battle by the island of Lade was imminent, one able officer managed by an impressive speech to get the allies to see that if they really wanted freedom they must take a hold of themselves and by rowing and manoevring prepare themselves for the fight. [22] All went well for a week but as it was very hot on the eighth day, the men said to the commander: "better slaves tomorrow than these fatigues today". So off they went ashore and lay down in the shade. After that, victory for the enemy was child's play.

Political conviction and readiness to sacrifice for the state were far more pronounced with the Athenians than with the related Ionian people. But they too deeply resented the coercion in the Spartan way of life, which they had got to know only too well during the war. A way of life that placed man from the cradle to the grave under the control of the state and compelled him to military discipline they found intolerable. Pericles, speaking with pride at the grave of the fallen, pointed out that the Athenians had made good the lack of continual training by the spirit which urged them to risk all for the fatherland of their own free will.

Bound up with the military character of Spartan life there were many other things that were utterly foreign to the Athenians. For example, narrow-minded isolationism from the outer world made it the normal thing to expel foreigners when military secrets had to be guarded, and a regimentation of life down to the merest details. It was meant symbolically when the ephors proclaimed on taking office: "The Spartan has to obey the laws and to shave his moustache." They kept suspicious watch on each other and any deviation from rank and file uniformity, even in daily life, was forbidden. And more important than such details was the whole way of life. The Spartan *kosmos* was a totalitarian state which took possession of the whole man, so pressing his interests into service that no room was left for any private life of his own. To everything of that kind the constitution of the Athenian state was the sharpest contrast. Pericles deliberately draws attention to that very clearly. He distinguishes sharply between the public and the private spheres, and emphasises as a characteristic of the Athenian state that it does not meddle with the private citizen's affairs, but grants him freedom to run his private life as he pleases. "With us there is

25

none of that state interference which, even when it does no material harm, is nevertheless unpleasant; and no citizen takes it amiss if another shape his own life in the way he personally considers right." (Thucydides, II, 37).[23] How much those words express the Athenian spirit can be seen in a little episode Thucydides describes elsewhere (VII, 69). After the defeat at Syracuse, when Nicias wanted to rouse in the fleeing Athenians, who were in the depths of despair, a last spurt of energy, he reminded them that it was in their fatherland that the greatest freedom reigned and each could lead his private life unhindered by administrative regulations. "In Athens everyone could live as he liked; in Sparta that was permitted to nobody," this antithesis dates from antiquity (Plutarch, *Lycurgus*, 24).

Particularly in the political sphere the Athenians became aware of this distinction. In Sparta too there was a General Assembly which decided the weightiest issues. But this was not a parliament where debates took place; it could only vote on proposals put forward by the leading officials. For the Athenian the free herald's call "Who wishes to address the assembly?" addressed to all citizens without distinction, was the bastion of democracy. Opponents might well ask scornfully how the peasant on the land outside the town could have the time and the mental equipment to decide about political questions (Euripides, *Supp.*, 420). But Pericles answers that the distinctive excellence of complete manhood in Attica lies in the fact that every citizen is in a position to follow his private occupation while at the same time picking up enough political intelligence to be able either himself to offer counsel to the People's Assembly or at least to form his own opinion about any proposal submitted to it (II, 40, 2): "The discussions preceding important decisions are quite as necessary for the state as is prompt action, and the sound common sense of the Athenian people ensures that word and deed are in true accord."

Point by point Pericles' portrayal of Athenian democracy brings to mind the antithesis of the Spartan *kosmos*. In the latter coercion reigns, completely dominating the individual for the sake of the state; in the former freedom which constricts him as little as possible. The contradiction in constitutional form results from conscious political decisions, but it springs from a profound difference in the whole outlook upon life, itself rooted in the nature of the two peoples.

Decisive in this respect are the different values attached to individual personality.

In Sparta too there were men of impressive strength and tenacity and more than one of them has by personal action, even outside of Sparta, left his mark on Greek history. But with rare exceptions they were acting as representatives of their world, as members of their nation, not as individual persons who had raised themselves out of the generality and whose importance was derived from inner strength of their own. In other parts of Greece we certainly meet even in the archaic period strong self-assured individuals whose personalities have shaped their nation's future. But even for them the traditionally revered *nomoi*, the outlook and customs handed down, remain the criteria by which their value was assessed by others and especially by themselves. What first changed this fundamentally was the impact of the Persian War. With a unanimity unique in the nation's annals, Themistocles was acknowledged by every Greek as the man whose personal ability had saved the nation from foreign domination[24], and still more weighty than the verdict of the crowd was that of Thucydides, who as a historian used his case to point out for the first time how much the genius of one individual can mean to the community (I, 138). In the grave conflicts being waged without and within many others were confronted with situations where no precedent could point the right way, nothing but the individual alone, the "self". Thus there also grew up in the masses an appreciation of the individual relying on himself. Nevertheless it remains a great thing that a statesman like Pericles drew from this situation its consequences for political life, and tried deliberately to secure for the individual the place rightly due to it in the traditional form of the community.

In Thucydides' history of the Peloponnesian War Pericles[25] starts with a clear exposition of what is to be understood by democratic equality. Juridically it means equality of all before the law, politically the abolition of all privilege due to birth or wealth, but not that all should have equal influence on the life of the community. Here, there is only one valid criterion, that of *arete*, the native ability by which the individual earns recognition in public life. Mechanical equality as expressed in voting in the popular assembly needs to be supplemented by some form of differentiation which given equal opportunity opens the door to talent, so that even the poorest may exert influence upon decisive political issues.

We must bear this programmatic explanation in mind if we are to understand the end of Pericles' exposition of democracy. He speaks there

27

of an Attic complete manhood by which a man, while performing his private duties, also concerns himself with affairs of state and politics. His concluding sentence is: "Our state is in its entirety the school of Hellas. For the individual it means that each carries in his own person the ability to act with versatility and grace in the most diverse domains."

Athens was to be the state that was to assume the cultural leadership of Hellas. The education of the whole man was to take the place of the one-sided Spartan training for war. This can only be achieved if the individual is allowed freedom for the all-round unfolding of his inherent capacities and therewith the development of his personality. An ideal was thus set up that has not only shown the way to modern humanism but was to exercise an enormous influence on the political thinking of modern times. Just as the French Revolution seized upon the slogan "Liberty, Equality", so modern liberalism is unthinkable without the freedom of the individual within the state that was formulated by Pericles. But we must not fail to recognise the fundamental distinction.[26] The liberalism of today grew out of an individualistic habit of thought concerned with the individual and "his human rights" and saw in the state a human organisation shaped by history, which was only a means to an end if not indeed a necessary evil. And as Wilhelm von Humboldt as a young man claimed in his *Suggestions for an Enquiry into the Limits of a State's Activity, (Ideen zu einem Versuch, die Grenzen der Wirksamkeit des Staates zu bestimmen)*, its only task is to enable the individual to develop his talent to the full. For Pericles it was something completely different. For him, as for his Greek contemporaries, the state comes first, being a society that has developed naturally and within which alone man can exist; it is the whole of which the individual is the part and upon its well-being his own depends. The statesman can afford to allow his fellow citizens so much freedom, for he is confident that they will of their own accord subordinate their own interests to those of the community. The individual is to enjoy freedom in society, but over him stands the city-state and it follows its own laws, to it belong freedom and sovereignty and also power. In his funeral speech, after declaring that the cultured state was the goal of his democracy, Pericles speaks with pride, in the second part, of the visible greatness of the fatherland for which the men who had fallen had gladly sacrificed their lives, of the un-dying glory Athens had won through the achievements of its citizens.

Only within the limits set by the interests of the community was the individual to enjoy his freedom. Yet attaching value to the individual personality brought an entirely new element into the political thinking of the Greeks – indeed, of mankind. It is not contained entirely in the idea of democracy. For that conception only meant: "All power emanates from the people"; and Isocrates is able to extol Sparta as the finest form of democracy simply because in it the principle of equality – even if enjoyed only by full citizens, the *homoioi* – is most completely achieved (*Areopagiticus*, 61). About the way the people exercises its power, or about relations between state and individual, that term says nothing – and today, too, it would be well to remember that fact. And it is precisely on this point that opinions differ, and not only in antiquity. In modern times, Liberalism was followed by Socialism. Particularly under the influence of Karl Marx the word has been used exclusively in the economic sense, and has become the watchword of the class war and the programme of a party. The complexities of modern politics have in the nineteenth century resulted, in practice, in Liberals and Social Democrats working together on a common front against Conservatism. It must not be forgotten, however, that originally the word "socialism" had a purely political meaning, and when Leroux coined the term "socialisme" the word was a fierce battle cry against reigning liberalism. It meant that the State and its interests must have priority over the individual and his rights.

Looking back in that light to antiquity, we can describe the greatest contrast between Sparta and the Athens of Pericles in these terms: in Sparta the idea of socialism made the deepest impression. The interests of the state are paramount, and the priority, indeed omnipotence, of the state is enforced at the expense of the individual citizen. Pericles, on the contrary, although setting out also from the pre-eminence of the community, is nevertheless convinced that it can achieve its highest goal only if every citizen is guaranteed freedom for the unfolding of his personality. Pericles thus became the precursor of the liberal ideal of the State. The linking up of the democratic ideal with the individual's personal liberty is his work.

One of the most noteworthy phenomena of the present age is the fact that even states which have proudly felt themselves the champions of liberalism are constrained by economic development and by temporary emergencies to adopt measures which imply a noticeable limitation of individual freedom. In the small Greek city-state, which for the sake of its independence had to consider economic autarchy, that necessity was felt even more strongly. If Pericles carefully avoided any incursion into the private personal sector, he nevertheless took it for granted that such laws as those on the supervision of the grain trade, to ensure the people's food supplies, were necessary like other social measures. The *politeia* was for the Greeks not a written constitution with clauses and detailed sub-clauses, but a way of life that a people worked out by itself and for itself. The democracy of Pericles, too, was a genuine fruit of the Attic spirit, but the ideal of freedom that it embodied had its roots in the general Hellenic sensibility, and so could have such a powerful influence on other Greeks that Athens, as Pericles proudly declared, became a model for other states. The Ionians, a related people, were particularly receptive to the new ideal, whereas the conservative Dorians remained on the whole reluctant to follow suit. And so it came about that together with the conflict in power-politics of the two great States dualism arose, although the two did not always share the same frontiers and the new ideas did not stop at city walls. Within the cities too, there stood, as a rule, two parties ranged against each other, one of them, the democrats, leaning towards Athens, and the other, the oligarchs, to Sparta. Everywhere the merits of the two political forms were hotly debated, and particularly the slogans "liberty and equality" were used with passion. To the "arithmetical" equality, which counted heads, was opposed the "geometrical" or "proportional" equality[27] which did not accord equal rights to the unequal people, but graded rights according to a man's achievements. The opponents count-ered the alluring cry of liberty with that of "common sense" or *sophrosyne*, which held steadfastly to tradition and in everything required training and order above all. Seen from that point of view, democratic freedom was lack of discipline, *akolasia* which induced arrogance and *hybris* in the common people, who were already inclined to excess and recklessness, and would render impossible all continuity in the life of the State.

That criticism really did find the weak spot in the ideal of democratic liberty. In Sparta free men felt themselves bound to a master, i.e. to the law, which prescribed what they had to do (cf. p. 15 above). In Athens in 458, Aeschylus spoke from the point of view of the new democracy in his *Oresteia*, but here not only the Erinnyes sing that a strict training in common sense is essential for the state: Athene also, the city's tutelary deity, explicitly takes up the words, and warns her citizens not only against the slave mentality which bows low before the despot but also against the indiscipline that acknowledges no master: "Who, being no longer afraid, will still observe the law" (*Eum*. 696).

No one ever realised more clearly than Pericles himself this intrinsic danger in democratic liberty. According to Thucydides he pronounces on the real significance of equality as well as of liberty (II, 37, 2). "Whereas in private life our relations with one another are not seriously restrained, in public life fear makes us carefully avoid doing anything illicit. We obey those who are in authority at the moment as well as the laws, especially such as protect those who suffer injustice and also those unwritten ones, the infringement of which disgraces us in the eyes of the community." The apologetic tone of these words is unmistakable. They are meant to blunt the point of the criticism of liberty that was already being made. And if Pericles does not hesitate to use so strong a word as fear at that point, it is no more mere accident that it reminds us of Aeschylus; like the poet, the statesman means not so much fear of punishment as a deep apprehensiveness to overstep the bounds imposed on personal freedom by obligations to the community, a moral apprehensiveness which Pericles firmly believed to be as deep-rooted in his Athenian people's nature as in that of the Spartan. He hates the coercion prevailing in Sparta; but something else must take its place, free obedience, doing of one's own accord what one owes to the state.

What Pericles has to say about this willing obedience was probably, even for him, meant as an ideal. For he could hardly be unaware that forces were already at work undermining the sense of the law's absolutely binding force. The active political life of a democracy in a state of continuous development gave daily evidence of the fact that written laws were man-made ordinances that might at any moment be altered. The same word *nomoi* was also used for conventional moral attitudes which were not set down in writing. They must therefore be of human origin, and the new class was much too self-confident to consider anything binding simply because their forefathers thought it right. Things which until that time were valid as part of a divine tradition were found to be rather a hindrance to progress. Nor did it help much if a pious old soul like Sophocles passionately supported the view that, at least for religion and family life, there were unwritten laws which were not created by man but had "originated in heaven and never could grow old" (*Antigone*, 450ff., and *Oedipus Tyrannus*, 863ff.). For the increasing acquaintance with foreign peoples could leave no doubt that the most diverse attitudes prevailed among mankind in this domain too. In the days of Pericles the philosopher Archelaus [28] had drawn from separate ethnological observations the general conclusion that human nature is admittedly inclined to state-building and law-making, but concrete moral attitudes had been developed late by individual peoples and so they had grown differently according to different customs. "Right and wrong are not derived from nature but are based upon convention." (τὸ δίκαιον εἶναι καὶ τὸ αἴσχρὸν οὐ φύσει ἀλλὰ νόμῳ, Vorsokr., 60A, 1, 2, 4, 6). This lesson was learned surprisingly soon, for it was in keeping with the spirit of the age and was seized upon particularly by those who had long been fighting against the traditional and narrowing influence of the *nomos*. For learning had now shown them that in eternal nature was the supreme court to which appeal might be made against historic customs. The fact that the state also was viewed from that angle was especially rich in consequences. From being a community which had developed naturally and was higher than the individual, it became an institution once created which could be measured against the 'nature' of man. Towards the end of the fifth century a theory had already developed about which we can learn from the Sophist Antiphon (*Vorsokr.*, 87B, 44 col. 4): "The actual laws of the State in many ways contradict human nature, which drives individuals to pursue their own advantage. Therefore they are not binding, they are fetters for men, and freedom resides only in what one's own nature determines." This dispensed with the curtailment of individual freedom by the laws of society and by a social ethic objectively effective in the community which Pericles with his feeling for the state had taken for granted, and the question simply became whether the law of nature would lead to any new inner obligation or if individual egotism should have full play. On that more will be said later.

Soon, however, another theory was advanced: The state is nothing but an assembly of the weak who want to protect themselves against the natural right of the strong – a theory from which forceful natures like Alcibiades were only too ready to draw practical conclusions. For Plato's Callicles [29] only he is really free who does not let himself be bullied with conventional talk about morality and justice but, like a young lion, breaks his chains and from being a slave of the masses rises to become their master. Naturally such ideas appealed mostly to educated young people. Nonetheless, a profound change of attitude was also taking hold of the whole community, and as a result the individual no longer felt himself a member of the whole, bound to it for better or worse, but a partner having rights of his own as opposed to the state.

That development was favoured by the long war which gave rise to a sharp conflict of interests between the peasants and the city-dwellers. Soon after the death of Pericles, in a work wrongly attributed to Xenophon, the *Constitution of the Athenians,* an Athenian oligarch unknown to us explains that Athenian democracy is by no means the rule of the whole people but the regime of the city *demos* which had risen as a result of the maritime policy and which was unscrupulously using its majority in the People's Assembly to promote its own interests at the expense of the best people. Although the writer is a party man, it is quite true that the optimism of Pericles who expected all from the voluntary obedience of the citizens did not stand up to harsh reality. Personal egotism and class consciousness proved stronger than that feeling for the state which thinks of the whole community first of all. Equality, which in the view of Pericles would enable quality to emerge and facilitate a proper differentiation, led to mechanical equalisation and to a levelling down, the envious taking good care that nobody should rise above the average. What the crowd understood by freedom was that nothing should stand in the way of the decisions of the all-powerful people, and any speaker in the Assembly who referred to the existing law was shouted down "for it would be mad to think that the *demos* should not have the right to do what it likes". [30]

It was not only the aristocratic Plato who described with biting sarcasm (in his *Republic*) how throughout the whole life of citizens in the fourth century the principle of liberty worked out and led in practice to the dissolution of all order and decency – a matter to be taken up later.[31] Even so loyal a democrat as Isocrates raises in the year 355, a time when the war against the former allies had clearly revealed the decline of Athens, a similar criticism of the existing constitution which "is condemned by everybody", and he knows only one way out, a return to the "genuine democracy" of their fathers, where *sophrosyne* still prevailed and liberty had not become licentiousness. But nobody was so painfully aware of the change as Demosthenes. He knew quite well the deepest cause of the political distress of his beloved Athens and also where the greatest obstacle lay to its advance toward the status of a great power and to its battle against Philip for freedom. It was the decline of the civic spirit in the

33

ictizens, who were still intoxicated with "liberty and equality", and dreamed of the greatness of Athens, but looked upon the *polis* only as a sort of public assistance body and had lost all feeling that they themselves had any obligation towards it or ought to do anything for its sake.

Pericles had once praised his Athenians for being obedient to authority and law, the unwritten as well as the written, not out of compulsion but voluntarily. It is no accident that Plato concludes his criticism of contemporary democracy [32] with words to the effect that the true democrat is extraordinarily sensitive to any kind of compulsion or servitude. "You know what this leads to. They no longer heed the laws, the written any more than the unwritten, so that they may have no master over them at all" (563d). In his *Politics* Aristotle described the various forms of democracy and their gradual radicalisation (1291b, 30ff.). The last stage is that wherein law no longer prevails but only decisions taken by the People's Assembly and born of the situation of the moment. That amounts to the dictatorship of the *demos*, now itself ruling as a despot. An organisation like this is no longer really a "State". A "State" exists only where there is law. Political freedom without obligation is monstrous.

The masses took self-government seriously and resented any kind of leadership as intolerable supervision. The People's Assemby, however, was quite naturally not equipped to conduct a purposeful foreign policy. Athenian democracy might thus hold together for a while so long as it had to contend only with the other Greek states, all the more so as they showed similar symptoms of decay, and not least Sparta. But when it meant coming to grips with Philip's stern monarchy and its disciplined army, there could be no doubt of the outcome.

Particularism prevented the Greeks from building up their strength into one united nation. The decay of civic spirit eroded the strength of the individual cities. The deepest cause of both was the exaggeration of the urge to independence which revolted against any obligation. The will to freedom, which had made the Greeks the first people able to develop a free political life at the same time concealed within itself the germ of its own destruction.

Freedom as a Formative Factor in Cultural Life

As a result of the exaggeration and debasement of the idea of freedom, the development of political life among the Greeks in the fourth century offers anything but a gratifying spectacle. That should not, however, blind us to the fact that it was this very freedom that gave the Greek spirit impetus enough to become the great teacher of Western civilisation.

"All the progress made by man is not simply brought about through pressure of external necessity, it has its origin in the spontaneity of the human *logos*, and it was individuals who used the natural freedom of the spirit to strike out new paths."[33] This is the thesis Posidonius the Stoic used to combat the materialistic conception of cultural development advocated by Democritus and Epicurus. The ancient Greeks thought along such lines when they always asked after the "first inventor" of even the simplest implements.

Creative minds of that sort the Greeks had in plenty already in the early days. Posidonius is thinking of the "seven wise men". But besides these there is the poet of the *Iliad* who in the wrath of Achilles gave depth and tragic sense to the old myths. So too the peasant Hesiod who in the face of the wealthy aristocracy proclaimed that labour was honourable and conferred human dignity; there are those who in Ionia discovered the idea of a physical science following laws of its own, thus releasing a whole new understanding of the world. There is the Athenian Solon, the man enjoying the confidence of his people, who recognised social justice as the foundation of the state and strove to make it a reality.

The independent spirit of the Greeks first found expression in individuals, whom it raised above their fellows. For this reason it seems surprising when in the fifth century a movement suddenly arose encouraging individual creativity in different fields and promoting progress. Without any doubt it was the great experience of the Persian Wars that gave the whole nation a powerful stimulus and led to the liberation of the spirit. We have ample evidence that this movement found its fullest expression and left the deepest mark in Athens, where Pericles, himself a creative personality of the first order, expressly laid down as his policy the awakening of the powers that were slumbering in his people and called upon every single citizen to exercise his own talents as a free personality for the well-being of all.

Pericles also created the environment where all those powers could work together and benefit each other. Places where intellectual activity was cultivated had of course already developed, especially in Ionia, but only small circles participated. But now Athens was becoming, as Pericles envisaged, not only the commercial crossroads, but also the educational centre of all Hellas. Other considerations were increasingly causing the allies to visit the chief city, and when in the Spring the delegates arrived to pay tribute, they attended the performances at the Theatre of Dionysus in their official capacity and consequently participated in the intellectual rise of Athens. Within a few decades the Piraeus had become a commercial port where ships from all parts of the world called to unload their wares. Even the oligarchic author of the work on the Athenian State[34] – stirred doubtless by words Pericles himself had uttered – reluctantly accepts the fact that, thanks to busy foreign trade, Attic speech had lost the character of a regional dialect and become a kind of Greek *lingua franca*. This marks the beginning of that progress which later raised the Attic speech first to the literary language and later to the colloquial medium for all Hellas. To Athens came all those who claimed they could satisfy the thirst for learning of the young men – Protagoras from the little town of Abdera, the Ionian Gorgias of Sicily, the Dorian Thrasymachus and also Hippias of Elis. Such men found here opportunities for intellectual exchange both with one another and with young men who were by no means merely receptive, but were also keen to develop for themselves what they had heard in lively discussion with the foreign teachers; after achieving success in Athens the latter themselves spread the new learning in the "Provinces". We still possess the transcript of a lecture given in a Dorian city, demonstrating the new dialectic, with discussion of the pros and cons of every item, applied to a whole series of questions of current interest ($\Delta\iota\sigma\sigma\sigmaο\grave{\iota}$ $\lambdaό\gammaο\iota$, *Vorsokr.*, 90). In Athens itself the whole tone of ordinary social intercourse grew much more free, and became later on a model of "urbanity"[35] for the Romans ($\dot{\alpha}\sigma\tau\varepsilonιό\tau\eta\varsigma$). And Plato took obvious pleasure, in the first book of *The Republic*, in contrasting it with the uncouth Dorian manners of Thrasymachus.

The intention of Pericles, however, was not that this education be the privilege of a small section of the population.[36] His democracy was to be a cultured state where, through the free play of their powers, all citizens – whether active or simply by enjoying – should have a share in the benefits of the full life.[37] For all his people the saying was true: "We love beauty but have simple tastes and we love wisdom while remaining energetic." Athens too knows poverty. But "to acknowledge poverty openly in Athens is nothing to be ashamed of, but it is shameful not to avert poverty by working". "Nevertheless we have taken care to provide recreations after work of many kinds through competitive games and sacrifices, which we organise in accordance with tradition, the whole year through, as well as magnificent private works, which every day are a joy to behold and keep discontent at bay." (Pericles, in Thucydides, II, 40, 1 and 38, 1). Pericles assumes in his Athenians not that anxiety, which many people like to introduce even into the Greeks of the Classical period, but joy, which is receptive for all beauty and magnificence and encourages constructive participation in it. Even Euripides, who found all superficial optimism thoroughly repellent, says that the poet must in the act of creation, enjoy contentment if he is to communicate it to his hearers (*Suppl.*, 180). We are still able today to feel something of the creative joy which filled the simple Athenian, when we see with what loving care even the tiniest details on the frieze of the Parthenon are executed, details which can scarcely be appreciated by an observer standing on the ground below. And when we admire how many different figures on that frieze, of men and gods in so many different attitudes, are all performing their proper task with the same skill and grace, we have the best illustration of the ideal of the Athenian as conceived by Pericles. Apart from the fulness of life, there is one thing in particular which delights us: the freedom of movement which reveals a feeling for life completely different from that in archaic art. We meet it again in the paintings on the vases or on the monuments. And just as the figures there gradually enter into closer contact with one another, so we experience the same in the drama. At the opening of Aeschylus' play *Seven against Thebes*, King Eteocles, his attendant, and the people still stand stiffly beside each other like a picture on an archaic vase, without ever arriving at real conversation. In the *Electra* of Sophocles, however, brother and sister have long been in spiritual communion before the actual recognition occurs.

Just as the works of architecture and the plastic arts were everyday experiences for all the citizens, so was good poetry to be. By providing the entrance money Pericles enabled even the poorest citizen to attend theatrical performances, and he managed to see that this possibility did not simply gratify a momentary desire for a show. Aristophanes could count on the interest and understanding of all spectators when in the *Frogs* he compared the art of the old master Aeschylus with that of the modern Euripides, alluded to a number of different plays and thus portrayed the whole history of tragedy.

The general educational level was higher than in many modern "enlightened" states. None of the Athenians was illiterate. Even the itinerant sausage-vendor in the *Knights* of Aristophanes who is the representative of the uneducated type, is able to read and write (189).

Moreover, the free democracy also avoided all interference with private life. There was no compulsory education nor state schools. It is therefore all the more remarkable that in all public affairs the State looked upon concern for culture as its own obligation. By far the largest items in the state budget under Pericles were the cost of the monumental buildings on the Acropolis, of sculpture and painting, the gymnasia, baths, religious festivals and institutions of general utility. Most fruitful of all was the stimulus arising out of the artistic competitions at the festivals of Diony-sus. It is hard for us today to imagine all that it meant in a time full of unrest and uncertainty, that dramatic art not only brought recreation and aesthetic pleasure to the whole society, but also tried to give moral and religious guidance, and that Sophocles' grave warning against lack of faith offered the common people a substitute for a philosophy that was too high for them, as indeed for the sermon which was unknown in the Greek religious service. During the festival of Dionysus the comedy developed from carnival extravaganza into state-regulated plays, which even in the sternest times could relieve depression with its liberating laughter and which, with its unrestrained impudence, could only flourish in a democracy, where freedom of speech was the supreme value.

The State commemoration of the fallen, introduced after the Persian Wars, provided the first opportunity to create works of art in prose, and the debates in the People's Assembly had much the same effect. The Athenians had such a discerning ear that they expected excellence of form from the speakers. Clumsy treatment of the mother tongue, such as we have experienced in Germany since the 1918 revolution, would have been impossible in Athens even in the most radically democratic period. The spoken word became the great wielder of power, which swayed minds in the Assembly, before the courts and in society as it willed. That, too, is what drove young men to the Sophists. But even more effective than schooling in the technique of rhetoric, was the regular discussion of the problems of man's life that were cultivated here and taught everybody to propound for himself his point of view, though at the same time opening the way to boundless subjectivity.

Out of that soil now sprang the most vigorous personalities, who in every sphere of life blazed fresh trails. In this period we meet such men outside of Athens too, in the arts as well as the sciences, and most of all in medicine, where alongside the great Hippocrates a whole host of independent scholars stand, most of whom we cannot even name. In the writings that have come down to us, we meet one outstanding characteristic, the enormous urge to independence which prevents any teacher from founding a school and the learners from becoming a homogeneous group who "swear by the master's word". That freedom was assuredly the force behind the steady progress of research.

It may well impress us even more that with the same freedom of spirit, such different men as Aeschylus, Sophocles, and Euripides in Athens, create their works from their personal attitudes to life. It is impressive too that Herodotus, without having any real forerunner, should lay the foundation of the art of historical writing and that then Thucydides, engaged in polemics against him and guided by a mind of his own, advanced further along that road and even undertook that hazardous enterprise of studying and writing down the history of his own times.

Self-reliance and liberty were the distinguishing marks of those men's lives and works. But that does not mean self-will. There is no room for that in art or in science. For the Greeks the formative element in art lies not in the free play of fantasy but in *mimesis*, the imitation of something objective and given. Polycletus of the Peloponnese even went so far as to write down dimensions for the proportions of the human body, and made it a duty for sculptors to observe that "canon". The plastic art of Attica is as inconceivable without careful study of man's body, as is medicine. The Greek artist is inspired by the object which he represents.

The same applies to poetry. Tragedy was objectively restricted by the fact that it was part of a state cult. Its external forms were thus for the main part firmly established, and so bold an innovator as Euripides himself could not consider eliminating the chorus although he makes play and chorus more independent of each other and so separates the choric ode from the dialogue. Similarly, unity of place and time – though by no means inviolable – was a rule imposed by the stage itself. Still deeper was the compulsion to represent in subject-matter nothing more than the myth itself, and we still can see clearly how Euripides was at pains to preserve his own freedom of invention within that framework and render the sacred story rewarding for his contemporaries. But we recognise also how conscious he remains of the limits imposed upon his art by the fact that it was presented during a religious festival. The spiritual significance which the personal faith of Aeschylus attributed to the myth was certainly given by him a new interpretation and a wider poetic range, but the tragedian's duty as moral and religious educator of his people remains his highest law, and he takes it no less seriously than his predecessors had done. It was only with such dramatists as Agathon that tragedy first became mere "play".

In science the Ionians had already discovered the guiding concept of *logos*, which presupposes the researcher's powers of synthesis while tying him down to the empirically observed raw material which he has to assemble and work upon. It is quite clear, however, that the earliest natural philosophers postulated, with the eye of genius, a basic element and proceeded from that hypothesis to explain the facts of experience. In the fifth century there were for a time men who even began airy speculations about the "basic element" of the body[38], but the empiricists immediately defended their position with success, insisting on strict observation of the objective facts and urging the anatomical study of the human body; we recall in that connection Polycletus, who probably was taught by doctors. In a work that has come down to us we find the dogmatic statement: "The nature of the body is the starting point of the doctor's art", and Hippocrates in one of his early writings proclaimed that the distinguishing mark of medical science against quackery was its recognition that the great teacher is nature, whose laws are the path that doctors must follow.

Heraclitus had already explained: "Wisdom is to say and to do what is true in accordance with nature, and to listen to her" (*Vorsokr.*, 22B, 112). In this context we must note that the Greek word *aletheia* means "naked truth" as well as that which in reality exists. Parmenides too aimed at showing man the "true" way (*Vorsokr.*, 28B, 8, 17; 8, 28; 1, 30). Thus the conception of critical scientific research has clearly been grasped and everyone who claimed allegiance to it given not only an objective but also an obligation precluding all subjectivity. When at the end of the sixth century Hekataeus of Miletus undertook to rationalize the mythical tradition, he was still able to set forth as his programme: "I am here writing what to me appears to be true: for the tales of the Greeks are diverse and in my opinion, ridiculous"[39] (*FGrHist.*, 1, fr. 1). When Herodotus decided to narrate the history of the Greek war of liberation, he was not only quite clear himself that that great theme set limits to his love of the fabulous, but also recognised something greater still: if he wanted to describe the war as it "really" had been, then he must put himself under the inviolable law of *aletheia* which imposed upon him throughout his research the most painstaking investigation of the facts and, in their presentation, absolute impartiality and veracity. By so doing he became the father of the historian's craft. And another consideration, which he practised intuitively, was clearly and consciously formulated by Thucydides: "The historian has not only the right but also the duty to form his own personal opinion about events; yet his subjective freedom is limited by the law of *aletheia*, which requires of him something over and above the will to truth, namely his adherence to a strict method which, so far as is humanly possible, leads to establishing objectively the actual facts." The natural philosophers had already been looking for a reliable way of penetrating "from the visible phenomenon to the invisible reality of the object"[40], and in mathematics the need for an exact method had long since been making itself felt. This demand was now applied to the humanities.

How anxious Thucydides was to observe these fundamental principles himself can be seen in every page of his work. But above all that objectivity which pervades the whole work has rightly been admired. Even when writing of events which concerned him personally and led to his unjust condemnation by the Athenians, his presentation remains purely factual, and the historian produces not a word in defence of his own case. Nowhere does any resentment or bitterness towards his native city appear.

The freedom to adopt a subjective point of view while voluntarily restricting oneself by observing the law of *aletheia* are both fundamental to Greek learning.

In these domains, too, the growing individualism naturally made itself felt. But if this proved on the whole destructive in political life – and by undermining the old patriotism it was in fact responsible, more than anything else, for the downfall of the *polis* – it was another matter altogether in the fields of science and of art. In the tragedies of Euripides there certainly were influences at work which not only led to the devitalisation of the old forms and transforming the odes of the chorus into musical virtuoso pieces, but also as a result of turning away from the old religious faith, threaten the very basis of tragedy. But the poet himself still intends to observe the highest law of his art, and there is on the other hand no doubt that the new development brings enrichment of poetry. The more the gods recede from the field of vision, the more prominently man occupies it with tragedies of his own. Figures like Medea, shaped entirely by the poet's own imagination, who out of boundless thirst for revenge kills her children and destroys her own life, would have been just as inconceivable in the old tragedy as the spiritual torments of the love-sick Phaedra. Sophocles himself in his youth had not known the psychological depths touched in the recognition scene in the *Electra*.[41]

The dawn of a new age is particularly evident in the attempt in the plastic arts to give individuality to the portrayal of the human form. Already in the early period the statues had certainly been intended to bring back to mind real people, loved ones who had died. But at that time people were primarily members of a society, and it was a tendency deeply rooted in the Hellenic spirit for the artist to try to penetrate the particular accidentals of outer appearance to find the inner essence and so, unintentionally, give to their figures common human traits. Gradually the piety of the bereft required that individual characteristics be more vigorously brought out. Admittedly the head of Pericles by Cresilas clearly shows the attempt to reveal the man's individual personality with its combination of great intellect and sense of moral responsibility, but it is still far from being a portrait in the modern sense. That came about gradually, only after the individual had long been prominent in real life. And, just as in poetry, the new way of looking at things led the artist to try to express character in ways unknown in the archaic period. In other ways too this new spirit expresses itself in the art of the fourth century. There is no thought, however, of disregarding the authority of the old rules. It is a further development but not in any sense decadent, like its counterpart in politics.

In Democritus science gained a scholar of universal interests who could build on the achievements of the Ionian natural philosophers and doctors as well as the ontology of Parmenides, and thus arrive at a quite new conception of the universe. How far the way was smoothed for him by Leucippus of Miletus we cannot, unfortunately, establish with certainty. But this much is assured: by employing a brilliant hypothesis, Democritus was the first to raise the atomic theory to a scientific account of the nature of the world by verifying it with untiring, exact, detailed research. He had also assimilated the views of his fellow-countryman Protagoras. But the measure of all things was for him not subjective man but the objective *aletheia*, which it was the scholar's business to discover.

In Athens, people were at first so much involved in the practical problems of everyday life (a matter we can look at in greater detail later on), that the world-wide outlook of the Ionians could only be felt marginally. As in art, so also in thought, man himself was becoming the centre of interest. The subjectivity of the Sophists indicates that man means to claim for himself complete personal freedom as opposed to external things. In consequence, however, individuals tended to lose all sense of direction in the conduct of their lives. The fact that this can be found only in acknowledging an objective good and submitting to its authority is what Socrates wanted to make his fellow Athenians fully conscious of, and Plato provided a metaphysical basis for his teacher's conviction by fitting man and the whole of human life into the whole world process and demonstrating that everything in our cosmos acquires value and significance only through participation in the idea of the good which operates in it. In matters of detail he was not too proud to learn from Democritus and the natural philosophers but gradually he worked out ever more sharply this fundamental difference of view. In his last work the central part is a vehement attack on materialism, which disregards the fact that not matter but spirit is the basis of all existence and all values and must also be the sole criterion of human behaviour (*Laws*, 889–899).

Thus the philosophic antithesis of materialism and idealism owes its inception to the freely expressed opinions of the Greeks. It likewise shows us how even men who are impelled by the same urge towards truth and recognize truth as their only law, can nevertheless arrive at contradictory conclusions. Such is the lot of man.

Over and above the commitment to truth and the laws arising from the nature of their discipline, there was yet another obligation laid upon those engaged in science and the arts. As political beings they felt that their achievements had significance only insofar as they somehow benefitted the community. Aristophanes [42] considered it self-evident that to better and advance mankind was the highest duty not of tragedy alone; of his own comedies too, he said, it was "proper" that they should serve the state by giving good counsel. Thucydides does not write in order to entertain his audience, but not for the pleasure of creativity either; his work is to be "a possession for all ages" where future statesmen prepared to learn from history can find bases for political discernment. Plato found it hard that his people did not want to listen to him, and he made it a duty for the philosophers of his ideal state to serve the whole community with their wisdom and abilities. The modern concept of a quest for knowledge for its own sake was completely unknown to the Greeks of the Classical period.

What, then, was the attitude of the political community to culture? Certainly Pericles was speaking from his heart when he claimed for all the Athenians the love for the true and the beautiful (see above p. 36) and, like the individual personality so too the arts and sciences were to be allowed complete freedom for their development. How liberal the state was in this respect may be best judged from the comedies which, with their criticism of public affairs during the national festivals, took liberties far beyond anything tolerated in our modern Fasching celebrations in Germany. There were, of course, various attempts to check their un-bridled impertinence on the grounds that it endangered the interests of the state but these were short-lived and had little effect. For us it is almost inconceivable that immediately after the rebel confederate city of Mitylene had been subdued, the young Aristophanes wrote in the year 426 a comedy in which the confederates – in the presence of their official delegations – were represented as Babylonian slaves. It is understandable that the leading statesman Cleon intervened and demanded in the Council that the producer responsible be punished.[43] But when the latter excused himself on the grounds that in his criticism the poet had not been attacking the state, but only the leading statesmen, the Council let him go. And two years later when Aristophanes, who had grown over-bold, launched in the *Knights* an extraordinarily pointed attack on Cleon in person, he was even awarded first prize. This freedom of the stage was part of the free-dom of speech, *parrhesia*, which accorded to the individual the legal right to say "whatever he liked to say"; and the people were of no mind to let that pillar of their democracy be undermined.

Still less was the government inclined to bother about the opinions which were expressed by the Sophists in private circles or circulated only in literature. Nevertheless, even in these cases, the interests of the com-munity might make intervention necessary. And there was one point about which the masses were extremely susceptible. However keen any individual criticism might be that was directed at the old popular beliefs, the conviction was equally firmly rooted that the existence and the prosperity of the state depended on the favourable disposition of the local gods, and that their ancient and sacred rites must therefore be strictly observed. Particularly in times of stress this led to legal prosecution on grounds of *asebeia* and these could become very dangerous, the more so if political factors were also involved. The respectable Athenian artisans might well be horrified when they heard that Anaxagoras, who had come from Ionia, considered Helios only a mass of glowing stone; nevertheless he might well have been left alone if his accusers had not seen in him the friend of Pericles.[44] Anytus and Meletus explicitly complain that Socrates wanted to replace the official gods by other "demonic" beings. However, they did not consider this accusation adequate themselves and therefore added that he exercised "a pernicious influence upon youth". That made their real motive clear. At a time when the sole object of the leading politicians was the material reconstruction of Athens, they might consider it a danger to the state if the young men were listening to someone who argued that all the things they were striving for were worthless if the spirit of the citizens did not fundamentally alter.

The freedom of learning was an integral part of democratic freedom. But for the authorities the interest of the state was more important; and on the question whether this was being damaged it was not specialist lawyers who had to decide, but a court of sworn jurors who could be swayed by their feelings and the prevailing atmosphere.

INNER FREEDOM

Introspection

The bourgeois-democratic ideal of freedom did not end the distinction between free men and slaves existing in private law. The economic prosperity following the Persian Wars resulted in a vast new increase in the number of slaves. In the big concerns, the mines and in shipping, manpower was urgently needed. Rich people like Nicias found it more profitable to invest their money not in property but in slaves, whom they then hired out to contractors. The final result of this was a sharp cleavage between social classes. But the gulf was not unbridgeable. Among the slaves were a good many who, working on their own though under their masters' instructions and for his profit, earned enough to be able after a time to buy themselves free. And so an ever-increasing number of people could give thanks to Zeus Eleutherios for their personal freedom. Once this goal had been achieved the way was clear for rising still higher. The freed men joined the social class of their free fellow-citizens; but in the fourth century there were so many former slaves, particularly in banking concerns, who had earned for themselves through their business capacity considerable fortunes and had acquired not only civic rights but also a distinguished standing in society, and it did not much matter if their appearance and manners were strikingly unhellenic.

At a time when all human institutions were being examined as to whether they had originated in nature or in human custom, it was to be expected that this scrutiny would extend to the institution of slavery. Admittedly it is not until 366 that the orator Alcidamas proclaimed "God conferred freedom on all men, and nature made no man a slave" (1S), and his purpose is only to defend the natural right of the Messenians in their war for liberation from the tyrannical Spartans. But clearly his formulation is based on the general discussion of the origins of slavery, and public discussion of this kind had been going on long before Aristotle discussed in detail in his *Politics* (I, 4–6), whether there were men who were 'slaves by nature'. The reasons for his affirmative answer and his justification of slavery from the ethical point of view must be considered later. But even his opponents never seriously considered the abolition of slavery. Slave and freeman, like man and woman, is one of those antithetical expressions which describe the self-evident contrasts which make up the whole of mankind.[45]

On the whole slaves were very well-treated. Thus in Athens the oligarch mentioned above (p. 33) was shocked because the slaves shared in the democratic freedom in word and deed[46], and that you could not box the ears of somebody's slave for impertinence without running the risk of action in a court of law. The fact that it was usual in Athens to use the familiar term "boy" ($\pi\alpha\tilde{\imath}$) when addressing a slave was noticed in antiquity. As children grew up for the most part under the care of suitable servants, a relationship of close devotion often developed. In the new drama, both the pedagogue who guides the boy as he grows up and helps him play tricks, and the nurse who accompanies the girl to her new home after marriage and remains her confidante, became typical stage characters. Aeschylus presents us, at the beginning of the *Agamemnon*, with the trusted servant whose one wish is to shake his master's hand again when he returns. Similarly, in order to make his Athenians realise that this is a human problem, Euripides takes pleasure in introducing as a character the "noble" slave.[47]

> Some slaves are servile only in their rank;
> In spirit they are freer than the free.

In his plays the thought occurs no less than six times. And so with Sophocles:

> The flesh may be enslaved, the mind is free.

Homer's Eumaeus complains that servitude robs men of half their powers. Attic humanity goes far beyond that. From behind the external juridical concepts of slavery and freedom there emerges a new freedom, the freedom of the mind which alone determines a man's real worth. And this freedom the slave too can have within him.

Such ideas are all the more compelling because the Greeks always see a thing together with its antithesis.[48] Among the women characters of the Homeric saga there is one in particular who appeals to Euripides. She is Hector's wife, Andromache, who, according to the epic is handed over by the harsh, unfeeling victors to the son of Achilles, her husband's murderer, as a slave captured in war. In the play that bears her name we see how she is forced as the concubine of Neoptolemus to share his bed and has even borne him a son, but in her heart of hearts belongs only to her Hector, even in slavery never loses her queenly dignity and as a mother is prepared without faltering to lay down her life for her child. Opposed to her stands Hermione, the lawful wife of Neoptolemus, whom she must obey and who believes herself entitled, because of all her wealth and ostentation, not only to "speak freely" and abuse her rival in the basest way but also attempts treacherously to bring about the death of mother and child. In her "kingly" father Menelaus she finds a helper who is even more unscrupulous (if that is possible) than herself. Euripides' hatred of "perfidious Sparta" is seen unmistakably in his sketch of both of them. But elsewhere too, he portrays free men who are vastly inferior to the "free-minded" slave, and that type of man was so numerous that the language had to find a term for it. It was not for genuine slaves but for men of that stamp that the term "unfree" (ἀνελεύθερος)[49] was coined, as a foil for the ἐλευθέριος, the "men who lived freely", who were not only free legally but who, because of their whole appearance, and still more, of their disposition, gave evidence of deserving that honoured title. The word was particularly current in aristocratic circles, where (as later in the Latin word *liberalis*) it signified in particular the generosity of the noble man and his liberality. Such nobility of mind (*eleutheriotes*) could be applied to that freedom of attitude which according to Pericles characterised all Athenians and made them equal to the old aristocracy. This Athenian society was, after all, the soil in which the idea of 'spiritual' freedom had grown, even if the antithesis to slavery had caused the crystallisation of the concept.

The new conception of liberty however created new problems. The citizen of a free democracy ought to be able as the formula soon ran, "to live as he likes".[50] Was not that too high an aim? Just at the time when the new ideal was making Athenian hearts beat higher, they were surprised to hear from Aeschylus in his *Prometheus*[51] the significant words "Nobody is free but Zeus" (50). They are spoken by one of the new ruler's magistrates. Even the god Hephaestus has to recognise them as only too true. And even the freedom of Zeus was to be restricted later on, for there was something that bound him also. That was Necessity, "whose course is steered by the three Fates and the vengeful Furies" (515). We are not, of course, to imagine that the real government of the world is in the hands of old women. We may remember the words of Heraclitus (B 94) "Helios will not depart from the path prescribed for him: or else the Erinyes will find him out". The Greeks knew no transcendent creator God. For them the cosmos comes first and Zeus himself is bound to a world-order and lives within it. Only this attitude explains how Aeschylus could have in his tragedy the theme that Prometheus takes up a weapon against Zeus, for he knew that the new ruler of the world was, like his predecessors, threatened with the danger of being overthrown by a stronger son in the event of his taking the goddess Thetis to wife. There can be no doubt that in the last part of the tragedy, after Prometheus has revealed this secret, Zeus renounces the desired union. In doing so, he is bowing to the law of necessity. He recognises that his freedom, too, is limited, and he is then called upon to become the guardian of the world-order.

But if the ruler of the world is himself bound to some higher order, how could men be able to live as they please? Soon we hear not only Aeschylus warning his Athenians not to overstrain the idea of freedom (cf. p. 30f.); Pericles too expected his citizens to obey the authorities and the law. We have had to discuss how the new generation tried to shake off these heavy chains. But did that make them really free? There is no need to consider straight away the limitations imposed upon them by the worldorder and the avenging gods. Was the poor man really free when it was his everyday experience that "The poor are powerless although they are free", and when for the sake of his daily bread he was compelled to enter into service and do whatever his master required? In the *Phoenician Women* of Euripides, Polynices gives his mother a description of the bitter lot of the emigrant, who, like a slave "dare not utter an unguarded word", and must, despite his better nature, humiliate himself before ignorant men. And how then do the mighty of this earth fare? Are they free?

Euripides [52] shows us in his *Hecuba* how the old, sorrow-laden queen finally learns of the treacherous murder of her only surviving young son by her guest, the Thracian King Polymestor, for money. The crime is so atrocious that even the victorious Greek commander Agamemnon would like to help her in her understandable designs for revenge. But he does not, for the Greeks would take it amiss if he gave support to his enemy against the official allies. Hecuba knows enough about human life to understand:

> Truly no mortal man is ever free.
> He is the slave of money or of fate,
> Or pressure of the people or the law
> Prevent him acting as his will decides.

Man's whole life is caught up in a network of conventional views and social obligations that keep even the most powerful from moving freely.

Is man in a position to escape all these restrictions and to preserve his freedom of action?

Whereas in the *Hecuba*, Agamemnon retains his kingly dignity in spite of everything, Euripides shows him in quite another light in his last play, *Iphigenia in Aulis* [53], written some two decades later. The situation is the same as the one Aeschylus had placed Agamemnon in before. But whereas in Aeschylus' play, having once submitted to the yoke of necessity, he represses his paternal love with iron resolution and offers up his daughter in sacrifice, since he regards this as his unquestionable duty to the army, the picture painted by Euripides is entirely different. When Calchas insists upon Iphigenia being sacrificed, her father's first reaction is "Impossible!" But under the influence of Menelaus he quickly decides to do the impossible. And in order to get his daughter into the army encampment, stoops to a disgraceful lie to his wife, pretending Iphigeneia is to marry Achilles. But the message is hardly despatched before he wants it recalled and keeps being torn between conflicting feelings; when at last he does "submit to the yoke of Necessity" – the allusion to Aeschylus is obvious – he is compelled not by obedience to the goddess or moral obligation to the army, but fear of the Greeks who will call him to account: "For we are simply slaves of the masses."

The heroic king of the saga and the dedicated leader of his army has become a pitiful weakling, who lets himself be swayed because he does not have within himself the strength to act according to his own judgment, the sort of caricature which Euripides could certainly model on certain political personalities of his time. It is their own inner weakness that robs men of their freedom.

The sketch is the more striking because, as so often happens, Euripides shows the opposite in the same play. Pious Chiron has nourished in young Achilles the simple robust frame of mind which keeps him self-reliant among life's turmoils and recognises only *arete* as his guiding star, and is determined now, as he will be before the walls of Troy, to defend his "free way of life". Unperturbed by the opinions of the Greeks or his own people, who even threaten to stone him to death, he alone champions Iphigenia, and his idealistic energy carries Iphigenia with him. She recognises that she, a weak girl, has the high mission of ensuring the Greek victory over the barbarians, who must become their subjects, and as a free human being she willingly embraces death. It is a person's inner attitude that matters, for this can give a man freedom of choice, even when he is unable to alter the outer march of events.

If in this matter we are to understand the poet fully we must carry our study still further.

The Self

There has been a tendency to assert that Homeric man has no awareness of the self[54] because he has not yet realised the unity of the psyche but only speaks of the various organs and functions, like the heart and the dia-

50

phragm, reason and passionate rage, *thymos*. Yet when Odysseus sees the shameless behaviour of the maidservants but restrains his angry heart and warns it not to indulge in hasty retribution and endanger the main object, the overpowering of the suitors, then precisely that "self" is speaking, which lies behind and above the several organs, the "man" of whom the muse in the introductory lines is speaking to the poet, the man who, with his plans and his actions, holds the whole thing together as an integrated personality. That self is in evidence ever since Hesiod, whenever an individual consciously sets himself against the great majority, because he is capable of revealing a truth that others do not know. In lyric poetry the self comes out with such force that the poet dares to express in front of others what moves him most deeply. It enables Archilochus to formulate perfectly clear principles to arm himself against fate in the varying fortunes of life (fr. 67a). The decisive turning point, here too, came with the Persian Wars when more and more individual personalities rose above the general mass, so that Pericles could now advocate for every citizen the independence of the formed personality which, conscious of its responsibility, moulds its life to its own measure.

The time was not yet ripe for theoretical discussions about the nature of personality – that first came with Hellenism – but the time had come for the great art of expressing the spirit of the age in living characters and events.[55] The great achievement of tragedy was to interpret mythological events in terms of human experience. This might cause events themselves to puzzle the religious thinker and incline him to a private interpretation of their meaning, but the poet saw in them men of flesh and blood and so, in drama as well as in sculpture, man was in the centre of the picture.

It may be asked whether Greek tragedy presented "characters" as that word is understood in modern aesthetics. There can be no reasonable doubt that the poet saw complete personalities in whom, as art criticism in antiquity already required, word and deed sprang from the inner core of their beings. The deeply moving impression of tragedy depends after all upon its not simply presenting "tragic situations" into which any random mortal may be flung who through some momentary decision succeeds or fails, but showing how a man's fate is bound up with his whole being, and that it is this whole, responsible man who proves for Aeschylus the truth of the old saying: "Whoever acts must suffer". With a poet who uttered the proud words: "I think differently from the world, even if alone"[56] we

51

can well understand why he was attracted by those powerful personalities of the myths who each experienced as an individual his own fate to the full.

"After the battle of Thapsus", writes Cicero, "many Romans surrendered to Caesar; only Cato could not, because – he was Cato, and that Cato could not survive the fall of the free State".[57] Here the Roman is indebted to the Greek Panaetius, who was the first to appreciate the moral significance of individual personality. But Panaetius himself had learnt from the tragedy and drawn attention to Ajax who would never have been able to do or to countenance anything conflicting with his own nature and his conception of honour. "Nobody will say you ever uttered a word not coming from your very self", Sophocles has the chorus say when it hears of Ajax' decision to die (*Ajax*, 481), and nobody knows better than Ajax himself that he must take that decision just because he is Ajax, because his own personality will not let him bear a life of shame. He is destroyed by his own nature. That is his tragedy. Even so, he remains a free man, himself determining his fate.

The superstition that Greek tragedy is a fatalistic tragedy where an invisible hand controls men like puppets will presumably not disappear as long as dilettantes speak about Greek tragedy on the basis of their sixth-form knowledge of Greek poetry. In reality the tragic hero of the Greeks is in conflict with Fate which threatens him from without. In the fight he may be crushed physically, but that does not mean that he is handed over defenceless to external forces. He has within himself something to set against them. It is the lot of man that he must always be prepared for suffering. That fact he cannot change. But he has in him the power to decide how he will bear that suffering. That inner attitude is what matters and it can enable him even in physical defeat to save what is most precious in him, his personality, his self.

Precisely that is what the tragedies enable us to experience most profoundly.

In Aeschylus the desire to grasp the significance of suffering often leads to the conclusion that man's will to independence leads to *hybris*, overstepping the limitations imposed upon him by the divine order, and the attempt to do this brings certain disaster. But just as the Titan Prometheus fulfils himself only by voluntary submission to the authority of Zeus, so too can man master his fate by willing surrender to what the world order requires of him.[58] The Theban trilogy ends with Eteocles' departure for a civil war that fills him with horror and from which he knows he will never return. He cannot escape his father's curse – the most crushing human fate imaginable. And yet the situation has for him a most elevating effect. This the poet achieves through the preceding scene where the women of the chorus passionately implore Eteocles to abandon his plan, but he refuses to do this, since his honour as a soldier will not let him (677–719). The Athenians in Aeschylus' time knew nothing about the problem of free will and all that they could feel, or were meant to feel here is that Eteocles chooses his own path and that the decision he takes comes from his own personality. The external events are prescribed by his father's curse. But by making this course of events part of his own will Eteocles transforms it into a moral act redeeming the sin of his ancestor Laius. We have already met him as a prince with only one aim, one mission in life: the preservation of his native city. In deciding to go to his death he fulfils himself. Physically he is destroyed, but what he saves is not only Thebes but his true self as well.

Sophocles makes Antigone, as she is going to her death, break into heart-rending lamentation because she has to die for her pious deed. Yet not for one moment does the conviction leave her that she has acted rightly and she has had to act that way. The chorus[59] can object: "You yourself have chosen... It is your own ruling that you will be the only mortal to go down into Hades alive." To this one young girl the expression "autonomous" is applied, though it generally expresses the right to self-government of the free city-state. Antigone herself had previously appealed to the ancient unwritten law which made it her duty to bury her brother. But when, unlike her sister Ismene, she summons up strength enough to translate her religious conviction into action, this is her free decision; and, just as for Eteocles, the death she takes upon herself is the fulfilment of her personality.

The Antigone of Sophocles, unlike Anouilh's, does not confront life with weary scepticism. She loves life with all its joys and hopes and for her to give it up is a real sacrifice. She does it nevertheless because the inner voice tells her that there is something higher than this life. That is what gives her the freedom and the conviction to choose her own path and she is triumphant, although she is physically destroyed.

The idea of sacrifice also inspires the oldest play that has come down to us from Euripides. Alcestis too finds it extremely hard to surrender life. She nevertheless spontaneously declares herself ready to die for Admetus

53

not out of any passionate upsurge of love but because she considers it her obvious duty to save her husband's life. That is why the chorus recognises that she has given proof of the highest virtue as a woman. And when the funeral procession has left the stage[60], we hear a hymn which tells first of the inescapable power of *ananke*, which destroyed this woman like others before, but closes with the prospect that Alcestis will live on as a blessed spirit and be honoured like the gods. Thus even iron necessity does not touch the inner core of man.

From then onwards the voluntary sacrificial death[61] becomes for the poet a favourite theme which, regardless of the repetition, he uses time after time. In the old saga a divinity very often claimed a human sacrifice as the price of her assistance. Euripides seized upon this theme, sometimes even introducing it himself, but altered it radically. Already in the *Children of Heracles*, and similarly in the *Alcestis*, we can clearly see what he is aiming at. The Attic King Demophon is ready to protect the children of Heracles from their persecutors, but Persephone claims as the price of her assistance the sacrifice of a virgin. The eldest daughter of Heracles has no sooner heard this than her mind is made up. She offers to sacrifice herself "of free will and not through persuasion by others", and will not consider the suggestion that lots be drawn between the sisters. "Freely do I sacrifice my life and not by force. For only the deed freely done has merit" (531, 548, 551). Some years later the *Hecuba* was first performed. Then the shade of Achilles demands the sacrifice of Priam's daughter Polyxena and for reasons of state the Greeks decide to give her up. Thus for Polyxena there is no choice between life and death. But she still has one thing: the possibility of dying honourably. "Loose my chains", she implores the Greeks, "so that I may die free", and her bearing makes such a deep impression that even the simple Greek soldiers vie with one another to pay the last honours to her when she dies (550ff).

The same thread runs through the *Phoenician Women*, where Creon's young son even uses a stratagem in order to sacrifice his life against his father's will, and on to Iphigenia's free willingness to die in Aulis for the sake of the army. The Athenians will have recognised in this the poet's farthest deviation from the popular saga, which regarded Iphigenia as an object with no will. But they must also have felt what actually led Euripides to write scenes of that kind: what in the saga had been divine compulsion, was for him the freely willed action of man, the passive suffering of one's fate had become an act of one's own, a moral deed, arising from a man's free decision, and precisely this is what lends these scenes their tragic character.

The tragedy has its deepest roots in the painful feeling of the Greeks that their innate urge to master their lives comes up against the opposition of external powers which determine what happens. For them "I will" and the saying "nobody can escape his fate" are fundamental experiences. That does not however lead to fatalism or resignation. For they know that they hold in their hands a weapon to deal with fate that none can take away. That is the freedom of their own attitude to events. Man has the power to remain true to himself even in the face of death. He can preserve the best part of him, his individual personality, even in physical destruction. Therein lies his freedom and his greatness. That is what still moves us in Greek tragedy today and what moved the ancient Greeks in such figures as Eteocles, Antigone and Alcestis.

Freedom of the Person and Its Religious-Ethical Limitations [62]

Attic tragedy was part of the official religious observance and did not aim at entertaining a random collection of the public, but at the inner development of the citizens as a whole and was intended to "make the people in the *polis* better citizens". This is how Aristophanes in the *Frogs* makes Euripides answer Aeschylus' question as to the purpose of tragedy (1009), and the comic playwright can assume that he is expressing the attitude of all his fellow citizens. For precisely that reason in an age not yet ready to think through rationally the general problems of life, tragedy could take upon itself the guidance of the people in intellectual and ethical matters. It did this by reinterpreting the old myths and making them alive and instructive for the new age. The essence of the tragic art was to bring before men's eyes the fate of individual human beings. But for the new way of thinking there was one feature which always seemed the most significant: man is not merely an animal but has within him something which raises him above the animals. He is a personality acting on his own judgment, responsible for his own acts and having to bear the consequences. Responsibility however presupposes freedom of decision. For the tragedians therefore the freedom of men is self-evident, even if in the archaic period – of which more later – higher powers might interfere, and they have contributed most of all to awakening and crystallising in man the consciousness of his freedom.

But for them human freedom is not absolute. For that age a man has not yet become an individual, he is a member of a community with which he is by nature inseparably bound up and towards which he has binding duties. As we have heard already (p. 30f.) even before Pericles, Aeschylus had warned through the lips of the goddess of their land against such misuse of freedom as would cast off all fear and obligation and repudiate obedience to the inviolable laws. But above the city state and its commandments there was for him a higher authority. Like Heraclitus (B 114), Aeschylus is deeply convinced that "all human laws are derived from the one divine law". His Oresteian trilogy reaches its climax in the glorification of the city state, which dares to risk, through a court of free men, to settle the disputes that break out even between the gods. But this they only dare because God himself has entrusted them with this duty, and the free judges must remain aware that they are responsible to the power that gave them authority. The state, too, which has defended its freedom against human threats, is not absolutely free. It is not an arbitrary collection of men in their own right; it is part of a whole and its nature is determined by the divine world order to which it owes its existence. In this cosmic order it is laid down that each being has its alloted sphere which it may not with impunity overstep. And as Zeus the ruler of the world binds himself to this order of his own free will (cf. p. 48), so he requires as much from mankind, from the individual and from the *polis*. It is the tragedy of man that his urge to independence also contains the urge to overstep the bounds set by nature, and that he has to atone for this. The mightiest of mortals, the Great King Xerxes himself, has to experience this. Such suffering is painful; but for Aeschylus it has the deep purpose of saving man from *hybris* and leading him to *sophrosyne*, which remains well aware of human limitations. Whoever has grasped that deep sense of suffering will not consider it an arbitrary dispensation but a means of education used by God to lead man along the right road. He will not therefore grumble when he comes up against difficulties, but will bow to God's will. At the same time he will not live in eternal dread of God's anger but will look up in pious reverence to him who rules the world firmly but kindly.

That is the faith which the prophet poet, not without a struggle, had won for himself and preached to his people. He too remained fully aware of human freedom but he combined with it the insight that not only outward success of actions can be thwarted by the higher powers, but that man's freedom is beneficial to him only when he remains mindful of the limits imposed on him as a man.

Sophocles too had firmly proclaimed all through his life faith in Zeus and his meaningful ordering of the world. But whereas the brooding Aeschylus could find no peace until he had found in the old myths a meaning which satisfied his moral sentiments, Sophocles considered it presumptuous for man to try in every single case to probe the thoughts of a god or to call him to account. He was satisfied with the knowledge that man is a finite being, that he must be ready to face disaster at any moment and dare not ask why. In contrast to a family given to *hybris* and imagining that man is the measure of all things, he presented on the stage a terrifying *Ecce homo* by showing how even Oedipus, the wisest of men, and Heracles, a hero of supreme physical strength, are suddenly hurled from their deceptive heights to the depths of misery. Never was the outward impotence of man more devastatingly demonstrated. And yet even these men retain the innate freedom to adopt their own attitude to fate. It may appear greater to us when the young Antigone sacrifices her life to serve a sacred cause, but it is also a free action when Oedipus by blinding himself expiates his unwitting crime, a sacrifice required of him only by his own feeling and not by any man or god. It is not Sophocles' intention in presenting these incomprehensible destinies, to arouse anxiety and despair. The devout poet retains his trust in the God who means well with men, and in his latest works it is perfectly clear that he, like Aeschylus, was striving for a solution in reconciliation. And when as an old man he shows how old, sorrow-worn Oedipus becomes a hero in death, we find in it a compensating act of divine grace corresponding to man's moral experience. It is nowadays often said that it was not on his own incentive that Oedipus offended nature's most sacred laws and that morally he is not to blame. He nevertheless has had to suffer, for he was a man. But that suffering now becomes the preliminary stage for a still higher form of being. And in his death the sufferer proves his human greatness.

For Sophocles too man's whole existence can only be understood on the basis of his right to free decision. But he is also so deeply aware of its dangers that he feels under even stronger compulsion than Aeschylus to warn his fellow-citizens against its misdirection and to remind them of the limits placed on it in the divine order of the world.

57

His passionate condemnation of the spirit of the age that wanted to free itself of all religious and moral obligations could nevertheless not prevent its development. It was no mere frivolous superficiality or pride that started the struggle against the traditional ideas. In these ideas there still survived too much of the primitive conception that the gods were simply the bearers of life and, like life itself, could not be measured by man's moral standards. It was a new religiosity governed by moral demands that made it for Euripides a pressing duty to show clearly to his Athenians how base were so many of the old myths. "A god who acts disgracefully is no god at all." Admittedly there was another problem which worried him much more. He would have shared only too gladly Aeschylus' faith in the just government of the world by Zeus. Yet in one choral ode in the *Hippolytus* there is an impressive complaint that such faith was constantly contradicted by human experience (1102ff.). That did not make him an atheist; he remained all his life a seeker after God. But could he really be positively effective as a religious teacher of his people, when he could never overcome his own doubts?

In his last works he is no longer concerned with divine justice. The poet wants to understand human destiny in purely human terms. Like the historian Thucydides, he flays mercilessly the deterioration of manners brought about by the long war and he observes with sorrow that in the place of the freedom of Pericles' day a licentiousness has grown up that recognises no limits to individual indulgence or any responsibility to God or man. He still believes in the goodness in man, and we have seen how the voluntary sacrifice of their lives by young people becomes one of his favourite themes. But he can hardly have surrendered himself to the illusion that he could have a general effect on the community either by putting such models before them or through the simple appeal to listen to one's own inner voice.

He nevertheless still wanted to be the people's teacher, a role to which he was called through his activity in the holy place. This comes out most clearly in the theoretical discussion of everyday questions which he brings up more and more in his later plays. But precisely these discussions show us that although he could shake up people's minds and make them think for themselves, he was unable to give them the firm basis they needed. His contemporaries already felt that these discussions of the "stage philosophers" had brought a foreign element into tragedy. Certainly they bear witness to the tacit recognition that poetry was no longer able to play its old role of fostering the community's moral progress. The new generation needed as its guide some other power which did not appeal to the religious sentiment; it expected an intellectual solution for every problem in life. The old question, what use could man make of his innate freedom, had again to be asked and answered.

The Self and the Good

Just at the time when tragedy was at its height, Protagoras appeared in Athens with a new educational programme. He did not aim at the whole community, but pledged himself rather to educate individual young men by giving them a better intellectual training than had been usual, in order to "make them better" – meaning thereby that they should become capable of playing a worthy part in public and private life. Neither he nor the other men who took up after him the lucrative calling of the Sophists were revolutionaries. Their goal was purely practical and took existing conditions into account. But since, in their teaching, they concentrated on the act of "persuasion", which ensured their influence on men in the courts and in the People's Assembly, and since to that end they accustomed their pupils to discuss every possible problem in terms of pro and con, they only too easily got into the habit of looking at things in a purely subjective way and the individual person became for them the "measure of all things". These discussions offered great stimulus and lots of old prejudices were discarded, but its great danger lay in the perpetual criticism which shook the old political and religious authorities and the community's ethical values without putting anything in their place. Only too many people consequently felt entitled to follow their own personal whims and this caused in the community a serious moral crisis.

The man who realised the full significance of this was Socrates. He too was a modern man who did not think of simply accepting tradition but recognised as binding only what stood the test of his intellectual examination. But he quite clearly saw not only at what point the new education broke down, but he learned to recognise the fundamental reason for the spiritual crisis of the people.

After the Persian Wars Athens had not suffered a period of reckless speculation, but there had been unprecedented progress, which resulted in a general quest of power, prestige and wealth. This tendency of the age received its greatest support from the Sophists who sought to help young people to succeed in their own efforts. But the whole trend filled Socrates with the deepest misgivings. Behind the brilliant exterior he felt the developing crisis in the lives of the people, and so he found a question, of which his fellow-citizens and the Sophists were equally unaware, namely whether his people's whole attitude to life was right or a mistake leading away from man's true goal.

Are the "good things" that men naturally strive for really good? Experience teaches daily that power and money are by no means always good for man but even do him harm when he tries to acquire them unjustly or makes bad use of them. It is not things themselves that matter, but the attitude a man adopts towards them. But this attitude cannot be left to subjective choice, for what use is it for a man to choose something that seems to him good but in reality does him harm? Good must be independent of any individual judgment, for it is equally sought by all. But only he can attain it who knows what is really good for man. Only he can live well and prove himself a good citizen in public and private life. Efficiency, ἀρετή, must not be sought in chance outward success or in the possession of wealth and power, but it lies in the inner nature of men.

This is the first time among the Greeks – or in the history of mankind – that an individual has examined fundamentally the naïvely conceived values accepted by his people and tested their validity. For Socrates the outcome is that a completely different attitude must be adopted if the intellectual and moral crisis is to be surmounted and the people's spiritual troubles resolved. Man must not pursue external good things but must himself become good, and that he can do only if he is conscious that the good is an objective value, above the individual, a value, too, which determines the value of the individual and it must be a guide in all his actions. That knowledge of the good is the only thing that a man really needs.

But this raises the hardest problem. How is a man to arrive at that knowledge? The Sophists could not help, because they could not see the problem at all, like most other people. But Socrates himself did not have that knowledge and his social sensibility even told him that no single man could attain such knowledge by himself. And so he tried, in frequent conversations with other men to get at least nearer to the intellectual common property of the Greeks and be clear about these fundamentals. But in spite of unremitting efforts he did not reach his goal and at last had to acknowledge that ultimate knowledge is only available to God. For man there remains only the age-old search for truth ($\varphi\iota\lambda o\sigma o\varphi\epsilon\tilde{\iota}\nu$). Nevertheless, for the immediate problems of everyday life many statements could be made that would stand rigorous examination. The fact that not life, but the good life, was important had been proven by the death of many a Greek. What the content of the good life was Socrates learned from the old Hellenic sense of the *polis*, which he too, as a modern man still felt as strongly as his ancestors: Man can exist only in society, and it is not an external law that prescribes for him that he must subordinate himself to that community, but an impulse of his own nature; it is the whole of which he is a member and on whose well-being his own existence depends. No society can last, however, without law and order. The individual citizen's first duty is therefore to support it himself and never to want to endanger it to his personal advantage. To act thus constitutes his moral behaviour, the beautiful, the *kalon* which already in the old city-state constituted the highest human value. This ideal of the moral and beautiful has certainly been disregarded through the egocentric motives of men, but particularly for the modern thinker it is clearly man's real good. For whoever thinks only of his own interests, whoever disregards the rights of his fellow-citizens and the social order, is not only undermining the stability of the state but also the very basis of his own existence, and does himself the greatest harm. Acting unjustly is not only disgraceful and hateful ($\alpha\tilde{\iota}\sigma\chi\rho\acute{o}\nu$) but the greatest evil ($\kappa\alpha\kappa\acute{o}\nu$) for the evildoer himself, a greater evil than suffering unjustly.[64]

Such statements might sound paradoxical; yet for Socrates they contained the knowledge of the true good, and how prepared he was to apply their consequences in his own life, Plato has shown in the *Crito*.

As a result of an unjust court sentence Socrates was condemned to death. Friends made every preparation for him to escape from prison and no Athenian would have considered it morally blameworthy of Socrates if in self-defence he had taken advantage of the opportunity. But Socrates recognised one problem only, whether flight would be in keeping with the principles he had advocated all his life. He heard the voice of the law speaking to him in the name of his Athens. "Your whole physical and spiritual existence you owe to us, much more than to your parents. Your

61

debt of gratitude will not be cancelled if you suffer injustice in a single case at the hand of your native city. Even then you may not repay injustice with injustice or suspend the authority of the laws, without which the state cannot exist, through your unauthorised flight." Socrates thus clearly tells where for him lies the true good, and his decision is made.

Pericles had built his democracy on the conviction that his Athenians would without compulsion devote all their energies to the community. This hope was false. The selfish urges that sought only personal advantage proved stronger than the social sense. This is where Socrates begins. He was deeply convinced that such a conflict does not really exist. For the true "advantage" of a man can only consist in his fulfilling his highest vocation, and that goal can only be reached if he integrates himself in the community by his moral conduct. That is the "good" for him; in doing it man expresses his own nature. Subordination to the state was thus no longer a matter of patriotic feeling, but of self-interest properly understood, so that the need for social sense had rational roots. The relation to the whole, however, which the individual man imposes on himself is no fetter. It rather gives him the true freedom where the external restrictions, which beset him in the pursuit of success, disappear. Only so does man find it possible, even in circumstances that seem the most difficult, to reach decisions suited to himself and to get a firm basis for the conduct of life that threatened to be lost for the new generation.

The tragedians had already felt that there was something higher than physical existence. Here too Socrates put in the place of mere feeling the clear recognition that a man must care only to preserve his humanity by adopting the proper attitude in every situation and that under some circumstances it may be the greatest value for him to sacrifice life and limb if he can thereby save his real self, his moral personality.

Socrates had an irresistible sense for what was right or wrong for him personally. Consequently, in his philosophising, in his constant discussion with his fellow creatures, he restricted himself to the practical problem which the spiritual crisis of his people presented him with, the clarification of the issue of what was really good for a man. He kept away not only from natural philosophy, but from all metaphysical speculation as well. Even the question whether the good he was searching for was anchored in some divine order, does not seem to have concerned him. In this it was not merely a feeling of personal inadequacy that counselled reserve to the man who does not know, but his general conviction that man's understanding was incapable of solving such questions. He was at all events determined to concentrate his investigations wholly upon the questions on which he could hope to achieve some progress by dint of the strength of the human intellect.

But for all that his attitude was not purely intellectual and he was far from denying the certain knowledge of experience when it could not be grasped by reason. He was of a deeply religious nature and if he went his way with unshakable certainty, and even in the face of death preserved an unperturbed peace that revealed no trace of anxiety, it was thanks to his firm conviction that he had a divine mission to fulfil and that even in death God would not abandon him. The idea that he was departing from the conception of God prevailing in the minds of the people was aroused not least by his feeling that he was in a personal relationship to God who in moments of decision spoke to him directly. What is significant, however, is that the divine voice he heard, the *daimonion*, only gave warnings. For positive actions Socrates had to seek his way alone. When he felt the irresistible urge to influence his fellow men, he might readily believe it something divine (θεῖον), but in his philosophising he followed only the instructions of his own reason. It was part of the world order that he as a man had that reason and ought to use it. The freedom of the human intellect was thus not hampered but furthered by that higher order. But his own intellect also shows man that there are limits that may not with impunity be exceeded.

That was the faith to which Socrates firmly held, even when he experienced to his sorrow, that he, living wholly in and for the *polis*, was in ever sharper opposition to contemporary Athens. He did not seek martyrdom. Death, however, held for him no terror. "Anytus and Meletus can kill me but not harm me."

The Soul and the Problem of Freedom

When in the imperial age, the former slave Epictetus proclaimed the glad tidings of men's inner freedom, he repeatedly drew his hearers' attention to the example of Socrates, who was the first to recognise this highest good and to realise it in his own life. We too can say without hesitation that Socrates not only led the life of a man inwardly free and "cast off all the fetters which enslave the ordinary man" (Epictetus, IV, 159–169), but also laid down the theoretical basis for that ideal by showing that the true values reside within man and thus ensuring his superiority to external things.

It may seem surprising that so far as we can see, the idea of freedom was by no means the decisive factor in Socrates' thought.[65] In the opening of his *Memorabilia*, Xenophon gives a list of subjects on which Socrates liked to converse. He makes no mention there of *eleutheria*, and his later writings, like the Socratic dialogues of Plato, do not give the impression that the idea of freedom was for Socrates the central problem.

To understand why we must remember that at that time the word freedom was the great political slogan, the party programme of democracy, and that the freedom in private life advocated by Pericles was taken by too many people to mean freedom from all fetters which restrained egotism. In this attitude lay the danger to the moral life of the community which Socrates wanted to overcome. That must have made him disinclined to make use of the concept of freedom himself; it is clear that he, like most of the young people who flocked around him, had more sympathy with the Spartan conceptions of strict discipline and order. In his nature these were deeply rooted. For, however emphatically he advised his young friends to follow their own convictions, uninfluenced by men or things, and live a free and independent life, he felt deeply the objective limitations imposed upon man alike through his nature as a social being and through the divine world order. He did not, like Epictetus, look upon freedom as the essence of personal *eudaimonia*, but freedom gave him the right position from which he could play his part in the *polis*. He wanted to arouse the same attitude among his fellow citizens. They needed to consider their obligations much more than to be roused to liberty.

Socrates felt very strongly that his divine mission was to guide his Athenians away from their false attitude to life on to the right road. For that reason, he explained to his judges, so long as he lived he would never cease to confront every one of his fellow citizens with the question (*Apol.*, 29d)[66]: "Good man, you are an Athenian, a son of the greatest of cities and the most esteemed for intelligence and energy; are you not ashamed that you care only for getting as much money as possible, for appearances and honours, whereas for understanding and truth and for making your soul as good as possible, you are not interested and take no care?" The one absolute essential is care for the soul.

64

For us modern people the notion of soul is so feeble that we hardly realise the importance of that sentence. For the contemporaries of Socrates it was something new and embodied a programme. To appreciate that fact we must first take a backward glance at the history of the word.

Homer knew nothing of any unified "soul" [67], but only of organs and functions of the spirit, most of them not yet really different from those of the body. He knows about a *psyche*, but this is only the breath of life, whose function is realised only when it leaves the body and then leads a shadow existence as the soul of the dead. We meet quite another conception, probably derived from foreign influences, in the religious movement that makes its appearance in Orphic and Pythagorean circles. Here the psyche is an independent being, connected with the body only for a time and able to develop properly only when wholly independent of it. That is the first time that the antithesis so familiar to us between body and soul was formulated in the West. It was so suited to Greek sensibility that it gradually gained general acceptance. As early as 432 the epigram on the Athenians fallen at Potidaea says that the Ether has taken their souls, the Earth their bodies; and that is clearly already a widely-known image. We find it expressed more than once in Euripides too. Otherwise the tragedies show how great was still the influence of the habits of speech and thought in Homer's epics. And despite the development towards conceiving the life of the soul as a unity, terms like *thymos* and *phrenes* compete with *psyche*. So it was really something new when Socrates started, here as everywhere, clarifying the conception, and the content he gave to the idea of the soul was also new. In the cult of Orpheus the *psyche* was already not merely a life-force, but had an ethical-religious flavour as well, in that it became a duty for man to look upon the soul as his true being and keep it during his earthly life as unsullied by the flesh as possible. But through being linked to ritual and ascetic rules this conception took on a sectarian character which in the enlightened fifth century only awoke response in isolated circles. Socrates was the first to introduce into the idea the spirit of the new age. For him the soul is not only the vehicle of life and consciousness: but it is that which makes a man into a thinking and acting personality. What the tragic poets had found obscure, becomes for him a clear concrete image: man possesses something which raises him not only above the external world but also

65

above the body and constitutes his essential being. The Socratic "soul" is nothing other than the true self of man.

That is what makes "care for the soul" man's most compelling task. The goal is knowledge of the good, and upon this is built *arete*, the virtue of the whole man. For it is in the nature of this knowledge of the good that it cannot remain mere theory. Whoever knows what is good for him simply cannot fail to strive towards it and orient his whole activity in that direction.

Socrates did not hesitate to formulate that conception in the statement that the essence of all virtue, and to some extent of courage also, is to distinguish between what is good and what is bad for man. This statement was ridiculed by contemporaries as unrealistic, and we moderns wonder most of all why this definition takes no account of the will. The reason clearly is that, for the Greek, the will is not an independent function of the soul expressing its urge towards active engagement, but a reaching out to some more or less clearly defined goal that is or will be shown to man by his intellect.[68] So it is no high-brow eccentricity that is intended in Socrates' proposition about knowledge of virtue, but the conviction rooted in the general Hellenic belief that knowledge is the indispensable pre-requisite for right wishing and acting. The only thing that is his own is the exclusiveness with which he makes that knowledge the sole deciding factor in the life of the soul and concentrates his whole effort on that one point. In this his tendentious purpose of pointing to the one real essential certainly plays a part. The deepest motive, however, is obviously the unshakable faith that this knowledge necessarily leads to right acting. He is so confident in that belief that he wholly ignores many problems which not only bother us today but already occupied the contemporaries of Socrates.[69]

When he made the statement that seems so paradoxical to the average man, that nobody goes wrong or does wrong by his own intention, ἑκών, – an idea which must be considered later – this was only the negative side of his fundamental conviction that whoever knows what is really good for him tries to do it and therefore in his own eyes needs no other motive. We are all the more surprised therefore that, so far as we know, Socrates hardly alludes to the barriers which obstruct the knowledge of the good in the soul and inhibit the doing of good. Paul was certainly not the first to have the experience that the spirit is willing and the flesh is weak.

Euripides before him had repeatedly shown the terrible power of the passions to break out from the depths of the soul and prevent the recognition of the good. When, for example, Medea, who certainly does not lack a lively intelligence, is about to ruin her own life by killing her children, she expresses the result of her inner struggle in these words:

> The evil I shall do I understand
> But stronger than my reason is my passion.

Three years later the *Hippolytus*[70] appeared, where Phaedra explains that after long deliberation she has come to the conclusion that it is not lack of knowledge that leads men to mismanage their lives: "for we know the good and recognise it, but do not put it into practice, partly out of laziness and partly because some desire or other lures us from the right path" (377ff.). It has been suggested not without reason, that the dramatist is here engaged in a polemic against Socrates, and in another passage we read: "Awareness I have, but I am driven by the compulsion of my nature" (840).

Euripides is not the only one to entertain such ideas; he is in complete agreement with what his people were feeling. For however firmly the Greek spirit insists upon purposeful direction of life through its control by the intellect, it does not shut its eyes to the obstacles which the intellect encounters within the soul. Long before Euripides portrayed the conflict between the passionate *thymos* and reason in the soul of Medea, Heraclitus had proclaimed (B. 85): "It is hard to battle with the *thymos*, for what it wants it will pay for with the soul (life)", and Democritus took up the aphorism to develop it in his own way (B. 236): "To battle with *thymos*[71] is indeed hard, but it is the task of man, who considers things rationally, to master it."

That victory (κρατεῖν) over passion was regarded, despite the modern concern for self-expression, as just as necessary for the proper conduct of life as intellectual understanding. The idea that a man must master the lusts of the flesh, that he must be stronger not only than money and possessions but also than sensual appetites and sexual desire, that it is unworthy of a man to be a slave of his belly[72], these are basic principles of popular Greek ethics. Even in court Gorgias has the legendary Palamedes (15) defend himself against the charge of having betrayed the Greeks for money, by pointing out that he does not want it: "Money is

67

not required by the man who masters his sensual lusts but by him who is their slave"; and in practice a client of Lysias defended himself in 402–401 by affirming that he was a "decent, morally upright man who did not allow himself to be governed by desires" (or. 21, 19). In fact a fixed terminology for such things began to develop. *Sophrosyne*, which originally had the broad meaning of "common sense" and had hitherto had an intellectual flavour, became so far narrowed down to the moral sphere that by the time of Plato's *Symposium* (196c) the poet Agathon is able to say that in general usage it means "mastery of desires and passions".[73] And along with it two other terms gained currency, whose meaning could be felt in their structure. In early times alongside the word κράτος (strength, power) and its verb κρατεῖν the adjectives ἐνκρατής and ἀκρατής together with the related nouns ἐνκράτεια and ἀκράτεια (ἀκρασία) had been formed to express physical strength and weakness. Gradually these expressions were transferred to the purely spiritual sphere and just as already in the *Prometheus* of Aeschylus (884) Io, now insane, had said of herself that she was γλώσσης ἀκρατής: "no longer had power over her tongue", so it now became quite common, by the addition of a special genitive, to indicate whether a man had power over his tongue, his eating and drinking, or his sexual desire. This led to the idea of self-control by which a man has power over himself. It is this quality that Protagoras had praised in Pericles. The fact that this expression implies a distinction between a mastering and a mastered part was first clearly recognised by Plato (*Republic* 431a), and we shall see what far-reaching consequences for psychology he deduced from it. From what we have already seen we may say that this expression contains the feeling that in man there is a true self whose role is to control the whole man.

These widely diffused ideas exerted some influence, naturally, on the first writings which set out to consider in practice the art of living. While the materialist Democritus was writing his booklet on joy in living (περὶ εὐθύμης), usefulness was his obvious criterion for human actions, and the criterion for advantage and disadvantage was pleasure and displeasure (*Vorsokr.*, 68B, 4; 188). Personally he finds the genuine joy and pleasure in life in the research which is devoted to the eternal (189); for other people he recommends above all, in the old Hellenic spirit, the observation of proper moderation whether in enjoyment or effort (233). For him, too, the decisive question is the attitude to society. He certainly starts with the good of the individual in mind, but his own life of research leads him to the conviction that a man should, in his own interest properly understood, put the order and well-being of the community before his own personal interests since he cannot survive without the state (252). The deep impression made upon him by the Periclean ideal is unmistakable. He prefers poverty in the democracy to the so-called happiness of the nobleman's court (251). He extols the generous demeanour (τὸ ἐλευθέριον) of the free man who devotes his wealth to public ends (282) and praises freedom of speech which is characteristic of freedom but must not be used at the wrong time (226). He also values complete freedom in private life, but is against those who regard the laws merely as fetters; he claims: "The laws would not prevent the individual leading his own life to the fulness of his powers if one man would not try to harm the other" (245). Because of that he advocates the promotion by social behaviour of the harmony (ὁμόνοια) on which the community's well-being depends [74] (255, 250, 282). That is possible, however, only if the individual citizen exercises strict self-restraint. "Courage consists not only in overcoming an enemy but also in conquering one's own desires. Some men are masters of whole cities, but slaves of women." (214).

Closely linked to such ideas are the ethical theories of his contemporary, the Sophist Antiphon [75], (who must be clearly distinguished from the orator). He has become specially well known at the present time owing to some papyrus fragments of his work about "truth" and "real being", in which the well-known antithesis between *nomos* and *physis* is developed in an original way (*Vorsokr.*, 87B, 44, also page 32 above). With challenging pointedness he argues that the laws of the state are *post facto* human inventions which often contradict the instinctive natural law of seeking personal advantage, so that man is in perpetual conflict with authority and is urged by his own nature to break the laws if he can do so with impunity. But we have no right to regard this as Antiphon's last word or even his real meaning. For the purpose of that fragment is to prove that the prevailing opinion that righteousness is the same thing as obedience to the positive laws is inadequate and indefensible, and that the foundation of ethics must be laid anew with the help of ideas drawn from physics. And in the belief that this physical basis drives man to follow his own advantage, he is in complete agreement with Democritus. [76] Like him he is convinced, however, that a man's own advantage properly understood must prevent him from blindly following his selfish instincts. About that *homonoia* which Democritus had already rated so highly, he wrote a book himself where he showed it was mistaken to believe that a man could hurt his neighbour without being hurt himself, and it was wrong to set oneself against being governed when anarchy is man's greatest evil (B58–61). He too needs the state and expects the individual to be intelligent enough to contribute to the harmony of the community, which ensures inner peace. To that end a man must first of all establish order and harmony within himself. Selfish inclinations which tend to harm others he must overcome and "conquer himself". This power comes from *sophrosyne*, whose nature consists precisely in controlling unreasonable urges, fully expecting resistance within the soul. "Whoever has never at any time desired the disgraceful and evil or come in contact with them, is not σώφρων, for he has conquered nothing and has given no evidence of self-discipline" (B59). But the role of *sophrosyne* is to enable man to oppose the momentary desires of his *thymos*, of his passions and instincts, and to show strength enough to "master and conquer himself" (58). From this *sophrosyne* of the individual citizen flows the harmony of the community. It is at the same time the highest good for the individual himself, since it ensures for him peace in the soul and freedom from sorrow, the ἀλυπία he yearns for (A6).

Democritus is in this surpassed by Antiphon, who is not content with references to the real benefit of the individual and praise of *homonoia*; he also derives the relationship of the individual to the state out of human nature and attempts to found a new ethic on that idea. And whereas Democritus proceeds simply from the democratic idea of political freedom, Antiphon gives this a quite new meaning in that here too he refers to the nature of man. When he explains that what the law considers proper is only the restriction of natural tendencies, and that only what they command is free (44A, col. IV, 1), it is of course his criticism of another doctrine which has led to this formula. But his object is probably to prove that this very nature shows man that he ought to seek his advantage in voluntary subordination to the good of the state. This makes it seem likely that Democritus wrote first and Antiphon developed systematically the thoughts that Democritus had stimulated, making use of the conception of *physis*.

Antiphon also argues that a man who follows his sudden impulses is likely to choose the worse rather than the better, whereas a delay will make way for the intellect, the νοῦς, to overcome the impulsive desire (B58). But whether there is any clear psychological idea behind this is not clear from the fragments preserved.

It is natural that Socrates too knew these ideas. In his *Memorabilia* Xenophon even records a conversation between Socrates and Antiphon (I,6). But it only deals with a practical problem about asking for fees, and although Xenophon stresses the fact that Socrates urged his disciples to *enkrateia*, he provides no real indication as to how Socrates thought the conquest of the instinctive urges by the understanding of the intellect could be brought about. That is not solely due to the unphilosophical character of the narrator. We get the impression rather that Socrates was no more inclined to psychological studies than his contemporaries were.

He therefore concentrated on the one point, which for him was decisive, and he was able to do so just because of his firm conviction that knowledge of the good gives the power to act accordingly and to overcome any inner resistance that may arise. A fresh start was required to recognise the problems raised by the Socratic conception of the soul, which inevitably affected the ideal of inner freedom.

Freedom as Independence of the Outside World

Socrates had opened up for mankind the way to inner freedom when he placed the true values within the individual personality. He felt equally strongly the need for moral activity within the community. In him personally freedom and obligation could co-exist harmoniously. But it is quite understandable that the men of very different backgrounds and dispositions who were attracted by him were more powerfully influenced either by the one side of his personality or by the other. Alongside men who were wholly rooted in the Athenian tradition were others like Aristippus and Antisthenes who were not bound to the idea of the city-state, and these learned from his teaching only that what mattered for man was the proper use of things and that consequently any individual, whatever his circumstances, could attain *eudaimonia* which is the goal for all men. For such men freedom was very much a matter for the individual.[77]

Aristippus, who came to Athens from the wealthy and luxurious city of Cyrene, always had a certain regard for Socrates. But his own feeling for life and his way of life were of quite another kind. He was well versed

71

in the teachings of the Sophists, went about as a paid teacher, and, like them, led a wandering life. The nature of good, which Socrates took such pains to discover, presented no problems for him. Like the majority of people, he adopted the subjective notion that for man the good must lie in pleasure which all men seek. That was the point of departure also for men like Democritus and Antiphon. But he was no more inclined than they were to draw the conclusion that one should give way to the desire for pleasure every time. He too advocated the control of desires, which meant man must renounce many momentary pleasures, not out of any ethical consideration but for his own advantage properly understood. For it is a matter of daily experience that many pleasures have unpleasant consequences and lead to greater unhappiness. And that was the point where, for him too, the Socratic teaching acquired significance, not as recognition of some objective universal good, but as the practical understanding, as the *phronesis* (there can be no doubt that Aristippus coined this term which was then adopted by Epicurus), which by some kind of measurement can weigh up pleasures against each other and make the best choice. This *phronesis* is not an end in itself but a pre-condition of that proper conduct of life which will ensure for man the greatest measure of pleasure. By making him superior to each momentary desire for pleasure, it also gives him independence of the outside world, and thus inner freedom.

That freedom enables a man to secure happiness, *eudaemonia*, in any circumstances. Aristippus wants to enjoy life. But he is quite clear that whoever would reach that goal and stay there must while enjoying still retain control. Thus he was able to declare, while lying in the arms of the loveliest woman of Hellas: "I am holding her, she is not holding me".[78] And that famous phrase was the symbol of his life. He was a man who "could play every role on the stage of the world"; and yet, like Odysseus, always remained himself. He was adaptable enough to enjoy "the so-called *eudaimonia* of the princely court" which Democritus denounced as servitude (cf. p. 69); and whereas others travelling abroad were inclined to complain that they dared not speak freely, Aristippus was skillful, witty and self-assured enough to allow himself a joke. Even for Horace (*Epistles* I, 17, 13ff.; 1, 18) he is still the model of the man who upholds his freedom and his personality before the powerful ones of this world. If ever things got too hot for him anywhere, there was always room for him somewhere else. He did not have the attachment which Socrates felt to fatherland and community. He subscribed to the motto "ubi bene, ibi patria". And Xenophon in his *Memorabilia* (II, 1, 9, 13, 11) has him express his rule of life in these terms; "I gladly do without political power; I want to live comfortably and pleasantly. So I don't shut myself up in any particular land but live as a foreigner anywhere. My ideal is freedom".

Another man who had much in common with Aristippus is Antisthenes. He too could not share the civic sense of Socrates. He was the son of a Thracian woman slave and had settled in Athens, where he earned his living by teaching. He too had heard others before Socrates, but his meeting with Socrates meant for him something quite different from what it did for Aristippus. It was a turning point in his life. With absolutely fanatical veneration, indeed love, he devoted himself to the master, and his only wish was to become his real disciple. But his nature drove him to strike out on his own path. The unremitting search for truth was not for him. Philosophy was in his eyes a practical way of life that must rest upon firm principles. And yet it was like a revelation when he learned from Socrates that man has within himself the essential values, and that he need only let the moral good, virtue, have full play, to fulfil his human destiny and thus achieve *eudaimonia* in every situation in life. The sovereignty of virtue became the central idea of his thought.

But it was the personality of Socrates, even more than his words, that produced the strongest effect on Antisthenes. His complete supremacy over all external things, over his own body and the senses, and still more his ability to do without things, which was always in evidence, became the ideal for Antisthenes himself, and theoretically too *enkrateia* became the centre of the science of virtue. How that science can overcome the desires and appetites inherent in the flesh[79] was for him no more a psychological problem than it was for Socrates himself. Nor need we look for any definite psychological theory when he declares quite clearly that virtue is a matter of deeds not of theory and, in order to achieve *eudaimonia*, nothing more is required than the strength of Socrates.[80] There is behind it, nevertheless, a vague feeling that our conduct is determined not by knowledge only, and that the intellect requires a certain power if it is to overcome obstacles within the soul.

Socrates was not an ascetic, but the fact that he never surrendered to the temptations of pleasure and was always master of his senses was one of the most impressive traits of his character. It must therefore have seemed to Antisthenes like a betrayal of the master's memory when a man like Aristippus, who belonged to Socrates' own circle, set up sensual pleasure as a principle of conduct and degraded *phronesis* to the role of its handmaiden. "I would rather be out of my senses than live a sensual life."[81] "I would shoot Aphrodite dead if ever I got hold of her." Man is not made for enjoyment but for action. *Ponos*, toil and trouble are his lot, and he must train himself for it through effort and hardship, which alone bring real enjoyment. But not only is pleasure not good, it is evil, the basic evil of man, since it alienates him from his true nature and robs him of his highest good. For it is striving after pleasure that ultimately reduces man to dependence on things; and thereby he loses inner freedom, without which *eudaemonia* is unthinkable.

Antisthenes was the first to write a book on *Freedom and Slavery* (Περὶ ἐλευθερίας καὶ δουλείας, Diog. Laert., VI, 16). Only one sentence out of it is extant: "Whoever fears another is himself a slave, even if he does not know it" (Stob. III, 344, I H) but that is enough to let us see in what spirit it was written. Already in the fifth century the humane outlook of the Athenians was sufficiently advanced to see in freedom and slavery not merely a legal relationship but also an attitude (cf. p. 47). Antisthenes, whose mother was a slave, had every reason to develop such thinking and to define the concept of freedom more clearly in the spirit of Socrates. It is the Socratic *phronesis* that makes a man free, since, besides ensuring his independence of things and persons, it gives him through self-mastery the strength to do what is right, regardless of his inner sensual instincts. Along with that personal freedom goes voluntary service to the community. The wise man will acknowledge as the norm not simply conventional views and the laws that happen to be in force, but instead will live according to the law of virtue (Diog. Laert., VI, 11), and this law prescribes that he shall not be the slave of personal desires, but, despite trouble and effort, concern himself with the well-being of his fellow men. Heracles and Cyrus, who by self-discipline paved his own way to world power, are the great practical examples to whom Antisthenes dedicated special works (Diog. Laert., VI, 16). Even the ideal of the good king who with Socratic understanding and vigour leads the human herd (Plato, *Republic*, 267ff.) probably originates from him. Since he was not a full citizen, he was unable to take part directly in political life himself. Nor could he share the patriotism of Socrates; yet for him too it is self-evident that the individual has a moral obligation to the community.

In the early histories of philosophy Antisthenes is already made out to be the founder of the Cynic school. But that is true only in so far as he established certain theoretical conditions for Cynicism. He himself would have felt thoroughly insulted if he had been called a "dog". It was his pupil Diogenes who first adopted the abusive term *kyon* (dog), and defiantly used it to describe his own way of life. Not until after that have there been "cynics".

In antiquity it was already an established fact that cynicism was not a school of philosophy, but a way of life, *ἀγωγή* [82], like the Spartan *kosmos*, which without any theory at all provided a strenuous training for true manhood. Through Antisthenes Diogenes became acquainted with the new ideas of freedom, and his remark that the ability to do without was the right way to achieve it came from the heart. But all this remained for him so many empty words so long as it was not made good in disinterested action. In his opinion a complete change in the practical conduct of everyday life was necessary. Socrates had remained an Athenian citizen all his life and Antisthenes had felt himself at least a member of that community. Diogenes also needed it, if only as an object of his criticism, but he deliberately adopted an attitude of opposition to it and his desire was to lead a new life based on his own principles and quite outside it.

How did he come to this position?

Diogenes was a native of Sinope on the Black Sea, thus from the periphery of Hellenism, so that emigrating to Athens meant not only moving from the province to the capital city but being transplanted into a totally different intellectual atmosphere, into the centre of civilisation. The Greeks did not have a word which, like the modern word "civilisation", could embrace the complete realisation of human powers, both their technical and intellectual achievements within a community, but already in the fifth century there was a clear consciousness of the powerful achievements of the human intellect. Aeschylus had made Prometheus the discoverer of everything that first helped men to a really human existence, and from that time on there had set in a tremendous and rapid development which, particularly in Athens, the spiritual centre of Hellas, completely altered the whole life of the people. The new world Diogenes entered cannot have failed to impress him; but behind the brilliant façade

75

he also saw the drawbacks, the restlessness which did not let a man find himself in the pursuit of success which he had to engage in, the passions of political conflict and the contrasts between rich and poor, between luxury and misery. And so he was led to ask for the first time the question which has never since ceased to worry mankind: "Is civilisation a blessing for man? Has it not simply increased his needs instead of leaving him in the natural state of simplicity and content? Has all modern progress made men happier?" Socrates had shown that all external things had only relative value. Diogenes went very much further. Not just gold, power and material satisfaction, but also the so-called intellectual good things like art and sciences are nothing but phantoms of man's imagination (δόξαι), a pure swindle, a cloud of dust (τῦφος) that only obscures the view of the one thing that is really necessary.[83] It is right that Prometheus was punished by Zeus for bringing civilisation to men. For it has turned the world into a madhouse whose inmates chase delusions and fail to recognise the true good. To clear away the τῦφος is the most pressing task, and Diogenes means to accomplish it, not by theoretical precept but by his practical example, which will show men how renunciation of the goods of civilisation really makes for freedom and happiness.

Like the Hebrew prophets, Diogenes knew how to draw attention to himself and his programme by the use of symbolic acts and words. When people were streaming out of the theatre he "swam against the stream" and cleared a way for himself through the crowd. He described the essence of his work as "the trans-valuation of values"[84], not of coins (*nomismata*) but of current ideas and institutions, of *nomoi*. These were for him the embodiment of the whole civilisation and offered a new meaning to the old opposition between *nomos* and *physis*. *Physis* had already been thought of as not being simply human nature in the abstract but as the historical condition of man before the introduction of *nomoi* and the establishment of states and had first of all been thought a barbaric age, where everyone was at war with everyone else. Against this there had always been the old dream of a golden age. Diogenes was the first to present "nature" in quite a new light. He was anything but a Romantic, but he needed a picture contrasting with contemporary civilisation and so portrayed the happy life men had led when they simply followed nature and knew nothing of the needs of modern civilisation. Through him "back to nature" became for the first time an ideal programme.

When the Sophists, culture-proud, looked down compassionately on the animal condition of primitive peoples, Diogenes reversed the values here too. It had once seemed more important than Antisthenes' sermons on contentedness when he watched a little mouse come running, not in the least afraid, to take a few miserable crumbs and finally make his home in any random hole (Diog. Laert., VI, 22). There were other ways, too, in which an unprejudiced man could learn from animals what nature is. Animals did not know the cares that men foolishly allow to embitter their lives. Similarly they knew nothing of those rules of etiquette which prevent men from following their natural instincts. The sentence *naturalia non sunt turpia*[85] does not go back to the Greek medical men but, in meaning, to Diogenes, who applied it with provocative unconcern. He may well have cited as an example the dog, which had for Homer typified ἀναίδεια, shamelessness. But if he was abusively called a "dog" he was quite satisfied. He behaved like a dog, and those who laughed at him sided with him.

That is what made him a popular figure in Athenian life. He had inexhaustible humour and a ready wit that never failed him. But that was not all that attracted people to him. They felt that behind his joking there was a serious intention, and that this odd character was touching upon problems which concerned all of them. They might turn up their noses because he had no feeling for human dignity; but those democrats, proud of their freedom, also took note when in broad daylight he would wander about the crowded market-place with a lantern, and, when someone asked him in amazement what he was looking for, gave the answer: "I am looking for a man, a free man, who really lives free from all restraint and does as he will" (Diog. Laert., VI, 41). And then even the philistine might come upon the idea that there is a freedom other than that of the party programme, even if it takes so strange a form.

It was probably no accident on Diogenes' part that his behaviour reminded the Athenians of Socrates, though he exaggerated so much that he was called "Socrates gone mad".[86] But though he deliberately advertised poverty by wearing a shabby coat and even by not living in a house for a time but spending the nights in a big barrel, the impression he made was quite different. It can happen even nowadays in Southern Italy or Greece that one stumbles over people sleeping at night on an open square or under colonnades and in the daytime one can see on the beaches the

77

lazzaroni, who have for their midday meal a few figs, and they feel so very happy that highly-civilised people may be inclined, like King Ptolemy of old, to exclaim sorrowfully: "Oh why did I not come into the world like one of these?" Only in the warm South, only among a population with few needs could cynicism flourish as a way of life.

By his very nature Diogenes was not a man to teach philosophy or to found a school. But his way of realising his ideal of freedom and the return to nature made such a strong impression that others imitated him.[87] The most independent of his followers was Crates of Thebes. He once was a rich man, but he found the toil and worry of managing his property so burdensome that one day he made an end of his "slavery", distributed his money among his fellow-citizens and made out for himself a document declaring: "Crates of Thebes presents freedom to Crates". He went to Athens and chose the free mendicant existence of the Cynics. The missionary urge was even stronger in him than in Diogenes. So, as Diogenes did only in his old age, he took a knobbed stick and a satchel to hold the minimum necessities, πήρα, the forerunner of the modern rucksack, and he went wandering about to try to convert men. Wherever he suspected spiritual distress he would enter houses uninvited, but the intruder (θυρεπανοίκτης) as people called him, soon became a guest they were glad to see. It is true he could, if need be, speak sharply and use quite drastic means to rid people of their conceits and their τῦφος, but basically he was a much more humane and amiable person than Diogenes, and his genuine love of his fellow men made him a real minister to the soul in all troubles. This ugly and deformed man must have had some very special charm. The sister of one of his disciples, a girl with a good family background, was so fascinated by him that, against her parents' wishes and his own opposition, she insisted on marrying him, and from that time on shared with him his "dog's life" – an astonishing proof of the powerful influence of the idea of inner independence and freedom on young hearts, which was able to overcome all external considerations. For Crates himself, marriage though he regarded it theoretically as a purely man-made convention, implied no break with Cynic principles. He had, like Diogenes before him, called himself a cosmopolitan and declared that neither the walls of his native town nor any single house was his home. Every town and every house in the whole world offered him a place to live (Diog. Laert., VI, 98). But he was not a revolutionary, rebelling against everything. He only refused to let externals involve him in inner commitments.

Crates had also a poetical streak and enlisted in the service of his ideal poems which mixed humour with seriousness, and above all – itself a transvaluation of values – parodies of earlier works. The name of one of them was the *Knapsack*, *Πήρα* (Diog. Laert., VI, 85). This poem tells of an island in the sea of dishonesty. It cannot be reached by parasites, gluttons or lecherous people. Only cheap leek and thyme, figs and wheat grow there; but for that reason there is no quarrelling.

> Never bending to pleasure's yoke and never enslaved,
> There they worship only the highest goddess, freedom.

Following the example of Crates others arose to bear witness to the happiness inherent in restricted needs and inner freedom. But they were gradually absorbed by the *Stoa* which with its all-embracing philosophy offered a firmer basis, and it was only in the culture-saturated time of the Caesars that the Cynic philosophy awoke to new life. Then people who showed their contempt of all social convention in uncleanliness and coarse rowdy behaviour became part of the everyday scene. Among them there certainly were some who felt concern about the souls of others; but of others it was said that they preferred to obtain their livelihood by begging rather than by hard work.

In Crates' own time something else became more important. Since the city-state had lost its independence and the ideal of democratic freedom had become absurd, the new freedom preached by Diogenes appealed to many who would never dream of living a dog's life. A contemporary of Crates was Stilpon, who in the little city of Megara, without binding himself to any particular system, taught practical wisdom so sucessfully that he became famous throughout Hellas. He was a man of the world, at the very heart of civic life, and came out explicitly against Crates. But when his home-town was pillaged in the year 306, he was able to say that he had not seen anybody who could steal his property (Diog. Laert., II, 115). That was the old Socratic wisdom – that men carried the real values within themselves. But during the chaotic Diadoch period this saying spread so much that it became the motto of everybody who wanted to defend himself against the blows of fate. Even a man like the highly cultured Menedemus, who had liberated his native city Eretria from tyranny (Diog. Laert., II, 143) and who in other ways too played an important part in political life, paid homage to it in word and deed. A sceptic like Pyrrhon of Elis, seeking a peaceful life, could also set up ἀπάθεια as his practical goal, since it would defend him from influences from outside (πάθη).

This attitude took such a hold on society that business-minded people were able to make capital out of it. Bion, who was of South Russian stock, wandered around like the old Sophists, and delivered his public lectures on general human problems not to the proletariat in the streets but to a public well able to pay for them. These "diatribes" are not, as is frequently maintained, developed from the reasoned dialogues of Socrates, but derived from the rhetoricians, the only element of dialogue in them being that the lecturer was ready with a crushing answer to any interruption. In this Bion was a master, and if he was not gifted with the originality of Diogenes, he shared with him a sharp tongue and a quick wit – it was he who said that gold is the *nervus rerum*, that "One can find the road to Hades with one's eyes shut" and that "Beauty is a good for other people", and he was able to spell-bind his hearers through his brilliant style. He had considerable effect through his social satire and claimed to be the apostle of autarchy and inner freedom. In one of his writings he tells Antigonus the king[88], with Cynic frankness, that he is descended from the scum of the people, but concludes with the proud words: "You, however, must judge me by my personality." In himself he was as a matter of fact not much of a "Cynic". He divided his disciples into three categories, the golden ones who pay and learn nothing, the silver ones who pay and learn, and the copper ones who learn but do not pay.

Teles (about 240) is one who wanted to follow Bion, but this snappy dog became a tame schoolmaster and infant teacher.

There were also men who wanted to introduce the old brand of the Cynic philosophy into daily life. One of these who explicitly declared himself a disciple of Diogenes was Onesicritus, who became a high naval officer under Alexander and, in a historical work influenced by Xenophon's *Cyropaedia*, showed how the conquering Alexander had carried out a cultural and educational mission (*FGr. Hist.*, II, 134). The pleasantest link between the Cynic philosophy and practical activity appeared a century later in the Arcadian Cercidas, who was active as statesman and general in his native city of Megalopolis, and who is known to us as a man in some Meliambics contained in a papyrus. In these he praises Diogenes, who had no fear of death, and who being *Dio-genes*, offshoot of Zeus, has become the "divine dog". While calling himself *Kyon*, his work is not all negative and critical. Unlike Crates, he does not throw his wealth away as a burden, but uses it for the alleviation of social distress. The healing *Paian* and *Metados* giving freely of its own are the divinities he chooses as his leaders.

The Socratic freedom has thus stood the test in practice and has even become a requirement of plain common sense. Most of those who adhered to it assuredly saw in it merely the way to be independent of external circumstances and achieve happiness in their private lives, and the disciples of Socrates, accustomed to the traditions of the old city-state, could feel that only one side of this freedom was being expressed. They might be perplexed by the question as to how far this new freedom tallied with the old popular idea of freedom and how it could be made valuable for the whole community.

Yet still more important was the other problem which Socrates himself had not seen or at least had not raised: could his basic conviction really survive, that knowledge of the good necessarily caused one to act rightly, where everyday experience demonstrated the presence within the individual of powerful urges which opposed the intellect and even when a man had proper understanding prevented him from acting properly?

That was the problem most urgently calling for clarification.

Self-Control and Freedom of the Intellect

"Freedom is as precious as all the jewels in the world." [89] So speaks Agesilaus in Xenophon's *Anabasis* to the satrap whom he is trying to induce to desert his master. Before the battle of Cunaxa, the Persian Prince Cyrus spurs on his Greek mercenaries by shouting: "Now show that you are worthy of the freedom you possess and for which I consider you fortunate." He is not of course referring to the democratic freedom of Athens. Xenophon's heart hankered after the Spartan discipline which is necessary alike in the army and civic life. Even as an emigrant he retained his feeling for the *polis*. He particularly dislikes Aristippus, who cannot bear to have his personal liberty curtailed by any kind of state order.

He has a genuine admiration, however, for Antisthenes, who, poor in external things, vindicated the word of Socrates that man's wealth resides within him. He does not dream of carrying the praise of satisfaction with the bare essentials to its logical conclusion for himself. He is all the more willing to agree when Antisthenes finds the significance of Socrates above all in his combining moral strength with knowledge of the good and in urging men to self-control, *enkrateia*. For, as he explains at the very outset in his work on political economy (*Oeconomicus*, I, 18–33), there is no worse slavery than slavery to sensual appetites and the pleasures of the flesh, which not only keep men from striving after what is good and elevated, but also lead them into unworthy ways of acquiring the means to pleasure. These are enemies of freedom, which must be fought as vigorously as those who would enslave us by military force. He uses quite the same tone in another discourse on *enkrateia* included in the *Memorabilia*.[90] Socrates proceeds directly from the idea of freedom which, alike for the individual and the city-state, is a "great and lovely possession", and he defines it in these terms: "Whoever is dominated by the lusts of the flesh is not free." The unfree are those who have no self-control. Lack of self-control is the worst servitude and the greatest evil, for it makes men incapable of greatness. Only *enkrateia* fosters true manhood, *arete*, which alone brings true pleasure.

The nature of true freedom is here clearly grasped and so it is established that it is a mental attitude which by overcoming sensual urges makes man free to fulfil his highest duties. This concentration on the idea of freedom and self-mastery is quite foreign to the historical Socrates according to what we learn from Plato's early dialogues and Xenophon's other works. Yet it did not come out of Xenophon's own head either; that is clear from the way he treats it as well-known.[91] It is, as has long been recognised, Antisthenes' interpretation of the teaching of Socrates, which Xenophon here makes his own. As we have already learned, Antisthenes had made the Socratic teaching into a practical way of life and, in order to ensure man's independence of externals, he had advocated not merely subjective frugality, but control over bodily cravings and pleasures.[92] How this is realised through knowledge of the good and is put into practice in the soul is a matter about which Xenophon had worked out no clear psychological explanation, any more than had Antisthenes. It is worth noting that he says nothing about control by the intellect and makes no mention of the soul[93], but only of some indefinite subject like "a man", which conceals some vague conception of a self.

The problem which was thus posed, was first noticed by Plato.

Plato could not have been a Greek if he had not regarded his people's free city-state the only form of community life worthy of mankind. Even his ideal state is established on that assumption. If he brings a professional army into it, the basic reason for this is his conviction that arms are a part of full manhood; the practical task of this guard, however, is to ensure the independence of the *polis* from the outside world.[94] In the cases of certain states he criticised both the excess of a belligerent spirit which carelessly causes unnecessary foreign entanglements and pacifism, which seeks peace at any price, since both equally endanger the people's freedom (*Republic*, 307e). He recalls with pride the feats of war accomplished by the Greeks, more especially by his fellow Athenians, in defending their freedom against the barbarians. The battles his native city waged against the rest of the Greeks he certainly sees in another light; and when, during the debates in the People's Assembly or in orations on festive occasions, he had to hear *ad nauseam* how the Athenians had from time immemorial always fought for freedom, including that of the other states, regardless of their own advantage, this roused him after the Corinthian war to declare with biting sarcasm that the indisputable achievement of the particularist policy of Athens had been to set free and "liberate" even their hereditary enemy, the Persians (cf. p. 19). He was well aware that for small states the right to self-determination existed more in the propaganda of rival great powers than in reality.

The development of the internal politics of Athens after the Persian War could only appear to him, as well as to Xenophon, as a disastrous mistake. As an aristocrat he was convinced that men are different from each other and that the masses are not capable of government, and as a disciple of Socrates he could only regard it as absurd that in the democracy knowledge was not important either in the selection of officials or in the administration, or even in such questions as the ultimate objectives of state affairs. The criticism of Periclean democracy which had immediately set in (cf. p. 30) had already become so acute in the fifth century that it was possible, according to Thucydides, for Alcibiades in Sparta to say (VI, 89, 6) that democracy was "acknowledged nonsense" (ὁμολογουμένη ἄνοια) for which no new arguments could be advanced. The tone was embittered by the progress of radicalism. But about this "comic, uncontrolled, showy constitution" (*Republic*, 558c) nobody poured out mockery and derision more angrily than Plato. Where equality is concerned, he is satisfied with the well-known aristocratic argument (cf. p. 30) that it distributes equal rights equally to equal and unequal people. He spends more time on democratic freedom, which he needs as a foil to his strictly organised ideal state. "Freedom, as you can hear in the democratic city, is the wonderful good which it bestows, and whoever is by nature a free man can only live, therefore, under that constitution." (562b). "The city is therefore full of freedom, and everybody may do and say what he likes, may lead his life as he pleases. So varied and colourful is its constitution that it appeals to children and women." (557b, c). "This democracy is so generous that it does not bother about trifles like the education of youth or the preparatory training of officials, but only asks if a candidate is capable of having opinions." (558b). "Everybody here does just what suits him". "All that is inherent in the democratic system. But once the common people have tasted the heady wine of freedom, which wicked people have prepared for them, then all restraint and order are flung off. Officials who do not allow the citizens absolute freedom are called reactionaries and are punished. Whoever still obeys the authorities is regarded as a willing slave. Private life, too, is permeated by freedom. In school the teachers fear their pupils; at home it is the children who rule the household, not their parents, the wife, not the husband. The slave is as free as his master. Even the animals claim freedom and equality for themselves. An Attic donkey will not get out of the way for anyone. And the upshot is that nobody now bothers about the laws, for people will no longer tolerate constraint and allow no authority over them." (562c–563c, cf. p. 34 above).

In that last description, Plato is thinking about the situation of his own experience when liberty had become licence. But he also explicitly maintains that from its inception the democratic form had an inherent defect. And his criticism there strikes not only at Pericles' political principles, but at the Periclean ideal of the personality. For when he claims, as he here does, that the democratic man does exactly as he likes, today drinking water, to-morrow getting drunk, playing the politician one day, the soldier the next, or else the merchant, that is a clear caricature of Pericles' ideal, that in Athens one and the same man is in a position to engage in the different human activities (Thuc., II, 41, 1). And when we think how Thucydides makes Pericles extol as the pre-eminent virtue of his Athenians their ability to do this with grace and skill, we can fully understand why Plato stresses the bizarre feature (563a), that in Athens the elderly people themselves try to equal the young in skill and ability at games. There is little reason to doubt that Plato is here alluding to Thucydides. As a man of culture he must clearly have read Thucydides and found in it the sole exposition in literature of the Periclean ideal, which he could come to grips with.[95]

A passionate hatred of democracy shows through his whole account of it, but bound up with it is something quite different. It is the pain he feels at having to stand aside because his people are unwilling to follow him along his path to the right goal. And so, when age exercised its moderating influence and his deep love of Athens became more and more compelling, he made a great effort to judge democracy objectively. Already in *Politicus* he counts democracy without question as one of the mistaken forms of government, since the masses are incapable of attaining to knowledge of the good and consequently of self-government. He does, however, concede that it is better to live in a democracy than a self-seeking oligarchy or even a tyranny (303a), provided, of course, that the people stick to the laws. The laws are admittedly imperfect because their general character prevents them from doing complete justice to individual cases – the ideal monarch should be able to rule authoritatively without being bound by any laws – but in the actual state the laws are indispensible, since they are the sole protection against despotism and the abuse of liberty (*Politicus*, 292–303).

Whereas Plato had explained that in his ideal city-state the right spirit in the citizens renders laws superfluous, the blueprint of his "second best state", laid down in the work of his old age, the *Laws*, is a state founded on law. In this there is even an element of democracy. As an introduction to the actual laws he gives in the Third Book a historical survey of the development of constitutions and concludes: political principles are realised in their purest form in the Persian monarchy and the Athenian democracy.[96] These are diametrically opposed, but they are equally in danger of becoming radical and of degeneration. Just as in Persia a despotism gradually developed out of the patriarchal monarchy, so too

85

there was in Athens at the time of the Persian wars a moderate democracy where moral restraint, *aidos*, was the dominant authority, and the stress of danger from without compelled unity and proper subordination to the needs of the whole community. The *demos* at that time was not master of the law; it was prepared of its own accord to make itself a slave to the law. Only gradually was this restraint lost and radical democracy developed, where only one kind of freedom mattered, that which cast off as intolerable servitude all obedience to the laws and their officers, to parents and elders, and even to the gods.

The lesson which Plato learned from that development was how dangerous it is when a single political principle is applied in a one-sided way and overstrained. That constitution which, like the Spartan one, combines diverse elements, must therefore be better and more enduring. It too contains freedom, which Plato now sees in quite a new light. "For a state to be sound and have stability, it must unite three elements – freedom, mutual consideration between citizens, and control by the intellect".[97] Freedom is needed. Freedom, of course, but only in the sense used in ancient Athens, where it was bound up with law and morals, and if he accords this to the masses, it is now only as a concession to the real world. In a state that knows only rulers and subjects, reciprocal love cannot last for ever. Consequently he approves that the right to vote and participation in the people's courts be accorded to the masses; reluctantly he agrees that beside proportionate equality (which alone is just) there must be the head-counting equality, and to a limited extent he would even allow ballotting for official posts. But all this ought to be permitted only in so far as to make the masses feel they are participating in the government of the community. The real government should be in the hands of the best men, who are selected through a complicated electoral system, and exercise their function as far as possible independently of the masses. Over them is the law itself which in turn derives its authority from God. The absolute norm is God, to whom men are bound.

After the murder of Dion in the year 354–353[98], Plato warned his friends in Syracuse as much against tyrannical ambition as against anarchic liberty. The right road was indicated by Lycurgus in mingling different elements in a constitution. Slavery and liberty in excess are both the greatest evil, whereas in proper measure they are the highest good. The proper measure lies in subjection to God, the extreme in subjection to men.

For men of wisdom, God is the law, for fools it is desire (*Epistles*, VIII, 354).

In his old age Plato remained opposed to the Periclean ideal of freedom. Plato does not recognise in principle that the individual should be free to choose his personal way of life.[99] His state is a Greek city-state which must be permeated by a single spirit, and he is convinced that within its narrow confines a change in one's way of life cannot help affecting the whole community. The exaggeration of the principle of freedom in Athens began, he maintains (*Laws*, 700–701), with the spectators at a play noisily showing their pleasure of displeasure, and then in political matters too began to make their own "free" decisions, regardless of what the experts thought. The general attitude of the citizens would be still more seriously in danger if the individual were allowed to behave just as he liked. "If anyone thinks of giving laws to the state, prescribing how men should behave in public life and communal affairs, and imagines that he need not bother about private life but that each may be free to live as he likes and need not have everything regulated for him – whoever leaves private life without legal discipline and imagines people will then follow the laws in public affairs, he is very much mistaken (780a). Following this principle Plato not only regulates the whole of economic life by means of strict laws, such as those on maximum prices and conditions of delivery, the kind of regulations that have only recently become known to us; he also provides for state education from the kindergarten onwards, and even if, in contradiction with his ideal city constitution, he establishes the family in its own rights, he nevertheless has officially-appointed women to supervise the lives of young married people and does not hesitate to intervene energetically in the private sphere. In place of that freedom of speech that the Athenian democrat looked upon as the bastion of the state, there came censorship of all public expression of opinion and of art.

Plato justifies compulsory education for all on the grounds that each child belongs more to the state than to the parents (804d) and he rejects freedom of inheritance, impressing upon the citizens: "Neither you nor your wealth belong to yourselves but to the whole race and still more to the state" (923a). The individual is a member of the community, in which alone he can exist. Only the community's interests are to be considered when shaping the life of the state. The individual man has to fit in with the whole, and must in consequence occupy the position in which he can best serve the community. In doing this his personal talents may and should reach fulfilment. But any freedom to shape one's own life can be permitted only as far as the advantage of the state allows.

That is the conception of the state which was realised in the Spartan *kosmos*, and Plato does not conceal his admiration of the latter, however much he disapproves of its one-sided military direction. It is clear that he was attracted to it through his opposition to the liberal democracy of Pericles, but basically it is a consequence of his whole philosophy. A man who always regarded the individual phenomenon as only an imperfect copy of the universal and eternal, could not in human affairs recognise as the supreme goal the free unfolding of individual personality.

That the citizens must, if they are to lead a life in accordance with human dignity, be exempt from the roughest labour is self-evident for the aristocratic Plato. Slaves cannot therefore be dispensed with, and he lists them with other items of property without asking whether slavery as a social institution is really just.[100] He takes it for granted that the master has certain moral obligations to his slaves, and must avoid *hybris* when dealing with inferiors, but he equally considers it necessary to maintain a sharp distinction and gives a warning against too much familiarity. In penal law he goes farther than does the law of Athens, and in the event of a slave being killed by his master, he deems ritual purification sufficient atonement. Only one thing does he expressly forbid, namely, keeping a Greek as a slave.

Plato's attitude to his country's ideal of political freedom was thus one of unconcealed opposition. But for this very reason there arose for him the problem of that other freedom which his dealings with Socrates had led him to recognise; for him, as well as for Antisthenes and the other disciples of Socrates, the most powerful experience had been to witness that inspired human being confronted like them with the problems of daily life and yet towering above it because, being truly free, he fearlessly went his own way untroubled by men and things and preserved, whether in the clash of battle or in the tempestuous People's Assembly, his perfectly unshakable peace and confidence.[101] His power to do this lay in the fact that not only was he superior to external things and had his body firmly in control, but he was master of his inner self, master of the sensual urges and desires which caused other men such trouble.[102] Socrates was really free because he was master of himself.

We have seen how in Plato's youth this self-mastery was a part of popular morality. When it took visible form in Socrates himself it was firmly grounded in his inmost being. But what puzzled his disciples was how that self-mastery was related to the knowledge of the good, which the master had impressed upon them as the one real essential. A man like Antisthenes might be satisfied with the vague idea of "Socratic strength". Plato, however, wanted perfect clarity on this point. In fact we can still see that it was precisely at this point that his philosophic investigations started and how he was led from this thought to a new formulation of the idea of freedom.

Plato clearly realised that the heart of the Socratic philosophy was the teaching of the knowledge of virtue, the conviction that knowledge of the good is not only the prerequisite of right action but that it constitutes the reality of every virtue, because it necessarily brings in its train right action. This thought of the master's is thus the central problem he was dealing with in his early dialogues, and we can see clearly how anxious he was to clarify it and to defend it against criticism. He was well aware that this came not only from theorists, from the Sophists, who at least would have to accord primacy to knowledge, but also from the laymen, "the many", who – like Euripides – considered it common experience that man clearly recognised the good but does not do it, because other motives deflect him from it and he gives way to pleasure which he is too weak to conquer.

This popular opinion Plato takes up in the concluding passage of the *Protagoras*, where he argues that even the essence of courage consists in knowledge of the good (351b–360e). He starts with an account of common opinions which at once recalls the *Hippolytus* of Euripides (352d) and asks what "the many" can mean by being conquered by pleasures which divert men from their goals, since they see in these pleasures precisely the good most worth seeking. It can only mean that man yields to a momentary pleasure although it has harmful consequences, since the gratification results in a greater measure of displeasure, as in the case of illness. This interpretation is in keeping with the views put forward by the Sophist Antiphon and most pointedly, in all probability, by Aristippus (cf. p. 72). In the latter Plato could find the notion that a criterion of measurement is required in order to measure up pleasures against each other. He takes up this idea, however, only to draw from it the one conclusion which he needed for his argument: even the popular conception assumes that a man can lead his life properly only when he knows what is harmful or what is profitable for him; and only that knowledge can constitute the essence of that quality which enables him to achieve his purpose in life. This is necessarily also true in the case of courage which as a human moral attitude is quite distinct from the purely physical courage of animals. That courage is proved not only on the battlefield, but also in the struggle with one's own desires, Plato, agreeing with Democritus, had already demonstrated in the *Laches*.

People have expressed surprise that Plato should proceed from the arguments of "the many". But although in the *Crito* he emphasises that one should not be influenced in one's judgments by the opinions of the masses (48a), he was by no means the doctrinaire, who simply sets himself above the views of other people, and this was particularly true when such views could help in the elucidation of an important practical problem. When the people commonly spoke of "being overcome by pleasure", this was based upon an experience which Plato himself could not deny – namely, that the intellect with its awareness of what is good encounters obstacles in the soul itself. From that fact Socrates had drawn no conclusions. Plato as a young man was already independent enough to recognise that there was a problem here, but still attempts to solve it from the Socratic point of view by interpreting the processes of the soul intellectually and deriving them from a mistaken estimate of what is good. The notion that man must be guided by knowledge and ought not to become the slave of sensual desires is a fundamental conviction which his Socrates has confirmed right at the outset by Protagoras (352c, d).

For us the real difficulty of that passage lies in the fact that Socrates does not only make pleasure the average man's goal, but declares as his own opinion that it is in itself a good (351c). Protagoras, admittedly, at once makes the reservation that there are bad pleasures, and we are meant to get the impression that here a problem is mooted that calls for further discussion. But the idea that pleasure as such is something good is adhered to later on (358b). Plato is not of course thinking of the sensual pleasures mentioned by Aristippus; his mind is much more on the "pure" pleasure which he recognises later, the joy in the good and the beautiful that can have no unpleasant consequences.[103] The good must remain the supreme value. But it must soon have become clear to him that even with this limitation he had made too great a concession to pleasure, for as early as in the *Gorgias* he adopts quite a different attitude.

In this work pleasure and the good are the two alternatives between which man has to choose when determining his way of life. The "superman" Callicles is introduced as the radical advocate of the pleasure principle. The goal for him is to get the utmost pleasure, since this is the natural right of the strong, who dominate the others. "And what about himself?", asks Socrates (491d) "being a moral man ($\sigma\dot{\omega}\varphi\rho\omega\nu$) who as the "many" assume, masters himself and is master of his inner desires and instincts?" But this only gives Callicles an opportunity to set out with complete frankness his own view of life. "Do you mean the block-heads, the "polite" people who allow themselves to be ruled by the gossip of the masses and conventional notions, and would you set these up as examples? No, only the free man is happy, who enjoys life and allows his desires free play and satisfies them without bothering whether other people call it disgraceful or not. What is disgraceful is only the failure to make use of the law of the stronger; luxury, license and liberty – in these lies virtue and *eudaimonia*. All the rest is empty words and accidental conventions, which are in contradiction to nature" (491e–492c). At first he sticks to this view when Socrates talks of the contentment offered by modest living and compares the full life of staggering from pleasure to pleasure with the cask of the Danaids. Lengthy discussion is required before Callicles recognises that some pleasures are wrong and harmful, and the criterion for life can only be in the good.[104] But he is obliged in the end to concede that, both in the whole world, the vast kosmos, and in its individual manifestations, the best and enduring condition will only be achieved where lawfulness, order and harmony prevail. That holds also for man, for his body and for his soul. The best human condition consists not in loose living which recognises no order but in disciplined self-control. The virtue of man and his worth depend upon that self-control.

Here the superman Callicles comes upon the scene as antagonist of Socrates. But he says himself that he is only expressing what "the many" secretly desire. The power which he deliberately strives to get is in fact a worldly joy that the average philistine might in his imagination dream of. For he can in reality think of nothing better than the absolute power either to do or not to do just whatever he likes. And if he did not feel within himself the superman's power to raise himself above the rest, he would at least wish to live his everyday life as he wanted to, and that was not the smallest attraction of democracy, that it promised that freedom. Plato was also aware of that, and he was not thinking only of Callicles when in the spirit of his master he pressed for clarity on that point too and introduced a detailed discussion of the question: "What does "will" mean, and what does man in reality wish for?" His conclusion is that true willing is not a momentary subjective fancy but a striving towards that which a man by his nature ultimately desires, because it is the real good for him that helps him to fulfil himself and thus brings him *eudaimonia*, which he longs for. This good resides for man in the moral life of the community. For Socrates objective good is what man really does "will". Only that can be the norm for life, and knowledge of the good is therefore the first essential for man.

We can see what lies behind that quest – coming to grips with the popular conception of freedom as expressed in the ideal of democratic freedom. Plato is by no means able to finish with that many-sided question within the space of this particular dialogue; and another still more important question is only mooted, without any conclusive answer being arrived at. We are certainly told that the *sophrosyne* and self-mastery needed by man, if he is to lead the good life, must depend upon order and inner harmony, but what these consist of we are not told.

The reason for this was probably that Plato himself had reached no satisfactory solution, and that to find one he must not confine himself to purely ethical questionings. But after the publication of the *Gorgias* a long period of enquiry soon set in, which was to lead Plato to a quite different outlook on the nature of the world and of man. He recognised in the non-material that which really exists and this led him to the problems that had been encountered in connection with the concept of the soul which Socrates had introduced. In the *Phaedo* he makes of the Socratic distinction between soul and body a profound metaphysical theory and takes over the old religious conception of the soul as an independent immortal being that belongs to the immaterial world and is only temporarily attached to the mortal body. He does not fail to draw ethical conclusions from this idea and to correct explicitly the views which he had advanced earlier propounded in his *Protagoras*.[105] Then he had not hesitated to interpret self-control, as the "many" do, as a kind of art of measurement, helping to suppress momentary desires because of their unhappy future effects. But now he sees the popular virtues of *sophrosyne* and of bravery as a kind of bartering shop where one wishes to master sensual desires only in order to acquire other material benefits. Above these goods he now sets another, the true virtue, springing from the soul's very essence, and completely liberating him from the shackles of the flesh and the outer world.

Yet even so that was not Plato's last word. As a result of the sharp cleavage between body and soul which he puts forward in the *Phaedo*, the sensual desires as in popular opinion belong to the sphere of the flesh; they develop out of its material necessities and fix the soul to it as if with nails.[106] But even so no clear psychological image emerges. That first appears in full in the *Republic*, where he undertakes to solve the ultimate problems of human life, of the individual and of the city-state, on the basis of a new insight into the nature of the human soul.

Once again he takes as his starting point the popular conception of *sophrosyne* (430e). According to popular opinion this is a certain order, a mastery of pleasures and desires, whereby man is said to master himself.[107] That immediately recalls the *Gorgias*. The new element however is that this self-mastery now becomes problematic, and – as was the case with the victory over the pleasures in the *Protagoras* – the question must be asked, what does it mean? The expression must at first sight seem ridiculous, for how can the same man at once be the master and be mastered? Yet it contains a hint of the truth. It must mean that within the soul of man are diverse elements, the better and the worse, and that the better must have the mastery.

This explanation certainly brings Plato into a certain opposition to Socrates who had represented the soul as a unity. But it is borne out in the study which follows. For the sole object of the question about self-mastery is to lead on to the main point of the *Republic* where Plato sets out his new psychological discovery, which also lays the scientific foundations for the setting up of his ideal state: in its earthly existence the soul is no unitary being.[108] For the sensual appetites which man had attributed previously to the flesh are also psychic processes. They are the lowest layers of the soul's life which have to do exclusively with the material needs arising from its being attached to the body. Together they constitute the desiring part of the soul, the *epithymetikon*. This is quite separate from the *thymos* which embraces the higher manifestations of the soul like fortitude and the sense of justice. High above both, however, is the *logistikon*, the intellect, whose task it is to curb the urges of the spirit's lower tendencies and thus to point the way to the proper conduct of life, *eudaimonia*. For that is true self-mastery, that within the soul the intellect should be master.

This threefold division of the soul is borne out, says Plato, when we turn our attention to human society. For the population of the state falls by its natural composition into three layers corresponding to the parts of the single soul, the social classes of the philosophers, the armed guard and the producers who see to material needs. The fact that here too the philosophers, who are intellectually the highest, must be dominant if the state is to be healthy and happy – that is the ripe fruit that falls by itself into one's lap in the course of the investigation.

There also emerges one other fact that is likely to direct man's pursuit of happiness along the right lines: the much praised tyrant, whom the masses envy, because he has power over others, to do or to leave undone whatever he likes, is in reality the most unhappy and unfree of men, because he is not master of himself, but, like Callicles, he makes himself the slave of his own pleasures, which keep him from following the knowledge that the better part of him has and from being really free. He does not do what in reality he "wills".

This line of thought [109] culminates in the passage that finally enlightens us about the nature and the origin of the soul and shows that even in the older conception of the unity of the soul there was a grain of truth. There we learn that only in the earthly existence is the soul something pieced together, a sort of fabulous creature that consists of a man, a lion and a many-headed monster. Only through association with the body does the soul develop the *thymos* and the *epithymetikon* and only when we have overcome these things is the true original nature of the soul revealed. That is the intellect, the νοῦς, the inner man, ὁ ἐντὸς ἄνθρωπος. It also becomes clear what the highest duty of man is: he must do all he can to keep this inner man pure and prevent him from being dragged down by the body to the earthly sphere (*Republic*, 588a–592a; 611b–612a). That is possible, however, only if within the soul the intellect is absolute master. Only then can its own being fully unfold. Only then can man prevent "the most godlike part of him from being enslaved to the most ungodly" (589d). Only through the intellect's control of the senses can man achieve his destiny, his *eudaimonia*, his true freedom. For only this makes him really independent of the external world, because it raises him above the earthly and shows him, by making him concentrate on his true nature, life's highest goal. It is in the freedom of the intellect that man fulfils his destiny.

In Plato's *Laws* we read: "The first and best victory is to master oneself; to be overcome by oneself the greatest disaster and shame – that applies alike to the individual and the community."[110] In the ideal state the citizens' natural attitude, which makes them concern themselves with material needs, prevents them from realising the freedom of the intellect in themselves. Their social virtue is their voluntary submission to the leadership of the "better" part of the community. Yet government of the community by the philosophers is exactly the same thing for the whole community as self-discipline is for the individual. It is the sovereignty of the intellect in the community and with it true freedom is achieved. The city-state of Plato, like that of Aeschylus, remains subject to the intellect of God. That, however, implies no limitation. For it is precisely the intellect of God that rules naturally in the ideal human state.

There is only one way for the individual to achieve that freedom: through intellectual training. In a famous simile in the opening of the seventh book of the *Republic* Plato describes how, so long as men are enslaved to sensuality, they are like prisoners in a dark cave, and they must adapt themselves completely before they can go out into the open air and be able to bear the light of pure reason. The climb is arduous and takes a long time, if the intellect is to get accustomed, through the disciplines of mathematics and dialectics, to freeing itself from the senses and finding true being in the immaterial. It was on that conviction that Plato framed the teaching in his own Academy, and in the *Phaedrus* (278) he proudly explains that this is the only education worthy of man, regardless of how extensive a man's practical activities are. Only the training of his own independent rational thinking capacity gives man the power to make his own personal decisions and keep his independence, uninfluenced by the views of the masses. Only that makes him truly free.

The idea of learning for its own sake no more occurred to Plato than to Thucydides. For him too there was no sense in investigations that did not aim at the advantage of the community. He went further still, however, and wanted the individual to recognise that his own freedom of enquiry must be defined by the limit of its advantage to the community. Admittedly, he says in the *Politicus* that no progress in the specific branches of knowledge is possible if individuals are cramped by rigid regulations (299); and again in the *Laws* he expressly lays it down that the highest authorities should see to it that foreign institutions are studied so that, when necessary, reforms can be carried out.[111] But the "private citizen" is allowed to study only to the extent that it bears upon the welfare of the state. False teachings like materialist atheism, which threaten the intellectual well-being of the community, must in no circumstances be tolerated. They are, in Plato's view, not learning at all. They are products of human *hybris* and come from disregarding the fact that not man but God is the measure of all things. (716c).

None of his disciples preserved the heritage of Plato so well as Aristotle. But that was partly because he regarded it as a divine commandment "to put truth higher than the men we love", and after Plato's death he even severed any formal connection with the Academy. He was born in the little town of Stagira on the Macedonian border, he did not have the advantages of Athenian citizenship, and so was without that warm attachment to the city which never left Plato. But he was at one with him in believing that a man can fulfil his destiny only in the organised community, and that it was only in the Greek city that this was possible. On Philip's invitation he went for two or three years to Macedonia to see to the education of the young Alexander and it is important for the course of world history that he introduced this young man to Hellenic intellectualism. But if Aristotle had made any attempt to win the heir to the throne to any political utopianism like the Platonic ideal state, Alexander would have vigorously objected, and Aristotle himself had no such intention. He was deeply convinced that the political institutions of the Greeks were indissolubly linked with their whole way of life and could not be transferred to other peoples. He does not use any general term for the idea expressed in our word "state" but distinguishes sharply between the barbarian tribal groups and the Greek *polis*, the perfect community[112], which alone made it possible for men to lead the good life founded on the ethical principles of justice. This goal can be attained, however, only in a limited area, and although Aristotle is convinced that the subjection of the barbarians with their inferior culture is to their own advantage and therefore morally justified (cf. p. 46), nevertheless the great empire was wholly beyond the horizons of his political thinking and he even took a stand against equalising the status of Greeks and barbarians, which Alexander considered necessary, in an open letter. In the lectures which at that time he delivered in Athens, he took no notice of Alexander's empire. All he wanted to do was to train leaders for the Greek *polis*.

The outward difference between Greeks and barbarians was particularly conspicuous in their attitudes to monarchy. Aristotle of course considered theoretically possible the ideal monarchy in which one individual so far surpasses the others in knowledge and moral capacity, that these willingly acquiesce. In practice monarchy as a form of government might well suit the barbarians, who are suited to service, but not the Greeks, or at any rate not at the present time (*Pol.*, III, 14–17). For the Greek *polis* is a "community of the free", "a living community of the free and equal".[113] He also naturally dismisses the democratic "head-counting" equality and unbridled freedom, but he requires not only that all citizens should be equal before the law but also that all should have a certain amount of political freedom and be entitled to participate in major political decisions in the running of the state.

Thus for Aristotle freedom and equality are of the very nature of the Greek city-state. It is customary to see in them special features of democracy[114], for freedom is generally regarded as the foundation of the democratic constitution. There is a tendency to say that only in that form of the state does man enjoy freedom, and also to associate with it in practice the mechanical levelling which helps to raise the majority of people without means to power. But that is true only in so far as democracy has developed these principles in a one-sided way. Yet even so there arises the danger of a radicalisation which would destroy any gradation of privileges according to a man's contribution to the community and which undermined respect for the laws required in order to preserve the state because they were considered a curtailment of liberty. But as Aristotle and, in his later years, Plato maintained, the state's welfare lies not in the one-sided application of a single principle but in the proper combination of different elements, and in normal circumstances the best constitution is a *politeia*, a moderate democracy which accords to the whole of the citizens the rights which are indispensable to a free people but, through aristocratic institutions, like the elections of officials instead of casting lots for them, gives it a counter-balance. Another advantage is a sound social structure, free from the dangerous contrast of rich and poor, and preventing the total community from being ruled by the numerically superior poor. A powerful middle class is the best foundation for the state.

It is the system of Solon which, as for Plato and Isocrates, is here chosen as the antithesis of the radical democracy of the present. For Aristotle, Solon is the only practical law-giver who followed the policy of the middle way which was so well suited to the Greeks.

Aristotle not only coined the famous saying that man is a political animal, ζῷον πολιτικόν, a being made for living in the *polis*; he also showed that theoretically the State is of greater antiquity than the individual man, since the latter can really only be a man in society (*Pol.*, I, 2, 1253a, 7–19). It was quite in the spirit of Plato when he also said: "We must realise that a citizen belongs not to himself but all citizens belong to the state, for the individual is part of the state" (*Pol.*, IX, 1, 1337a, 27), and this justifies state education. But he makes these proposals only for the ideal state, and however unequivocally he insists that the state is the all-embracing organ and that it must take precedence over the interests of the individual, he is also fully aware that the citizen body consists of very different individuals and that these have a right to an individual life and to the free development of their personalities within the framework of their community. [116] He turns explicitly against democratic freedom, in which "each may live as he likes", and he extols as a virtue of the Spartan *kosmos* that it takes care of the whole of life and carries out in particular the public education of youth. It is obvious, he points out, that order must reign in a household and the wife must not do just as she likes. But for him there is no question of that strict intervention in the private sphere which Plato advocates in the state constitution. He not only recognises individual personality as a fact, but considers it in his ethical theory.

In the introduction to his lectures on politics (*Pol.*, I, 4–6) Aristotle explored the economic foundations of the life of the state and in this context discusses systematically the question of slavery. That slavery is not brought about by some sort of accident, but a necessary component of the structure of society was for the aristocratic Aristotle a foregone conclusion, since the free citizens require "animate tools", to do the rough work, so that they may themselves be free for their real tasks. As we have seen (cf. p. 46), however, he also believed that slavery could be justified from the ethical point of view. For however willing he was to recognise that in individual cases servitude was a consequence of an act of violence, he was also fundamentally convinced that there were men who were "slaves by nature" because they were intellectually very much inferior and needed to be supervised by others and that this supervision was therefore to their advantage. As a Greek he was of course thinking of the barbarians. In fact in discussing high politics he quoted the words of the Iphigenia of Euripides (*Iphigenia in Aulis*, 1400):

> Mother, the Greeks must rule, and barbarians must be slaves,
> For Nature made them slaves, and the Greeks she created free.[117]

This domination is inwardly justified only if it is really exercised in the interests of the slaves. It does not alter the fact however that the slave is by right a chattel who may not look after himself, but belongs to a master.

For Aristotle civic liberty is such a self-evident prerequisite of the good life that in his Ethics he barely mentions it at all. He does, however, mention among the virtues *eleutheriotes*[118], the free behaviour of gentlemen who in all money matters observe the happy mean between wastefulness and meanness, and this is a consequence of *megalopsyche*, magnanimity, which is above all petty considerations and derives from the consciousness of its own worth its superiority over men and things.[119]

He was particularly concerned about the problem of self-control, *enkrateia*, and of its opposite, *akrasia*. For, as he explicitly emphasised, that was the point at which he most sharply conflicted with Socrates. The latter believed that from knowing the good, doing good necessarily followed and that therefore the question of "lack of control" did not arise and the only valid cause of wrong action was ignorance of the good. This contradicted what in Aristotle's eyes was the obvious fact that very often the proper knowledge is really present in the soul but cannot prevail against irrational desires. With Plato he recognised the conflict within the soul of man and, with certain modifications, he took over from him the separation of the soul's several capacities. For him self-control was an important psychic phenomenon. He distinguished it however from perfect virtue, or *sophrosyne*, where the instincts are in harmony with true reason,

99

ὀρθὸς λόγος, and he held that the essence of *enkrateia* lay in the intellect being in conflict with the instincts and overcoming them, whereas in the man lacking self-control, the ἀκρατής, the intellect is defeated by them and in the case of the dissolute man, the ἀκόλαστος, the opposite of the σώφρων, it surrenders to the instincts without a struggle.

Aristotle's own way of thinking tended entirely towards the theoretical. For him the gulf between the mind, νοῦς, and the soul's lower powers grew ever wider, and this has consequences for his Ethics. Situated far above the "practical" virtues, concerned with regulating instincts and passions in daily life are the "dianoetic" ones where the mind itself unfolds. The idea that in this man attains his highest goal Aristotle had maintained enthusiastically already in his early writings. Even in the *Nicomachean Ethics*, which in other respects is so sober and matter of fact, quite a different note is suddenly heard when he comes to speak about this point (1177b, 19): "The active engagement of the mind upon theoretical thinking, which is its supreme object, brings a perfect pleasure of its own kind and brings along with it everything that man otherwise identifies with perfect happiness." "Such a life is far beyond the measure of man. For a man who lives like this is not living according to his humanity but according to a divinity which is within him. Then in so far as that is higher than his whole being, so much higher is this activity than the activities appropriate to the other virtues. If therefore the intellect is divine compared with man, then living according to the intellect is divine compared with human life. We must not listen however to those who advise us as men to be merely human and as mortals to behave as mortals; we must on the contrary try as far as we can to make ourselves immortal and to live in accordance with that part of us which is the best.

In order to appreciate those words fully we must remember that Aristotle could envisage God's blessedness only in terms of purely theoretical thinking. To partake in that divine bliss is consequently the highest that can be vouchsafed to man. The proud feeling of joy that comes over Aristotle at that thought is heightened by his consciousness that this utterly superhuman life is in reality the complete fulfilment of human nature. For the mind, which makes it possible, is the true nature of man. Already in the *Protrepticus* he had maintained that the ruling part of the soul which includes understanding and thinking, exclusively, or at any rate for the main part, constitutes our very self, our true being (6, p. 34,

100

11W) and this thought is so firmly held in the *Nichomachean Ethics* that, in the course of a train of thought with quite another object, he can twice make use of it as an indisputable fact: "Each one of us *is* the spirit; that is the true self" (1168b, 34ff.; 1166a, 17).[120] So it will not surprise that our extract concludes thus: "One may well say that the mind is the man himself inasmuch as it is the dominant and better part" (1178a, 2).

Thus the identification of the spirit with the real self of man is purely Aristotelian, but it is unmistakably Plato's "inward man" which, transformed through the disciple's personality, survives as the νοῦς. It would be easy to understand if Aristotle had abandoned Plato's term since it had sprung from a specific analogy (cf. p. 94) and for that reason had not become widely used. But in all probability the Academy was ahead of him in this. So we may conclude from the first *Alcibiades*, which certainly was not the work of Plato himself but was written by a Platonist about the middle of the century.[121] The author's intention is to give an introduction to ethics from Plato's point of view. He gathers together all sorts of related thoughts of the master's and puts them, quite often superficially, under the general theme that concern for oneself is man's most important task. The position he personally adopts can be seen in this extract from his concluding section (128–133c) where he starts out from Apollo's command: "Know thyself", and goes on to say that "this self is not man's body nor even his whole being but the soul – more exactly his best, most godlike part in which knowledge and thought have their seat". The religious phrasing is certainly important for this writer, but it is clear here, as throughout the dialogue, that he is working with ideas learnt at school.

This "godlike" part of man is however nothing more than the "inner man" of the *Republic* and from Plato himself is also derived its equation with man's real self. When Plato speaks of burial rights in the *Laws* he impresses upon his readers above everything else: "The soul is quite distinct from the body. It is the soul which during life constitutes the true being of each one of us, whereas the body accompanies us only as the external appearance. Instead, therefore of designating, like Homer, the souls as copies (εἴδωλα), it would be better so to name the bodies of the dead, and to bear in mind that the truly existing self is the immortal soul which goes to the gods."[122] It is only conditioned by the special theme that Plato speaks here of the soul instead of its "godlike" part.

Through the *Alcibiades*, whose wide circulation was due to its introductory nature, this conception became commonly known. "When Apollo
tells us "know yourself", he does not mean the parts of our body and our
outward form. What he is telling us to do according to Cicero (*Tusc.*, I, 52)
is "know your soul, your mind" [123] and this idea has travelled further and
further, especially through the Neo-Platonists and the Greek Fathers of
the Church."

Socrates had shown man the road to inner freedom by pointing out that
the true values lie in his own soul. But people gradually became more and
more conscious that within the soul itself there are powers which threaten
that freedom; these are the sensual pleasures and desires which Plato
recognised as processes in the psyche. That these can lure men into the
vilest servitude the common people had already dimly felt in popular
morality (cf. p. 67ff.). As a result of his new psychology Plato was led to
recognising clearly that real inner freedom can exist only in the mind's
absolute mastery of the lower instincts. The self-mastery which even
popular opinion required is that freedom of the spirit which represents
man's true self. Aristotle's natural tendency made him give to that reasoning the interpretation that theoretically that intellect, in raising man completely above the daily round, realises the divinity in man.[124]

Plato like Aristotle used the expression "freedom" with caution because of its too political overtones. But objectively they both developed
the idea to the point of philosophical clarity. Inner freedom fulfilled itself
in the freedom of the intellect which not only guarantees man independence of external things but also is the only thing that enables him to
develop freely his real self.

To that freedom there is only one barrier, but an immovable one. It
lies in the nature of the intellect itself, which is subject to strict laws and
can only desire what is good and true. That is what binds it to God. And
"God is the measure of things".

"Education for Freedom" as a Community's Cultural Ideal

Among the young people who came under the influence of Socrates was
for a time Isocrates, born in 436–5, who soon, however, went a different
way. It is true that he adopted the teaching that man's most important
task is the care of his soul and he even wanted to practise "philosophy"

himself.[125] But all he meant by philosophy was an above-average education and from personal inclination he realised this in the cult of beautiful form. When he then opened a school of his own dedicated to that idea he expressly formulated its antithesis to Plato's Academy[126] by declaring that he did not aim at an intellectual training concerned with the quest of truth, which could never be attained by man, but sought to prepare his pupils for practical life and inculcate in them a way of thinking that conformed to generally accepted views (*doxai*). That does not, however, mean that he had no opinions of his own.

Isocrates was an Athenian body and soul, equally proud of the cultural and the military achievements of his city and he liked to speak of the willingness to self-sacrifice of their ancestors who at the expense of their Attica had realised that "freedom was the fatherland" (*Archid.* 43). As late as the year 380 in his *Panegyricus* he maintains that Athens is entitled to the hegemony in Greece at least on the sea. In that pamphlet he equally pointed out to the Greeks that there was still a greater fatherland than the single city-state.[127] When these continued to tear each other apart in endless civil wars and the great powers among them were only striving to bring into their power and enslave the very compatriots they had once liberated from the Persian yoke, Isocrates then became the spokesman of the Panhellenists. The unification of the Hellenes by means of a great common task, fighting the hereditary Persian enemy, became the political programme which he followed with extraordinary tenacity and which ultimately made him see in Philip not the threat to Greek freedom but on the contrary the one man in a position to put to an end the splintering up of the nation.

That led him in his old age into the sharpest opposition to Athenian foreign policy and to its present democratic form of government. For, the imperialism which his native country was still pursuing in spite of its weakness was for him part and parcel of its maritime policy, and this was also the cause of the ominous developments on the home political front. That fact was as evident to him as to the oligarchic author of the work on the *Constitution of the Athenians* (cf. p. 33) and for Plato and Aristotle. As an Athenian he saw in the democratic constitution of Athens a claim to glory. He even seized upon the legend from the age of Pericles that it had been introduced by Theseus and he coined the happy expression that Theseus had thus "made free the souls of his fellow citizens" (*Hel.*, 35).[128]

But it had been a democracy very different from that of his own age. For in it had still reigned the true freedom, where willingly accepted obligations had to be honoured, and the genuine equality, which still had a place for merit. It was only after the Persian war when, instead of the indigenous conservative population of the countryside, the restless undisciplined elements who earned their livelihood in the fleet won decisive influence in the state that radicalisation set in which destroyed discipline and order not only in politics but in the whole way of life of the citizen body (cf. 34).

Isocrates agrees almost word for word with Plato in his criticism of the contemporary situation. But whereas the latter breaks completely with the democracy and takes refuge in his ideal state, Isocrates wishes to remain within the community of his own people and he levels at the men of culture the reproach that they do not pay any heed to the opinions of their fellow citizens (*Panathenaicus*, 29), whereas his own pupils are to learn "to become honourable men and to be held in respect by their fellow citizens" (*Speech on Exchanging Property*, 278). He proposes to teach in his school not merely beauty of form but also beauty of thought and action. When almost a hundred years old he summarised in his last work (*Panathen.*, 30–32) in four points what he considered the right education. These points are the practical skills of daily life, correct and tactful dealings with one's fellow men, spiritual poise which remains the master of pleasure and does not surrender to the blows of fate and finally, "the greatest quality", the sense of the proper measure of man, which does not allow good fortune to create arrogance and which values spiritual qualities as highly as material possessions.

Those last words may remind us of Socratic ideas to which Isocrates does occasionally refer. He can introduce them at this point because they are for him part of that outlook which had been long since accepted by the best of his fellow countrymen. What he is here developing as an educational programme is by no means the fruit of an ethical system of his own. He only wants to be the interpreter of the feelings of his people, although he boasts that he personally is called upon to develop that lively Greek feeling for proportion and the golden mean in the conscious approach to beauty, and in that way to become the herald of a purified popular ethic.

In that context freedom is not mentioned, probably because for Iso-

crates too the word sounded too political. But at the back of his programme we are aware of the "free education" (ἐλευθέριος παιδεία), which
had become in his time an educational slogan. Even Aristotle had wanted
for his "best" state an education which was not determined by practical usefulness and external necessities, but is "worthy of a free man and beautiful"
(ἐλευθέριος καὶ καλή, Pol., 1338a, 31; cf. 1339b, 5). In *Areopagiticus*
(43) Isocrates himself describes, in contrast to the riotous living of the
present, the situation found in ancient Athens where young men were
"brought up with a free intellectual attitude" and were accustomed to
high-mindedness. But already in *Panegyricus* (49) he had used the same
term to praise Athens as the house of true philosophy where men, brought
up from the outset with a free mind, were not judged by their physical
strength and money but by their education. The words reflect his patriotic
pride, and it is true that the idea of "free education" could fully flourish
only on Athenian soil where the free attitude of mind of all citizens had
already been the ideal of Pericles and the conviction soon spread that
freedom itself was a matter of one's attitude (cf. p. 47).

This "education of the free man" was quite different in its inspiration
and nature from the Socratic inner freedom. It knew nothing of an objective good that man must know if he is to lead a good and really free
life. It held naturally to the traditional estimate of the value of material
wealth and made no attempt to foster a personal moral attitude, in
accordance with Socratic teaching, which could be independent of the
opinions of the "many".

All the more suited was it to become the collective educational ideal
in Athens. For if even the genuine democrat understood freedom to mean
above all a man's right "to do or not to do whatever he likes" in his own
life, then it could seem to him to be only right that the word should also
include the idea of a "free", higher education.[130]

That was fundamentally of course what Pericles had envisaged. Of the
high idealism which had led him to the concept of the free personality
there was now very little left. And the freedom of the spirit propounded
by Plato and Aristotle was too high for the broad masses and was anyway
not intended for them.

CHAPTER IV

THE HELLENISTIC AGE

POLITICAL AND LEGAL FREEDOM

"For the man of Hellas there is nothing greater than freedom", says an inscription from Priene of the third century, honouring the commander of the citadel for his valour in defending it. "Let us fight for freedom, man's finest possession", still was the cry to spur soldiers on before battle.[1] Freedom and the independence of the fatherland were on everybody's lips all the time; and countless men had given their lives for that ideal. But that could not halt the progress of historical development which was pressing on towards the annihilation of Greek independence. Admittedly Aristotle had still divided mankind into Greeks and barbarians, citing with approval Euripides' words that nature itself had ordained that the Greeks should be lords over the barbarians (cf. p. 99). But it soon became clear that Greece was a small part of the whole world and the course of world history was being determined in quite another place. The geographical position of Greece, its commerce, its mercenary soldiery and above all its intellectual superiority, which made it a high school for the barbarian lands and enabled it to determine opinion all over the world, all these were of no small significance for the practical politics of the country. But the only consequence was that the new great powers were speculating on how to make the country serve their own interests, and as the narrow minded separatism of the Greeks continued, hampering political unification and even undermining such loose confederacies of states as might arise, Greece became inevitably a plaything in the hands of the great powers, especially as these well understood how to use Greek ideology for their own ends. Just as Athenians and Spartans had once used the right of small states to self-determination as propaganda, so now did Macedonians, Ptolemies and Seleucids in turn. Similarly, just as the Ionians had celebrated Lysander after the fall of Athens, so now Antigonus' son, Demetrius, was honoured by the Athenian democrats as liberator and god because he had set aside the moderate constitution that had been introduced under Macedonian influence. But such "liberations" did not last long, and even when the presence of foreign garrisons was not drastically drawing attention to the real situation, in most Greek states freedom was only a word, since the inhabitants were no longer in a position to defend themselves by their own means.

That situation was not changed when the big brother from the west took a hand in Greek affairs. The Romans came, after the second Punic War, as champions of Greek freedom against the Macedonians and when at the Isthmian Panhellenic Games Flamininus, in the year 196, proclaimed freedom and autonomy for all the Greeks, there was tremendous jubilation and enthusiastic gratitude to the liberator. "There still is one people in the world which with its own money and effort and at its own risk, fights for the freedom of others", wrote Livy (XXXIII, 33). That was the boast that Athens had once made (cf. p. 83). But this time the "liberated" were soon disappointed and it was partly their own fault. For quarreling between the city-states, as well as internal tensions, never ceased. More and more delegates went to the Roman Senate asking for intervention, but there, instead of the genuine philhellenism that inspired men like Flamininus, quite other interests prevailed. So it could come about that in the year 146 Corinth, the most flourishing city of Greece, was destroyed with a degree of cruelty that made Cicero blush for shame. The other Greeks gradually became more and more dependent on Rome and Augustus only put the finishing touch to the process when he officially made Greece legally a Roman province.

Among the men who had suffered personally from the brutality of Rome was Polybius of Arcadia, one of the thousand distinguished Greeks who were deported to Italy as hostages in the year 166. But through that very circumstance it became his fate to undertake a mission of great historical importance to the world. As tutor and fatherly friend to the younger Scipio he came into close contact with the better Roman aristocratic circles, who experienced a deep need to enrich their own way of life with the Greek intellectual qualities. They were however most of all receptive to the political ideals of the Greeks which they got to know through Polybius and which helped them to understand in theory how their own state worked.

Ever since the publication of Plato's *Laws* there had grown up a wider recognition in Greek political theory of the fact that success was not to be expected from one-sided application of a single political principle but in a combination of elements of different kinds of constitutions. And when, in his conversations with the great men of Rome, Polybius was himself confronted with the question what was the fundamental cause of the swift rise of Rome to world power, he found his answer not simply in its general military and moral ascendency which he as an unprejudiced historian was quick to recognise, but more especially in the constitution which it had developed, not without serious internal conflicts but nevertheless by itself and of its own nature, with its particularly happy blending of democratic, aristocratic and monarchic elements.

The democratic element was freedom.[2] But the Roman *libertas* was different from the Greek ἐλευθερία. Just as the head-counting democratic equality of the Athenians was contrary to the Roman spirit which required that a citizen's influence be commensurate with his worth, his *dignitas*, so the unbridled freedom of the individual citizen "to live as he likes" was for the ancient Romans out of the question. This was, in their eyes, not *libertas* but overstepped the proper measure and was *licentia*, the term they used to render Greek ἀκολασία. The Periclean ideal of freedom, permitting to each the unfolding of his own personality, was also quite foreign to the Romans. They too respected a strong personality, but their ideal was manliness, the *virtus* of the *vir bonus*, and this *virtus* was determined by the practical duties which every citizen had to perform in public and in private life. *Libertas* was not so much the individual expression of a man's striving after independence as a component part of a legal order which had for every individual a proper place in society. The Romans had a pronounced sense of law, order, strict organisation and discipline in the field and in the home. Even within the narrow space of the household a dividing line was therefore drawn from the start far more sharply than in Greece between the unfree servants and the free, the latter embracing, apart from the master of the house, his family and the children, who were explicitly called *liberi*. The *libertas* which distinguished them from slaves guaranteed them security of the person and freedom of decision in purely private matters, and the right to take part in the *res publica*, the people's affairs[3] – it took centuries for this to develop into the rigid concept of a state – but the popular feeling was that this *libertas* has its natural limits not only in the obligation to conform with fixed laws but also in the *mos majorum*, the traditional moral ideas, and also in *auctoritas*, the authority of individual persons and corporations whose superiority was willingly recognised and heeded.

How little the Romans thought that this *libertas* excluded the strict supervision of the citizen's private life is best seen in the institution of censorship and the laws on luxuries. It is true, however, that their practical effect gradually diminished, and opposition to them grew so strong that at about the year 100 an opponent to a law of this kind declared it an intolerable constraint incompatible with liberty.[4] He could even risk the quip: "What is left of liberty if a man who wants to ruin himself with luxury is not allowed to?" – an impertinence which the censors punished by expulsion of the speaker from the Senate.

This concept of *libertas* did not develop until after the overthrow of the monarchy and then as a contrast to it. But the inborn sense of discipline was strong enough to give the higher officials, who now ran the affairs of the state, a degree of authority which the Greeks would have felt appropriate only to a king. It was quite compatible with this *libertas* that the Senate developed into a sort of corporation and for centuries or more controlled in practice the whole administration. In the eyes of the aristocracy the people's *libertas* was organically associated with the authority of the Senate, and its members defended themselves with all their might against the claims of the "popularists", who rebelled against the Senate's rule in the name of *libertas*. Naturally Scipio and his friends welcomed the fact that Polybius and his compatriot Panaetius, who supported the historian's ideas and generalised them philosophically, gave them a theoretical basis for their own aims, by arguing that a composite constitution is the best. As Plato had already recognised, civic unity is possible only when all citizens enjoy a certain modicum of freedom.[5] But this must be confined to the most essential basic rights and must be counterbalanced by a permanent political body which is able to pursue consistently a purposeful policy and by a body of officials possessing the full authority which is essential to the executive.

Through this translation into Roman terms the Greek idea of the composite constitution had considerable practical significance in political history. For a long time it offered the aristocracy the ideological basis for its programme, and Cicero could still hope to succeed in restoring on this basis the old Roman constitution; to him that seemed the only way out of the crisis the state was going through. For a long time past, however, a factor had come into political life which did not go with the old scheme of the mixed constitution. Panaetius had recognised well enough the innate lust for power of the great men in Rome to teach them to respect not just the control of an individual over the community but leadership which caused men to serve the community of their own accord. But as a result of growing individualism the whole of political life became a struggle for power between individual men. Caesar came to recognise clearly that the old Roman constitution had been good enough for a small Italian state, but that for the new world empire it must be changed basically and must have a monarch at its head. He was victorious, and so the time of the *libera res publica* was over.

The change in the times was made felt particularly by one act which seemed symbolic. When Cato, so often ridiculed by his fellow-citizens for his principles and still unconquered after Caesar's victory, chose suicide while still free in preference to servitude, everybody had the feeling that the old champion of liberty could do nothing else. "By divine law they were indissolubly united. Neither did Cato survive freedom, nor freedom survive Cato."[6]

Augustus maintained the old forms of the state as far as possible, and he begins the account of his activities with his having given freedom to the community which had been repressed through the dominance of one party; (*rem publicam dominatione factionis oppressam in libertatem vindicavi*).[7] And on his coins he calls himself the liberator, *vindex libertatis*. Later emperors were glad to do the same thing. But it only meant that they had destroyed one ruler to put themselves in his place. In practice, the privileged position of the first citizen developed into absolute monarchy, *dominatio*, and the *res publica*, the republic, as we call it today, changed into *imperium*.

People quickly got accustomed to the new situation and the opposition fell silent.[8] It had always had its real basis in a few aristocratic groups in the Senate who could not get over the fact that their own political role had come to an end and as upright men were on moral grounds not prepared to obey every command of a capricious tyrant. In the capital after the loss of their political liberty the great majority were satisfied

110

with bread and circuses. In the provinces too people were quite content and glad that law and order now prevailed. Above all they enjoyed gratefully a boon the world had hardly known before, blessed peace, the *pax Augusta*. The Greeks reacted in the same way. The most celebrated orator of the day, Aelius Aristides, delivered in the year 156 an address of praise to Rome. In it he extolled the blessings of peace and praised the world-wide empire, in which the same citizenship was available to all men without distinction of nationality or place of residence provided they showed themselves worthy of it. And if Thucydides, speaking about the democracy of Pericles, had said it was in reality a monarchy with the first man of the people at its head, Aristides now dared to remark about the empire: "We have one common democracy covering the whole earth under the most excellent man in it as its law-giver and administrator".[9]

The ideal of freedom of course was not forgotten.[10] And when at the Olympic games Nero romantically proclaimed once again to the Greeks the freedom they had never really possessed – "For you were always subject either to foreigners or to each other as servants", – the Greeks, of course, once again paid him the honours of a new Zeus Eleutherios who "conferred upon them the freedom which through their own nature and through the land they lived in had always been their heritage", but the discerning people realised that this was a farce and in no way changed the real situation.

The old civic sense remained very much alive and, just as in present day Greece, generous endowments given to the town of one's birth bore witness to it.[11] Plutarch as a true Hellene and highly esteemed in Rome, remained faithful to his little home town, Chaeronea and did not consider it beneath him to take on official posts there. But he urgently warned a high-spirited young friend who took on a similar post never to forget that a stroke of the pen of the Roman governor was enough to deprive him of it, and that the Greek cities had just as much freedom as their masters decided to leave them. He also treasures freedom as the highest good and is proud of his people's great past achievements. But he cannot conceal from himself that the enormous power which the Hellenes had engaged in the war of liberation against the Persians, had afterwards been used by them for mutual mutilation and enslavement, and that the Romans had to come to put an end to the eternal dissensions of the Greeks. The subjection to Rome was not only an unalterable fact in his eyes but also a historical necessity; its deeper significance lay in the fact that only in that way could the Greeks partake of the blessings of the peace which, left to themselves, they were unable to obtain.

Plutarch is fully aware of the tragedy inherent in his people's longing for freedom.

At that time there was a vast increase in the number of slaves.[12] The vigorous economic prosperity and the development of capitalism, investing its money in large-scale agricultural and industrial concerns, intensified the demand for cheap labour, and in order to meet it the most brutal methods were adopted. In the year 167 B.C. no less than 150000 inhabitants of Epirus were sold into slavery as prisoners of war by the Roman conquerors.[13] In the East especially it was not only pirates who openly indulged in capturing men; even tax-gatherers organised systematic manhunts with the tacit complicity of the authorities, and in the greater markets like Delos there was a roaring trade in this human merchandise. The kind of life which many of these unfortunate beings had to expect is described by the Stoic Posidonius as a historian. During a journey to Spain in the last century before Christ he saw slaves in the silver mines living under the most miserable conditions and compelled under the overseer's rod to do very hard labour without resting so that their owners in Rome might pile up incredible riches. What emerges from his picture is not only his deep compassion and moral indignation but also his concern at the danger threatening the social structure of the world. In various different places, particularly in the west, despair had already driven the tortured masses to bloody rebellions in which their repressed hatred was released in inhuman atrocities that were only suppressed by force of arms in an equally inhuman manner. Posidonius clearly saw that all these rebellions sprang from the same cause and were symptoms of a developing ill-health in the whole economic system. It was only the Empire with its strict administration and more reasonable measures that established internal peace.

Much happier was the lot of the slaves working in the smaller concerns or in the households, and here the spirit of the new age even exercised a beneficial influence. Aristotle had still tried to prove that barbarians were naturally born to be slaves, but with the mingling of peoples in the

Hellenic period and more particularly with the rapid rise of Rome, the separation of the world into Greeks and barbarians lost its meaning, and its place was taken by the belief that all men are equal by nature.[14] The recognised champions of the new conception of humanity were the Stoics, who had at the head of their school Zeno and his followers, drawn principally from the Hellenised non-Greeks. In explicit contradiction to Aristotle their doctrine was: "No man is a slave by nature", and the saying soon became a dogma which in theory nobody dared refute. Chrysippus distinguished slaves from free labourers only by the life-long nature of their service conditions. During the empire Epictetus, himself a former slave, develops that thought in a religious manner: "You have the soul of a servant"; he once retorted to a nobleman who complained of his slaves, "you don't want to be on good terms with your brother, who is no less descended from Zeus than you are, who is begotten of the same seed and is of the same heavenly origin."

The numerous anthologies that offered the general public a sort of guide to behaviour could not be without a chapter on "Masters and Slaves", containing a collection of the humane sayings of poets and philosophers.[15] There was plentiful material, particularly in the new comedy which in Athens had become the mouthpiece of the Hellenic spirit.[16] It adopted the new conception of man, which we shall soon have to consider, and from that standpoint saw slavery also in a new light. In one of his plays the poet Philemon took up the old thought that in reality no mortal is free, that even the power of Zeus is limited by *ananke*, the law-abiding nature of the universe (cf. p. 48ff.), and he has a slave address his master in these words (fr. 31):

> I am my master's slave, who says what I must do;
> You and your equals are the slaves of city law,
> Others a tyrant rules, himself enslaved by fear,
> He must obey the king who does as God commands.
> And God himself must yield to universal laws.
> There is for every man a power above himself,
> And he must, as a slave, accept it as his master.

Consideration of that kind no longer meant, however, dissatisfaction with the prevailing lack of human freedom; their goal was to make sure

113

that the legal bondage of slaves should not be the occasion for regarding them as inferior members of the human community. The same poet has another slave say (fr. 22):

> If someone is a slave, my lord, he still remains
> No less a man for that, if he is human.

To recognise and respect the human being in a slave was for Hellenism a recognised moral obligation, to treat him humanely a sign of good breeding and culture. Seneca wrote a whole letter on this subject to his friend Lucilius (*Ep.* 47). He knew perfectly well the old Roman saying "So many slaves, so many enemies". But as against it he maintains "Numberless are the slaves who have died for their master. We make enemies of them only if we treat them inhumanly." He knew too that many of his equals in rank considered it beneath their dignity to sit down at table along with their slaves. "Why, then?" "They are slaves." "No, they are men, comrades, friends of a lower class, fellow slaves, no more subject to the power of destiny than we are."

We must not of course assume that it was usual for Nero's minister to take his meals with his servants or believe that it was a general custom, but there can be no doubt that slaves were by no means generally despised socially. In the community of Epicurus slaves were treated as members having equal rights, and in Rome, where the tendency was in other respects towards a sharper cleavage, those who were not free had always belonged to the *familia*, whose head was not the "master" but the *pater familias*.[17] Within this household it became more and more customary later on to find Greek slaves who, because of their better education, seemed suitable for educating the children as well as for social intercourse with the grown-ups. In Rome the increasing number of slaves who were set free also reduced the social distinction. For, whereas in Greece the former slaves only lived on as settlers, in Rome they became real Romans, with only very slight limitations to their full citizenship. Horace, of course, had to put up with envious aristocrats turning up their noses at him as the "son of a freedman"; but that was something he could easily get over so long as he was really friendly with Maecenas and Augustus personally appreciated his company.

In the ensuing period freedmen attained to great political influence because for the rulers they were more convenient helpers and tools than were the nobility, and the aristocrats might then compete for the favour of the all powerful minister.

The legal situation was unaffected by this change of outlook. Roman jurists took over from the Stoa the thesis that by the law of nature all men are born free, but supplemented it with the rider that according to *jus gentium* the difference between master and slave was everywhere recognised as a legal institution. The Stoics had no occasion to call for the abolition of slavery in practice; to have done this would have been contrary to their fundamental view that happiness does not depend upon externals. Similar views were held by the new religions that sought to bring salvation to the individual man.[18] The small Jewish sect of the Essaeans abolished slavery in their own community as an offence against the divine and the human order. Christianity wanted to relieve the lot of the weary and distressed by active love of one's neighbour and united slaves and free men in the one community of the faithful founded on baptism, but it was far from considering any change in the social structure, if only because the end of all things was at hand. "Serve your earthly master in fear and trembling", Paul firmly impressed upon Christian slaves. For the slaves too came the good tidings that there is a freedom higher than that of earthly law, and that this freedom alone is what brings man happiness.

THE INTELLECTUAL SITUATION IN THE NEW AGE

Human Perspectives

The Greeks of the Hellenistic age are no longer the same as those of the Classical period. That is by no means due entirely to the mingling of peoples and the juxtaposition of races. Epicurus and Callimachus were pure Greeks by blood. The reason is much more the complete change in the conditions of life, which compelled a corresponding change in mental outlook.

If Aristotle as a Greek considered man πολιτικὸν ζῷον, a being made for a political community, we must not forget that for him that community is the Greek *polis*, the city-state, which alone enables men to lead the "good life".[19] Actually this *polis* means for the Greeks something totally different from the bureaucratic state that governs modern man. The *polis* is the society that has grown up naturally, providing for the

115

individual not only a place to live in, but content for his life. The Attic peasant, working out on his fields or vineyards, probably seldom took the time to attend the people's assembly; politically speaking nevertheless, he knew he was not a man of Marathon or of Acharnae but an Athenian, and was aware that as a free man he might discuss and help to decide on the important decisions concerning not only the community but himself personally. For him the city of Athens was not just the market place where he did his buying and selling. There on the rock was enthroned Pallas Athene whose strong hand protected alike his city and himself. And even the simplest peasant would certainly not miss the festival plays at the Theatre of Dionysius that were part of the glory of his native city. The *polis* was not only a political community but at the same time the cultural and intellectual homeland embracing all the citizens.

We have already seen how that community was threatened by increasing individualism and how much the individual was cutting loose from it. But when Plato fled the Agora for the Academy, he retained his conviction that a man can only fulfil himself in the city-state. And for Aristotle philosophy, his personal vocation, was fundamentally justified because it was a service to the community, the *polis*. Besides these men, there were of course others like Antisthenes and Aristippus who pointed to a goal beyond the society of the city, and it is even more noteworthy that in the educational syllabus drawn up by Isocrates in the last years of his life he thinks only about the development of the individual personality and has not a word to say about duties to the community. But that his pupils will fulfil such duties he takes as a foregone conclusion, and he himself claims to be a thoroughly loyal citizen. But immediately afterwards, in 338, came the Chaeronea catastrophe, and we know well the effect it had on the feelings of the Athenians. While immediately after the battle there came a movement for reform, urging that the state should educate the young to the service of the community, Epicurus was earnestly warning his young supporters not to take part in politics, because its excitements only upset the individual's balance. Menander and Philemon are at the same time producing their comedies showing Attic humanism and intellect at its peak, but the old civic sense is no longer alive in them. Together with their intellectual interests, men's lives were filled with wine, women and song; the state is hardly mentioned.

Whoever wanted to get on went out in the world and discovered there a wide field of activity where he could make a career as a soldier, official, merchant or man of learning. One thing, however, he could not find there – a home, to which he was linked by birth and tradition, a *polis* where, as a free man he could naturally take part in the development of the whole community. Instead, such success as he achieved was due entirely to his personal ability, and he could shape his life to suit himself.

That demanded a complete personal re-orientation. The Greek of the fourth century had already been demanding the right to live his own life. He remained nevertheless restricted by the *polis* in his thoughts and feelings. But now he had to make a new place for himself in foreign lands. From being a citizen, a member of the society of a small city-state, he thus became a man leading an isolated existence in the wide world as an *atomon*, an individual. The categories in which the new generation lived and thought were no longer those of citizen and city-state but of the individual and mankind. It was the relationship between these that had to be thought out anew.

Thus arose problems affecting not only individual theorists but all men everywhere, including the Greeks of the homeland as well. For, although faith in the binding force of established standards had long since been shattered, average people confronted with the practical problems of daily life had still turned to the conventional notions of happiness and morality prevailing in their *polis* and there found sanction for their own ways of life. Only when the *polis* had become quite insignificant did its old aura and authority vanish. Thus, even for those Greeks who had stayed at home the traditional standards were threatened. And yet they were needed more than ever in those very troubled times. For even the ordinary citizen became involved in the confusion of the wars of the *Diadochoi* and the less secure his life and property were, the greater was his longing to find within himself a state of mind withdrawn from the fluctuations of external fate. But, unlike his ancestors, he was not helped to achieve that either by the community of the city-state or the traditional religion. For the ancient gods of the city-states had never been greatly concerned about the needs of the individual and in the latest political crisis they had failed altogether. Only from philosophy therefore could any help be expected and indeed it did prove itself a living power competent to cope with the needs of the new age. To do so, however, it has itself to undergo a transformation.

117

Plato and Aristotle had in their day gathered round them a small circle of disciples looking earnestly for fundamental knowledge and truth. But now very many people were looking for a way of life which would show them how to become independent of external circumstances and to attain inner peace and happiness. Basically it is what men like Antisthenes and Diogenes had already been seeking and in certain cases had to some extent achieved.[20] When Demetrius of Phalerum, who had been the Macedonian Governor of Athens for ten years, was banished in the year 307 and was wandering around in exile, the Cynic Crates taught him through friendly conversation to overcome his disaster, and the words of Stilpon, that were soon to become famous, "No one can rob me of my assets" (cf. p. 82), had given many the strength to rise above material losses. But in such cases the effect was due mainly to strength of individual personality, and such maxims no longer sufficed for the men of the new age. They were looking for a real philosophy and although they had neither time nor inclination to think one out for themselves, they felt that they could achieve their ultimate goal, inner harmony and *eudaimonia*, only if they carried within themselves a clear, sharply defined picture of the world and of God and man.

The "free education", which in the time of Isocrates was the prerogative of the Greek citizen, now became the general training for everybody. Whether the subjects taught under this system, the *artes liberales* as they were called in Latin, included Philosophy is not at all certain. But in any case the educated man was generally expected to be in touch with philosophy, and that answered a basic need of many people.[21]

There were two men moved by the spirit of the new age who felt it was their mission to offer their contemporaries the philosophy they needed. In the year 307–306 the Athenian Epicurus put forward a new programme in Athens, and six years later the Phoenician Zeno began teaching in the *Stoa Poikile*, a hall adorned with paintings, after which his school soon became known as the Stoa. Zeno fully agreed with Epicurus as to the goal to be sought. For him too philosophy was not the affair of narrow intellectual circles but the one thing which all men required, and its value lay in the practical art of ensuring the individual's personal *eudaimonia*. But the path which his predecessor had taken seemed to him basically wrong and it was the opposition to Epicurus that contributed strikingly to the development of his own teaching.

In his youth Epicurus was tortured by the fear of death and of the avenging gods. That had driven him to the materialism of Democritus, and he consequently proclaimed that life and spirit are merely the product of matter, and the world is a purely fortuitous conglomeration of atoms that leaves no room for the intervention of overseeing gods, and that man at death, because of the disintegration of the atoms enters into a state of complete insensibility and nothing at all affects him. Zeno too was the son of a straightforward, realistic kind of Hellenism, and was quite unable to imagine immaterial being as Plato had taught. He did not however consider that mind is begotten of matter; it must rather be the principle which from the beginning was bound up with matter, shaping and directing it. The whole structure of the world as a well-ordered *kosmos* proved that it could only be the work of a creative *logos* conscious cosmos proved that it could only be the work of a creative *logos* conscious of its purpose. But Zeno was aware of that same *logos* in himself too. For man is not, as Epicurus held, an animal of a higher order. While of course sharing certain animal functions, he is by nature an intellectual being who by reason of his *logos* is sharply distinguished from creatures not endowed with reason, the *aloga*, and is on the side of the God, the cosmic *logos* which governs the universe. Zeno therefore firmly believes that we must start out from that assumption if we want to determine the goal of human life. If Epicurus sees that goal in sensual desire, since all living beings strive for this, he is thereby degrading man to the level of the animal and disregarding his specific nature. For man's nature requires him to master sensuality through his *logos* and freely to join the community of all the λογικὰ ζῷα – which is not the small Greek city-state but all mankind – and to work with it and for it. But that can come about only through moral conduct. Only that can be his goal. Only so can he reach his best state, his *arete*, and thereby attain his *eudaimonia*.

Such are the two philosophic systems produced by Hellenism and conditioning its intellectual image henceforth, systems sharply opposing each other and corresponding to two fundamental tendencies in human mental attitudes. Epicurus takes as his point of departure the animal nature of man; Zeno sees in him the reasoning being destined to a specific way of life. That opposition permeates the whole system and has its effect on every detail. No wonder that each of them has a totally different attitude to the problem of freedom.

HUMAN FREEDOM

Free Decision as the Characteristic of the Reasoning Being

Epicurus occasionally says that the value of philosophy lies in giving men true freedom.[22] For it releases us from conventional obligations and teaches us the happy contentment that enables a man to be satisfied with bread and water and be independent of external circumstances. Philosophy banishes fear, guards against perverted desires and teaches a proper assessment of feelings of pleasure. For the highest pleasure does not lie, as Aristippus taught, in a brief moment of enjoyment but, as Epicurus, who was for ever ailing, learned from his own experience, in the sense of well-being that comes upon us once we are free of bodily pain and spiritual agitation. In order to enjoy this highest pleasure continually a man requires *phronesis*, the practical insight that makes him superior to momentary desires. But since, for the sake of consistency in the conduct of life, Epicurus maintains that sensual pleasure, the "pleasurable sensation in the flesh" must be the ultimate motive for action, then for him *phronesis* cannot bring about complete independence of the external but can only set up a counterbalance to external influences. Consequently, the idea of inner freedom is not of central significance for Epicurus, and what he says about it is fairly conventional.

With the Stoics the situation is completely different.[23] The fundamental conviction of Zeno was that the goal of man's life can only be rightly determined by taking as starting point his distinctive nature as a reasoning being. His first purpose was therefore to draw the sharp distinction between man and animal which Epicurus tended to obscure. He recognised of course that they had in common not only the body but also the animal functions of the spirit. In that he was a true son of Hellenism, which rejected not only Plato's non-material soul but also the acquisition of knowledge *a priori* from reasoning. Like Epicurus he was an empiricist and convinced that the knowledge of external things was by way of sense perception. Even so he was sure that man's relationship to the outer world was entirely different from the animal's, and this conviction was so important that, in an effort to explain it, he developed a whole psychological theory of his own and did all in his power to prove its validity. His basic idea is consent, *synkatathesis* as he called it, borrowing a term from voting procedure. This is necessary if the external sense impression is effectively to appear in the soul of the living being. But, whereas the animal cannot choose but must consent to each impression, which can only be excluded by another sense impression, man's *logos* makes him able, after considering it from all points of view, to adopt his own attitude to the external impression. Only when he gives it his "consent", recognising it as valid and true, can it exert any influence on the total life of the soul; should he not accord his consent it becomes a meaningless illusion. The essential thing here is that this consent remains within man's power to give (ἐφ' ἡμῖν ἐστιν) and is a decision which the *logos* takes independently. The *synkatathesis* thus becomes not just one individual function of the reasoning being but the distinguishing feature that determines its whole form of existence. For *synkatathesis* not only operates on the objective images which the sense perceptions convey but also on the ideas of value which develop in all living beings from birth on, since all of them relate the things perceived to themselves and feel those which promote their existence as "good" and seek them, whereas those which impede them they feel to be "bad" and avoid. It is only because the *logos* here performs its scrutiny that man maintains his freedom to choose, his independence of the external influences rushing in upon him. He himself decides what for him is "good" and "worth pursuing", and the judgment which he passes guarantees not only the independence of his theoretical decision, but that of his practical action as well.

Free decision is the distinguishing mark of the reasoning being that raises man above the animals. It charges him with responsibility for his actions, but also calls upon him to live morally, and helps him towards the highest, specifically human good – to inner freedom.

In his own attitude to life Zeno fully approved the ideals of Socrates, and it is his own notion of *synkatathesis* that gives them a firm psychological foundation. He adopts the idea that the true values lie within man and goes much further in maintaining that for man only those things are good which foster his inner life and make him a moral person; everything else, the body and the externals, are irrelevant (ἀδιάφορα) as regards the goal of his life and his *eudaimonia*. Also the saying that knowledge of the good is the essential prerequisite of the proper conduct of life was for him an irrefutable dogma and he categorically maintained that such knowledge necessarily brought in its train right action. He was well aware of the objection that many who know the good do not practise it because

121

other urges in the soul keep them from it, but he nevertheless believed that a correct understanding of the life of the soul would overcome this argument. Plato had already compromised with practical experience by dividing the soul into several layers and recognising the primacy of the intellectual layer among these. It appears that Zeno went still further than this[24], for although so little has been handed down to us we have positive evidence that Zeno recognised in the central organ of the soul other urges alongside the *logos*. But it seemed to him that in Plato the intellect's absolute mastery was not assured. That could only be guaranteed if it had the power to determine the development of the instinctive urges. That however was precisely what Zeno believed he could demonstrate with the help of his doctrine of *synkatathesis*. For the *logos*, by refusing to give its consent to a nascent impression, thereby cancels the impulse it had given rise to, and only when out of weakness it improperly yields to it can an unreasonable unnatural disturbance develop in the soul, an "exaggerated impulse" that oversteps the limitations imposed by the *logos* and takes out of its power the control of action.

Even that assurance did not satisfy Zeno's second successor, Chrysippus, who introduced a profound modification which became a dogma of the school. He was a convinced monist who wanted to explain individual phenomena as different manifestations of one primal substance. He therefore saw in the soul's "directing organ" or *hegemonikon*, not various isolated capacities but one single *logos*, acting sometimes as intellect, sometimes as impulses, and sometimes imagining, choosing or desiring. Even the instincts are for him essentially intellectual activities, "consentings" or choices, which only differ from the theoretical ones in that they set practical impulses into motion. The greed for money that leads men to steal is thus no different in nature from the opinion that money is an all-important good which we must obtain at all costs; pain is the decision, exaggerated beyond the proper measure, that harm has been done to us.

The doctrinaire emphasis on intellect revealed in these views immediately aroused the keenest opposition and even, within the Stoa itself, was combated later on by Panaetius and Posidonius. If Chrysippus stuck firmly to his theory, the reason is clear. It destroys at one blow the possibility of there arising in the soul itself any opposition to the *logos*. If instincts and desires were interpreted as acts of the *logos*, then the *logos* itself had in them made its decision, true or false, and had thus determined the action which followed. The wrong acts of any individual could thus be traced to a weakness in his own personal *logos*, and that can only be explained by his ignorance of what is really good, while knowledge of this must necessarily lead to right and virtuous action. The whole theory of Chrysippus is simply a radical attempt, by means of a psychological substruture, to vindicate against all criticism the Socratic theory of knowledge and virtue.

If we wish to understand fully the motives guiding Chrysippus[25], and Zeno before him, in their psychology, there is one thing we must bear in mind. Zeno had coined for the feelings and desires that overstep the limits laid down by the *logos* the term *pathos*, which has developed, by way of Latin *passio* (the Romans also used the word *affectio*) into French *passion* and is often translated into German as *Leidenschaft* (passion). For Zeno the word *pathos* had a clear-cut meaning. It signified the "passive" suffering state a man falls into when his *logos* has become too weak to stand upright (ὀρθός) in the face of external stimuli although it is his nature as a reasoning being to be active and make his own free decisions. And that is where the danger for men lies in these irrational urges, the passions. For it is not external things as such that threaten a man's freedom; it is the false evaluation by men that causes these passions to develop in the soul and take control out of the power of the *logos*. The total elimination of the passions, *apathia*, thus becomes the most compelling task, not of course in order to achieve insensibility, but to quell such powers in the soul as might menace the freedom of decision and independence of the *logos*. The battle against the passions is the battle for inner freedom, and the whole psychology of the Stoa proves that by its very nature the *logos* is bound to win.

The individual man, of course, will achieve his freedom only if his own *logos* is strong and healthy. And this raises a great difficulty, which Zeno himself clearly recognised.

The function wherein the natural freedom of the reasoning being becomes a reality is the *synkatathesis*. It gives man no merely the possibility of rising above sense impressions and of forming his own mental picture of the world; it also equips him for bringing his practical life, according to his own judgment, into harmony with the universal *logos* from which his own *logos* is derived. It is the prerequisite of moral action, to which man as a reasoning being inclines.

Later on we shall see how the Stoic Posidonius took a much broader view of the importance of the freedom to adopt a personal attitude to things and found in it the basis of all the creative achievement that raises man above the animals. The old Stoa was more particularly concerned with the moral life. But it is precisely there that for them man fulfils his true destiny, his 'existence', and its realisation is inconceivable apart from the gift of free decision which is part of his general human nature.

Every moral judgment we pass on a man implies that he is free to decide. And yet we can observe daily and hourly that men are overcome by external stimuli and make their decisions under their influence. Zeno was thus necessarily confronted with the question – is this *synkatathesis* of man really free and in control in individual cases, so that a man is fully answerable for his actions? That is the problem which was first posed in all its complexity by Zeno, and since that time it has never been absent from the history of the human mind.

The Problem of Free Will

We moderns speak about the problem of the freedom of the will because to our way of thinking the will is an independent function of the human spirit which expresses its urge to activity.[26] As we have already seen (p. 66f.), the Greek attitude to this was different. For them the will was a striving towards some more or less clearly recognised or envisaged goal (or object) and so it was very close to the intellect. They also knew an instinctive desire, but the word βούλεσθαι[27], which signified for them the spontaneous will, is related to βουλή, reflection, and when it says at the opening of the Iliad that the βουλή of Zeus is fulfilled, the meanings of "decision" and "will" merge. So for the Greeks it was more a matter of freedom of decision and the Romans consequently coined the expression *liberum arbitrium*[28], which was still to be the bone of contention between Erasmus and Luther. The Greeks proceeded on the basic assumption that the course of events is not within man's power, and so arrived the conception of things "that are within our power" (ἐφ' ἡμῖν ἐστιν). They were so absolutely certain that among those things lay that power of decision taken by man as a result of reflection, that throughout the Classical period they never so much as raised the fundamental question whether or not anything at all does lie in our power, however strongly their other experiences may have suggested it to them.

As is well known, Homeric man had the feeling when important decisions had to be taken that a god inspired him with ideas and exerted influence upon him.[29] But when the poet describes in the first book of the Iliad the vivid scene where Athene appears in the flesh to Achilles in order to calm his rage (*Il.*, I, 216), he does not forget to stress the fact that it is the hero himself who decides to follow the goddess. Similarly, when Agamemnon later at the Assembly of the Greeks tries to put the blame for the conflict on to Zeus who had blinded him by sending the *ate*, this does not exonerate him from the responsibility either to the army or to himself. Plutarch once maintained that in such cases according to Homer the god only gives the external stimulus, while the decision rests with the man.[30] This is a later, philosophic interpretation. But this much is certain; it was not at all in the poet's mind to deny to man his power of free decision. The schism which we feel between divine influence and human decision did not exist for him.

Aeschylus makes Clytemnestra attribute the fact that she murdered her husband to the power of the curse upon the house of Atreus. This is bluntly rejected, however, by the chorus: the *daimon* of the family might well assist, but she herself is the doer of the deed (*Agamemnon*, 1505). Thus the dramatist's moral sense requires the murderess to bear the whole responsibility for her deed and he does not let the tradition of the influence of the curse deflect him from this purpose. At that time the two were still quite compatible. But soon it became necessary to put to the test and clarify the old religious conceptions. The administration of justice had been for a long time sufficiently advanced to distinguish whether the accused had done the deed of his own accord (ἑκών) or not.[31] In the moral sphere, the reflective Simonides had already said in a famous poem that we were not to expect absolute perfection from any man but to be content with one who had never "of his own accord" done anything blameworthy. Among the writers of tragedy it was here, as so often, Euripides who seized upon the moral problem and repeatedly treated it in his role of teacher of the people. In the *Cretans*, which was produced soon after 438, and from which there has come to us on a sheet of papyrus a speech by Pasiphae in her own defence, she proves that she could not "of her own volition" have conceived this unnatural love for a bull, but that she must be suffering from a divinely imposed fate. Unfortunately the answer, which must have been written, has not been preserved. But two of the poet's other tragedies allow us to reconstruct the sense of it. In the *Hippolytus* Phaedra's nurse is quick with her excuse that her mistress's love for her stepson was the work of Cypris (Aphrodite), and against her even Zeus himself is powerless. But Phaedra herself knows only too well that her passion is rooted deep within her. In a scene in the *Trojan Women* specially introduced for the purpose, Hecuba pointedly rejects Helen's accusal of Aphrodite. It was not the goddess Aphrodite, but her own unreasonable passion, her *aphrosyne*, that urged her of her own accord to follow the handsome Paris to Troy.

In the time of Euripides there must have still been people who thought as Phaedra's nurse did. But it would not have been much good for a man appearing before the court for adultery to plead that he had been impelled by Aphrodite; for educated people it was obvious that the source of all a man's actions is to be sought in his own soul.

Thus was removed the only impediment which the old Hellenic thought could raise against the freedom of man to choose and the belief in this freedom could grow into a firm conviction. That becomes plainest in the attitude to this question adopted by the great Attic philosophy.

Plato had of course already recognised the ultimate and hardest question that arises for anyone looking for the meaning of human existence and convinced of man's moral nature: morality requires free decision and responsibility; but can the individual man be free and responsible for his deeds if by his birth and without any effort on his part he inherits individual dispositions which at least play a great part in determining his way of life? How much Plato was concerned with this problem is shown at the end of the *Republic*. In that work he had shown from the nature of the soul itself that justice and morality are not only the most natural condition of the soul but also its happiest condition. That must be due to the immanent justice in the universe and this becomes more evident to us when we try to picture to ourselves the destiny of the soul in its non-corporeal existence. This leads Plato on to a myth which crowns the whole work.[32] But in this he does not speak only of reward and retribution after death but also of what occurs before a new entry into existence on earth. Before that happens, we are told, the soul is given the possibility of choosing its future life. "A life will not choose you but you will choose a life. The responsibility will rest with him who is given the choice; no responsibility will rest with God". We then learn that the decision that souls take will be determined by the way they have behaved in an earlier life on earth and by the degree of discernment they have thus acquired. That however only shifts the question of the reason for the choice back to an earlier phase; that in itself is all the more unsatisfactory because Plato includes those souls which are for the first time being linked to an earthly body. In fact the reader is meant to see that Plato recognises the problem but cannot and does not intend to offer a final solution. By adapting the device of a myth he has hinted that he is now entering a region beyond the reach of scientific knowledge which permits no rational answer to ultimate questions. Man's freedom in his life on earth and his responsibility for his actions are, for Plato, facts of experience, and are expressly pointed out in the myth. But how these facts can be reconciled with his inherited potential and his individual character remains a secret which cannot be grasped, except perhaps through religious faith. Only one thing is certain: for man's misuse of freedom, God the essence of the good, must on no account be held responsible. "Virtue has no master" and the burden of wickedness falls on man alone. In his actions man is free. That is the decisive fact, and one which for Plato is so certain that it raises no problem for him.

In the *Ethics* Aristotle discusses the concepts of ἑκών and ἄκων in great detail.[33] These terms are still often translated as "voluntary" and "involuntary", which brings the whole modern problem of the freedom of the will into the picture. But that is inadmissable. In the passage in question Aristotle is not concerned at all with the metaphysical problem of how the human decision is ultimately arrived at and whether it is free or determined; he is only concerned with the ethical and juridical question of assessing that decision and deciding if it is to be reckoned as the man's own act, for which he bears the responsibility. This is the case, Aristotle decides, only with such actions as he does not perform under external compulsion or in ignorance of the facts, but have their origin and point of departure (ἀρχή) within the man himself and are "of his own instigation", regardless whether the "instigation" is derived from the intellect or from the instincts. These are the actions which follow from his judgment of values and which, as distinct from bodily properties like health and strength, we recognise as his own merit, as moral (καλόν) and as virtue. For Aristotle it is obvious that the decision we take "lies within our power"; otherwise praise and blame, admonition and training, reward and punishment would lose all meaning. The very foundation of the whole idea of morality would be destroyed. For, as Aristotle clearly maintains, morality is a value-concept and decides whether acts are "praiseworthy" or "blameworthy". But such judgment implies that it is within a man's power to decide this way or that. Aristotle is well aware that a man's individual decisions just as much as his normal attitude are affected by his general disposition, upbringing and external factors. But the fundamental question as to whether man's freedom is thus restricted or even taken away from him altogether he does not raise. In his view this freedom is itself a fact of experience involving no problem, since without it the whole meaning and basis of human life would be lost.

The Stoic Zeno could easily applaud these arguments.[24] For him too it was quite clear that the morality, for which man's nature has fitted him, presupposes his freedom to decide; and the significance of his whole psychology, especially his teaching about *synkatathesis*, is that it should make that freedom, which to the feelings is an obvious fact, accessible to the intellect as well, since it ensures the autonomy of the *logos* in the face of both the outer world and the personal instincts.

Nevertheless, Zeno himself was the first man on Greek soil to see in this a problem and to ask the fundamental question: Is man, when he decides, really free? Is it in the power of the individual to choose for himself whether he grants or refuses in individual cases the *synkatathesis* which as a reasonable being he must give to external events? How can that be explained?

The only explanation is that Zeno was the first to see the contrary idea that might be raised against the hitherto unquestioned belief that man is free to decide. That was the idea of strict causality, which links all events together in a causal relationship.

The causal nexus had been familiar to the Greeks from the earliest times. Questioning about the cause of an event or an institution was in their blood and was the main driving force behind both their creation of myths and their scientific research. But Zeno was the first to follow up the implications of the idea of causality right through to the end. Every cause producing an effect must itself have a cause. It is therefore one link in a causal chain of events that can have their ultimate source only in an original principle, a first cause, which is greater than all the individual causal chains and is the source of all being and all happening. For Zeno with his religious sense, the world is a single organism filled throughout with the divine *pneuma* that penetrates to its minutest parts. From the divine being himself came "the unbroken chain of causes", the continuous causal relationship embracing all the single events and phenomena of the cosmos.

This side of the divine *logos* Zeno called by the ancient word *heimarmene* giving it however quite a new significance. The idea had developed among the Greeks out of the feeling that to every man is apportioned a part of the world's happenings. Gradually the tendency to generalise led to men's seeing in this *heimarmene* the power that determined all events. Progressive thought could then use the word to signify the immanent law which governs all happenings in the world. But *heimarmene* had nothing to do with the rationally held principle of causality. That belonged to quite a different realm of experience and feeling. It was the inescapable power of fate with which man had to come to terms. To fight against it would have been meaningless. It had its limits, however. It determined only external happenings, and man had both the duty and the power to assert himself against it as an independent personality. For it could not reach his inner being. Man still remains free to make his decisions about external events in the light of his own judgment.

That was the feeling of the ordinary Greek in the Classical period. It was moreover precisely the point to which Zeno directed his thinking on causality and so effected a far-reaching change. Into the relationship of all causes which contains all the happenings in the world the life of the individual human soul must be fitted. Even his most intimate decisions, even the *synkatathesis* which should be a guarantee of his independence of the external world, must be determined by preceding causal factors. Could then the belief in freedom of choice, which moral experience had postulated, still be maintained? How far Zeno himself realised the difficulties which followed from this and in what ways he tried to master them we can, unfortunately, no longer say with certainty. For our records have neglected his own words in order to record the lengthy treatment of the subject by Chrysippus. We see all the better, however, that the latter has formulated the problem quite clearly: "Is man's ability to decide freely compatible with the principle of causality when it is carried to its logical conclusions?" We also see that Chrysippus did all he could to find a satisfactory solution.

The way he sought to achieve that end was a scrupulous investigation of the nature of causes.[35] The Greeks had in the early days distinguished between the true cause and the mere stimulus. Thucydides wanted to penetrate from the apparent reason for the Peloponnesian War to its "truest cause" and as a critical historian he found it in the fear instilled in the rest of the Greeks by the imperialistic tendencies of ambitious Athens. In the time of Chrysippus medical men were teaching that the decisive cause of illness did not lie in the outer symptoms which provoked it but in the disposition of the human body which was to a greater or lesser extent susceptible to the particular disorder. On that analogy Chrysippus maintained firmly that in human decisions two causes operate together. One of these is the idea which comes upon us from outside without our intervention and is the last in a causal chain which determines external events. But that constitutes only the stimulus of the present moment. The decisive cause "which of itself produces the effect" (αὐτοτελὴς αἰτία) is the *synkatathesis*, whereby the *logos* either recognises the idea after testing it or else dismisses it and so prevents it becoming operative. In that way therefore man makes his decision on his own judgment availing itself of the rational being's privilege – granted to him by the order of the world, and thus by the *heimarmene* itself – that it has the freedom of decision and that "there is something which is within our power" (τὸ αὐτεξούσιον, τὸ ἐφ' ἡμῖν). Two causal series thus meet, but the decisive cause lies in the character of the rational being whose nature it is to be free. Chrysippus uses an image to explain his view.[36] Just as a cylinder needs a push from outside to start it rolling, but the real cause of its movement resides in its cylindrical form and thus in its nature, so, in the case of the human decision, the real cause is not the idea that stimulates but the ability which naturally resides within us to come to a free decision of our own.

In practice, that freedom is subject, of course, to considerable limitations. For only that man is truly free whose *logos* is strong and healthy enough to enable him to withstand tempting ideas that might bring him to false value judgments, to irrational feelings and desires, and thus bring him under the influence of the outer world. Whether he is able to withstand them in specific instances depends on the total constitution of his soul, and Chrysippus does not deny that this is determined by a multiplicity of causal factors. In specific instances therefore the decision cannot turn out otherwise than it does. But that only means that the man has lost the freedom of decision which nature endowed him with, and it is his own fault.[37] For, ready as Chrysippus is to concede the importance of hereditary factors, of environment and education in a man's development, he nevertheless remains firm in his conviction that man has not only the duty but also the power to keep his *logos* healthy and resistant to outside influences as a result of his own moral efforts and thus he can preserve his freedom. For that reason man bears full responsibility for his own acts, even if at the moment of a particular decision he can only act in one way. Praise and blame remain meaningful as moral judgments on his actual behaviour. Similarly, reward and punishment, admonition and training, are not merely necessary for the sake of society; even *heimarmene* does not make them superfluous for the individual. For the responsible purposefulness of man which they presuppose is, along with *heimarmene*, an indispensible condition for his self-fulfilment.[38]

The solution offered by Chrysippus is, as was already said in antiquity, a compromise between the causality idea and the consciousness of freedom. His real purpose is always obvious: the preservation at all costs of man's freedom, which for him too was the indispensible condition of all morality. Nevertheless, he came at once into the most violent conflict with his Greek contemporaries because they saw in his theory a threat to freedom, the importance of which as man's highest possession had been sharply illuminated by those very arguments. Epicurus sharply attacks "certain people" who would like to rob men of their natural freedom which allows no master ($τὸ$ $παρ'$ $ἡμῖν$ $ἀδέσποτον$), by making *heimarmene* their master. It was better to follow the old myths of the gods than to make oneself the slave of inexorable *heimarmene*. This polemic can be aimed at nobody but Zeno. Epicurus wrote a book on *heimarmene* and in his work on Nature he attempted positively to assure man's absolute freedom of decision on the basis of his own philosophy. Whereas he will otherwise only recognise a mechanical movement of atoms either by vertical fall which permits only slight variations or by collision with other atoms, he here introduces alongside this a voluntary, spontaneous movement which enables the mind of man to rise above the necessity imposed by his bodily constitution and its development, and to act as it will with the perceptual images and the notions these call into being. The papyrus that preserved for us part of his argument is unfortunately badly damaged,

131

and many of the details are not clear[39], but it is easy to detect in it an apologetic tendency and we can see against whom it is directed in Lucretius, who explicitly states that it is necessary to assume a free movement of atoms because we carry in our breasts something that breaks through the causal chain of *heimarmene*.[40]

We thus have confirmation of what was to be expected from this whole philosophical development. Epicurus had not by himself arrived at the defence of man's freedom to decide, an attitude that was not of central importance for his system. Instead, he considered this necessary because he believed it was threatened by Zeno. And Zeno is the one who first recognised the problem.

Soon afterwards the Academician Arcesilaus tried to prove that the Stoics with their teaching about *heimarmene* were unintentionally invalidating the idea of man's freedom to decide. And especially significant was the systematic criticism which the second-century Academician Carneades undertook with his usual acumen.[41] The latter frankly admitted that the Stoics had there recognised a real problem, and that by analysing the causes Chrysippus had pointed the way to a solution. His mistake, however, had been to apply the unbroken sequence of causes to man's inner life. For, as Chrysippus himself maintained, the "true cause" of our decisions lies in the *synkatathesis*, which is not subject to the law of *heimarmene*, since it is an act of independent choice, which is man's natural faculty as a reasoning being. Upon *synkatathesis* depends the whole freedom of man, which is the essential condition of his moral behaviour and a reality vouched for by immediate living experience.

Since that time the argument about the problem continued down the centuries till the end of antiquity. While on the whole the Stoics stuck to the position of Chrysippus, the Platonists and Peripatetics acknowledged the causal chain in the *heimarmene* but confined it to the material world, vigorously denying that it had any influence on the world of the spirit. But other men also took up the defence of the threatened freedom, even the cynic Oenomaus attacked Chrysippus for reducing man's fairest possession, freedom, to ἡμίδουλον, semi-slavery.

In the Christian era Clement of Alexandria[42] extolled man's inner freedom as a gift of God (θεόσδοτον τὸ ἐφ' ἡμῖν), and Origen emphatically defended the freedom of the will both as an ethical postulate and an obvious fact of experience. It was on Roman soil that the change first came and the complete break with the Greek outlook came with Augustine, who from personal experience was convinced that man is so burdened with original sin that the divine gift of free will works out in practice only as the will to do evil and that only through the grace of God can he regain the freedom to do good.

In modern times the problem was posed on quite another level when Kant transferred human freedom to the transcendental sphere. That naturally intensified the criticism of the solution of Chrysippus. But those who like to indulge in easy ridicule of his solution should not forget one fact: it will always remain a great achievement that the Stoics put forward for the first time a problem which still, thousands of years later, is occupying mankind and which, whatever progress may be made in psychology and atomic physics, will in all probability continue to engage it so long as there survives in the soul of man the conflict between the idea of absolute causality and the consciousness of freedom – the conflict which drove the Stoics themselves to pose this question.[43]

How did they arrive at that point?[44] What is the psychological explanation of the fact, that men who based their whole ethic and teaching about man upon the idea of his freedom of choice were the first to discover the contrary power which threatened to wreck that freedom? As we have seen, up to that time the idea of an unbroken chain of causes, which would also determine the life of the human soul, had never occurred to the Greeks, and despite all the efforts of the Stoics it always remained foreign to them. We are inclined therefore to remember the non-Greek origin of Zeno and Chrysippus, the founders of the Stoic school. But what we know about the soul of the Phoenicians and the Syrians is far too little to warrant here more than the merest conjecture.[45]

The Freedom of the Moral Personality

The Stoics were violently attacked from all sides because they wanted to deprive man of his freedom to choose. But for that very reason Greeks were first made conscious of possessing such freedom and also of its value. The Stoics themselves made the greatest contribution to clarifying the concept and giving it depth.

Because of their general conception of the world they were first of all led to define precisely the limits of that freedom. The free man of the Stoic school could do nothing to modify the fore-ordained progress of external events and for them the dictum that "none can escape *heimarmene*", which for Plato had been old wives' lore (*Gorg.*, 512e), becomes for them a valid scientific fact. But they also helped men to give quite a new kind of answer to the old question of what attitude they should adopt to fate. For them *heimarmene* is no longer the blind overruling power that thwarts the human will, nor the iron necessity which it is vain to oppose, but the divinely willed order within which man has his being. It is identical in fact with the *logos* itself, which controls all events according to inviolable laws; it is not a force that works mechanically but an intellectual principle that acts purposefully and turns all to the best. The *heimarmene* is for them also providence, the *pronoia* to which the beauty and the harmony of the cosmos bear witness even in the eyes of the most stupid people. It is this providence to which the individual man owes his physical and his spiritual existence. It determines his external fate but he must not for that reason be fatalist and do nothing about it. For *heimarmene* itself has implanted in him the urge to action and progress. But if success be denied him or if he suffers misfortune, then he must not grumble and turn resentful, or despair either, but hold fast to his conviction that all that happens in heaven or on earth is the will of God who means well for man and knows better than man does himself what is good for him. He will therefore gladly accept all that comes from the hand of God, and like the Eteocles of Aeschylus and the Polyxena of Euripides (cf. p. 53) will become master of his fate by himself willing it and transforming it into his own free moral action. He will thus overcome the contradiction between the compulsion of fate and man's urge to independence and preserve his freedom precisely by recognising its limits.[46]

The Stoics used a drastic image to illustrate their attitude. Man is like a dog tied to a cart. If it resists and sits on its hind legs it is dragged along by force, but if it is clever it runs happily along on its own and "combines freedom with necessity". More moving is the prayer of pious Cleanthes:

> Lead me, Zeus, and lead, Pepromene,
> Along my path which you have chosen.
> Unwavering I follow. To resist
> Is sin. And I must follow anyway.

Still more important was another barrier to freedom created by its own true nature.

The stern warning of Pericles that the limit to civic freedom is in the legal order of the state was by no means invalidated by criticism, and fear of a legal penalty was a corrective whose practical importance even Epicurus recognised in his ethics. Zeno did not have any inner link with the Greek city-state.[47] For him man was not a "being made for life in the *polis*" but one who could live only in a community; he was a κοινωνικὸν ζῷον, and precisely by living among a completely foreign people this Phoenician could become aware that there existed something which, overriding all geographical and racial barriers, united all men and placed obligations upon them. He might feel grateful for the fact that the Greek city-state sought to be a law-abiding state that offered protection to the foreigner. In the place of the single city-state he put the great community of mankind, but this grew automatically into a state-like structure on the Greek model, a *cosmopolis*[48] that embraced all reasoning beings. Because the gods also belonged to it, it gained a special religious quality, reminding men of their divine origin.

Like the little communities, the cosmopolis also had its law, that reigned within and held its members together. Heraclitus' dictum that all human laws are derived from the divine law (fr. 114, cf. p. 56f. above) was adopted by Zeno, who made it the corner stone of his ethics. For this "divine law" – like *heimarmene* and *pronoia* – is nothing other than God himself seen from a certain angle. It is the divine *logos* which according to unchanging laws governs both physical events and intellectual and moral life, "commanding what shall be done and forbidding what may not be done" as Chrysippus expressed it and as the Roman jurists did after him (*SVF*, III, 314). It is the unwritten law upon which all human morality is based, the law of nature which regardless of all individual laws is binding on all men eternally. Only insofar as the specific laws of individual states are in harmony with it have they any inner binding force for men even if they are a constituent part of the established legal order which men, as such, have to obey. He should do it, however, not through forced obedience, but in voluntary acceptance; and infinitely harder than the external punishment threatened by the laws of a state, is the other punishment, which necessarily follows from the breaking of the law of reason. For "he who disobeys this law is running away from himself and denying his human nature".[49] He is abandoning his humanity.

The law of reason confronts men everywhere with a rigid "thou shalt".[50]

That was something new in the moral philosophy of the Greeks. For although they recognised that there were rules a man had to follow they based their ethic on the idea that a man only needed to develop to the full certain natural tendencies within him to find the right way and fulfil himself. Zeno wholly shared that optimism; but he also knew the many evil influences that from the time of a man's birth menace and impair the individual *logos*. He therefore thought it inadequate to insist that man *can* be good, and so he referred man to the higher power to which he is answerable and which prescribes the way he has to act.[51]

What the law of reason commands is man's moral "duty". That idea too was first introduced into moral philosophy by the Stoics. They expressly referred to *katorthoma*, the complete fulfilment of duty, as "the law's command" (*SVF*, III, 520), without thereby intending to infringe man's freedom and moral autonomy. For this law only commands him to do what according to his own nature is in a given situation proper for him (καθήκει) and what, if he has remained true to his nature as a reasoning being, he would do of his own accord. The individual *logos* which each man carries in his breast is only an off-shoot of the universal *logos* governing all things and through the nature of its origin it is unable to will anything different. Only if it has been subsequently depraved and weakened can it happen that it consents improperly to misleading ideas, and this can lead to desires and actions contrary to the law of the universal *logos*. But those are "unnatural movements of the soul", symptoms of disease, which do not originate in the soul's proper being (cf. p. 124). If, on the other hand, the *logos* is strong and healthy, then it joyfully consents – just as it does in the case of *heimarmene* – to what the law requires. That is its free decision, given on the strength of its knowledge of what is truly good. Thus freedom and obedience to the law of reason are by no means contradictory. On the contrary, whoever sets himself against the law of reason, denies himself the freedom implanted in his nature and makes himself the slave of sensuality and the outer world. The obligations he himself chooses to accept are part of man's freedom. Only within this limitation does it become a living power leading man to his fulfilment.

When Zeno came to Athens, the first Greek to make an enduring impression on him was the Cynic Crates, who taught the young Phoenician by practical example that unaffected by the outer world, man can shape his life according to his own will and realise happiness in any situation.

But independence of the external world was first of all something negative and Zeno required life to have a positive content. He was no quietist like Epicurus, for whom undisturbed peace was the highest bliss. His nature impelled him to activity, but his field of action could only be the community of reasoning beings into which his human nature had placed him.[52] Zeno felt that it was not only personal inclination which urged men from birth onwards to join the society of other men, but also the objective order of the *cosmopolis*. And, just as the ancient Greeks regarded service to the small city-state as civic duty, so for Zeno it was the obvious duty of the individual man to incorporate himself into the *cosmopolis*, and work with all his power for its well-being. That, however meant that man was destined to lead a moral life. And since in that life the *logos* which has shaped his being achieves fulfilment, then that morality must also be his own best possible state, his *arete*, and therefore his *eudaimonia*.

The prerequisite of morality – that is as certain for Zeno as for Aristotle – is man's freedom. For an action is only "praiseworthy" and "morally good" if it originates in the free decision of the *logos*. Freedom itself is "the complete power to act according to one's own will", the ἐξουσία αὐτοπραγίας (*SVF*, III, 355; 544). It gives man the power not only to make individual decisions as an intellectual being but also to lead his whole life in harmony with the *logos*.[53] For, whereas the animal cannot help accepting its ideas and lives by sense impressions, man as a reasoning being can work upon these impressions, consider the past, present and future, see causal relationships, calculate the consequences of his actions, draw up general principles and make all individual decisions on the basis of rational consideration and with a definite goal in mind. Only man can shape his whole life consistently as a unique personality "in complete harmony with himself". He alone, by virtue of his *synkatathesis*, is in a position to lead a moral life in freedom and according to his own will.

The right decision depends upon the right evaluation of things. Only he who clearly grasps the fact that his real "advantage" lies in moral good and that compared with this all external things are quite unimportant has the power really to raise himself above externals and to make free decisions independently of them. He too is not only a being of the spirit and will concern himself in practical life for his health and his subsistence; but he will never let his body and externals gain power over him or put these on a level with moral good. He acknowledges the authority only of moral law and lets no power deflect him from it, not even concern for the consequences of his actions. And precisely that gives man his freedom. The Stoic could say with Theodor Storm:

> "Der eine fragt: Was kommt danach?
> der andre fragt nur: Ist es recht?
> Und also unterscheidet sich
> der Freie von dem Knecht."

(One man asks: What comes next? The other asks: Is it right? And therein lies the difference between the free man and the slave). The legal position is not the essential thing. Only the moral personality is free.

None but the man who genuinely carries within him the Socratic knowledge of the good as the power determining his life attains full freedom.[54] He alone is the perfect man, the wise man. In the picture of him which the Stoics never tired of painting in the most glowing colours freedom is the outstanding trait. He freely decides to submit to the law of reason; but precisely that makes him free for moral action and superior to all earthly things. He respects the limits imposed upon his will, and for that very reason can do what he wills. He follows undeviating the path the *logos* points out to him. He knows very well that no man can harm him, no fate can injure him. He follows only his own inner voice. "It is easier to force a pipe filled with air under water than to force a wise man against his will to do something he does not want to. For unconquerable is the soul which an upright *logos* has, through firm convictions, strengthened as if with muscles."[55]

The wise man remains free and master of his inner as well as his outer life. All the worries that torment ordinary men, all the pointless desires and unrestrained passions that disturb their souls, are kept out by his *logos*. He enjoys absolute *apatheia*. His entire life is in harmony with the universal *logos* and therefore with God, and thus he gains peace in the soul and assurance in his actions and is the master of all things.

At a time when the old myths about the gods had lost their force the Stoics created the myth of the perfect man, who with his own strength could through conscious striving climb to heights which raised him above all earthly things and placed him alongside Zeus himself. In him the idea of moral freedom attained plastic form.

The Further Development of the Idea of Freedom within the Stoa

Zeno gave the Greek idea of freedom a completely new basis by removing it from the context of the city-state and the citizen's way of life and developing it simply from human nature. Through him freedom became the distinguishing feature of man who, being endowed with *logos*, was able to apply *synkatathesis* and adopt a subjective attitude to external things and, uninfluenced by these, to lead the kind of life that was suited to his own nature. This also shows man his goal; it is his natural function to live morally within the community of reasoning beings and in that must lie his *eudaimonia*.

Zeno's especial concern was to enlighten people about the purpose of human life and thus to show them the way to their goal. He concerned himself mainly with the individual man and that remained the general practice in the Stoa. But in it there were also men who while agreeing completely about the primacy of the *logos* and wholly committed to the freedom principle, nevertheless from their own personal experience found new ways of looking at it.

Zeno, though he was warmly attached to the idea of *cosmopolis*, fully recognised the importance of the single states as necessary and natural institutions of human society; and, whereas Epicurus earnestly warned his followers against endangering their spiritual calm by playing any part in politics, Zeno explicitly made politics their duty "so long as there was no obstacle".[56] For himself there was indeed such an obstacle in the fact that he did not have citizen status in Athens, and this was the case with most of his pupils. But among them there was also the Macedonian Crown Prince Antigonus Gonatas, and when Antigonus later saw his vocation as king as a moral duty, he gave proof of it not only in action but also in a maxim that became famous: "Kingship is not a licence for the satisfaction of selfish desires but is service to the people", and, as he added with a deliberate sting, "an honourable servitude", ἔνδοξος δουλεία (Aelian, *Var. Hist.*, II, 20).

Antigonus was the first ruler who, like Marcus Aurelius and Frederick the Great, through his own personal inclination made the Stoic sense of duty the guiding principle of his reign. This became still more important

139

for the idea of political power when in the second century the Stoa entered into a new, more active relationship with the real state. The credit for this is due to Panaetius of Rhodes[57] who, as a pure-blooded Greek of the old nobility still kept alive the old feeling for the *polis* and later, as a friend of Scipio, gained practical influence on the aristocratic ruling class of the new empire, particularly upon their political thought, but then went back home, since he felt that only there could he live and work in complete independence and freedom. His own experience led him to comment upon the old conflict between the theoretical and the practical ideals. Not only the political condition of Greece but his own inclination and talents urged him to pursue learning, but he willingly conceded that the statesman's practical activity took precedence.[58] "Philosophers", he said on one occasion, "seek the same goal as kings, a life that knows no master, that freedom that consists in living just as one chooses". In this we hear again the old slogan of Athenian democracy, which had long been transferred to the ethical sphere. "But although in his private life the philosopher may more easily attain that goal, infinitely higher and more fruitful is the statesman's activity, which directly benefits the whole community."[59] That he is able to do of course only when he is filled with the philosopher's conviction that the morally beautiful is to man's real advantage, and when he possesses the greatness of soul, *magnitudo animi* ($\mu\varepsilon\gamma\alpha\lambda o\psi v\chi ia$), which equips him not only to regard all external things from a superior position but to remain in himself master over all his lower instincts. Panaetius rejected the doctrinaire attitude of Chrysippus, who traced all activities of the soul back to judgments, and he recognised an autonomous instinctive life in the soul; for him, however, it was obvious that its intensity and direction must be determined by the *logos*. Only so can the statesman too fulfil the old Platonic demand that the leader of the people must subordinate all his personal interests to those of the community.

Panaetius set out his philosophy in his work, *On Duty*, $\Pi\varepsilon\rho i\ \tau o\tilde{v}$ $\kappa\alpha\theta\dot{\eta}\kappa o\nu\tau o\varsigma$, which Cicero translated into Latin in the *De Officiis*. This was all the easier because Panaetius himself had written for the Roman aristocracy. He knew how much store they set by pride, which strove for power and precedence over other people. For just that reason he wanted to show them that there was something higher than selfish power over one's fellow-citizens; that is leadership which of its own accord places itself at the service of the community, thereby fulfilling its highest duty. Only this moral conduct brings man the true freedom that allows him to live the life his nature really desires.

Panaetius was a convinced Stoic and, with his respect for individual personality, a true Hellenist. He was also, however, the direct heir of the old Hellenic attitudes and, just as he took over into his "mixed constitution" elements from the early conception of political freedom (cf. p. 98), so he tried to convince the ambitious people that the modern ideal of the free personality could be harmonised with the old sense of the state, and there was for him no fundamental difference if it could no longer be realised in the small city-state but only in the empire.

Posidonius (about 135 to 50 B.C.), a pupil of Panaetius, born in Syria though certainly of predominantly Greek stock, was also a man who combined theory and practice. In Rhodes, where he lived later, he even held the highest political office. At heart, however, he was a scholarly man and his real spiritual home remained the cosmopolis, the society of all rational beings, to which he too must contribute. Man's goal[60], he maintained, lay in "a life which sees the reality and order of the universe and contributes to it with all its powers".

As a Stoic Posidonius was a monist and traced, with the precision of the natural scientist[61], the forms of life from the lowest rung of the ladder right up to God. That did not obliterate for him, however, the difference in nature between man and the animals. For, however much man has in common with them, there is one thing which distinguishes him sharply from them. That is the *logos*. Animals can create things of the highest perfection, like the honeycomb of the bee, or the spider's web. But these are the products of instincts of the species, designed to answer definite needs. Animals could never have created a comprehensive culture such as man through his *logos* has made possible. For *logos* gives him awareness of number and measure, of causality and universal laws, the capacity for theoretical thought and for purposeful action. And there is one other thing. All cultural progress is the work of creative individuals – among these are the traditional "seven wise men" – and the basic reason for this Posidonius formulates in a short sentence: "the rational being is a free being that acts with its own power" ($\dot{\epsilon}\lambda\epsilon\acute{\upsilon}\theta\epsilon\rho\upsilon\nu$ $\gamma\acute{\alpha}\rho$ $\tau\iota$ $\kappa\alpha\grave{\iota}$ $\alpha\dot{\upsilon}\tau\epsilon\xi\upsilon\acute{\upsilon}\sigma\iota\upsilon\nu$ $\tau\grave{\upsilon}$ $\lambda\upsilon\gamma\iota\kappa\acute{\upsilon}\nu$). Man is given in *synkatathesis* the ability to adopt an attitude in theory or in practice to the phenomena which come to his notice from outside. That is the freedom which distinguishes him from the animals. It belongs to the individual man and gives him the power to rise above tradition and his species, to find new ways of his own and thus produce the individual creative achievements to which humanity owes its progress.

Man's freedom is thus extended to become a principle of his whole intellectual life. But for Posidonius too its proper realm is that of morality.

Like Panaetius, Posidonius rejects the intellectualist psychology of Chrysippus. He attacked it in a special work, *On the Passions* (*Περὶ παθῶν*)[62], where he adopted the Platonic position that, alongside of the *logos*, there is in the central organ of the soul an independent, irrational, instinctive life with two layers, the *thymos* and the *epithymetikon*, both of which not only are ineradicable parts of human nature but, within limits drawn by the *logos*, perform invaluable services. But for that reason he most emphatically maintains in the same work that the *logos* must exercise unconditional mastery over these instincts and so preserve its own freedom: "The most important thing is that we must not let ourselves be led by what is unreasonable, unholy and ungodly in our soul". "The source of the wretched life is man's failure to follow in all things that daimon in his breast which is consubstantial with the spirit that pervades and rules the whole world, and his submission instead to the worse, animal side of his nature."

Mention of the daimon makes us think at once of Plato's "inner man" (cf. p. 95), and there is in fact a direct link from Plato to Posidonius. For, so far as we can see – and we are of course guided for the most part by our inferences from Latin writings – the soul is for Posidonius too an independent entity which is only temporarily linked with the body and only in that transient state develops the lower capacities essential to the maintainance of the whole organism. Its true nature is the *logos*, which in earthly life can only develop purely when it rises above the body, and can attain its full freedom only when it gradually casts off the lower functions after death. Being a Stoic, Posidonius did not recognise Plato's immaterial spirit. The daimon related to the spirit of the universe was for him a divine spark which radiated from the sun, the source of all physical and intellectual life, and which ultimately returned to it again.[63]

Thus for Posidonius too there was no transcendental freedom; but he too recognised in man a "real self". He too could say: "Each one of us is in himself neither anger nor fear nor desire, any more than flesh and blood, but he is the power by virtue of which we have thought and intelligence." Like Panaetius he felt himself a Stoic, but even the Stoa was for him only a part of that general philosophy that had reached its climax in Plato. He felt himself at one with Plato in his conception of the nature and the origin of the soul, of man's true self and of his highest freedom.[64]

The Concept of Freedom as Common Intellectual Property

Panaetius and Posidonius were undoubtedly the outstanding personalities of the later Stoa. But they were too independent and too great in stature for the framework of the school, which preferred to adhere to the established system of teaching developed by Chrysippus and based upon Zeno.

This orthodox Stoa and Epicureanism remained the opposing philosophies between which men of the Hellenic period had to choose, while the older schools of philosophy were pushed into the background. Some people might really feel drawn to the mechanistic explanation of the world and to the hedonism of Epicurus, others to the Stoic faith in the divine *logos* and the moral law. Fundamentally, however, it was something else that most people needed. Following the collapse of authority in state and religion, they wanted some practical guidance in life that would lead them firmly to their desired goal. And as Zeno and Epicurus alike promised such guidance, outsiders were inclined to regard that common ground as the most important thing and to leave to the professional philosophers the difficult decisions about the ultimate problems of life.

But even among the professional philosophers the conflict of ideas could not for ever prevent the consideration of practical problems. The rigid position of the Stoics, who in theory regarded all externals, and the body itself, as worthless compared with *eudaimonia*, was corrected by the practical reality of daily life, and the Hedonist Epicurus had impressed upon his followers that by following his teachings they could be happy with nothing more than bread and water. However passionately the Peripatetics and the Academicians fought the Stoic repression of the senses, they agreed with their antagonists that a man must be capable of controlling his instincts and keeping them within reasonable bounds. For a poet like Horace it was naturally compatible with his Epicurean outlook when, as a Roman patriot in the Augustan sense, he appealed to the *virtus* of the fathers and, like the Stoics, honoured the man who would allow no threat or danger to deflect him from acting on his moral convictions:

> Let the whole world collapse, its ruins
> will bury him but will not break him.

"*Si fractus illabatur orbis, impavidum ferient ruinae*". Even so convinced a Stoic as Seneca felt himself entitled to pick flowers in the garden of Epicurus.

Philosophers and laymen alike were agreed above all on one thing – man must be armed against changing fortune. And if he is unable to change the march of events, he must be able to form within himself a counterweight, enabling him to stand upright in the most difficult circumstances, and assuring his independence and peace of mind. Political freedom, for which men had once been enthusiastic, was gone beyond recall; what now took its place was the inner freedom of the individual, a possession not of the philosophic schools alone but of the whole educated world.

On the inscription of Priene political freedom was still extolled as the highest good of Greek man. In the first century of the Christian era Dio of Prusa, whose outlook resembled the Stoics' but who wanted to be an independent follower of Socrates, went about the world in order "to fulfil the true role of the philosopher, the leadership of men".[65] A theme he greatly liked to develop in his lectures was "freedom and slavery". He would begin in this vein: "Men strive above all else to be free, and consider freedom the greatest of all goods and slavery (δουλεία) the greatest disgrace and misfortune. But precisely what it is to be a slave or to be free they do not know and by this ignorance deprive themselves of their freedom." What they imagine – and here he echoes the old democratic slogan – is that freedom consists in being able to do just as one wishes. But what they "wish" in this way is often not at all good for them but is bad, and real freedom must consist in knowing what objectively is permissible for them and what is not. On another occasion he told his audience in a town in Cilicia that plenty of people are prepared to fight for political freedom and their country's independence, but are not concerned about the law of nature and thus through their own fault fall into a far worse slavery to stupidity, greed and the craving for pleasure.

144

Dio addressed an educated public. But there were on the streets at that time many wandering preachers who claimed to be the successors of the early Cynics and felt themselves called upon to care for the souls of the lower social strata (cf. p. 80). In one of his *Satires* (II, 7), Horace could already pretend that his own slave Davus took advantage of the freedom of the Saturnalia and served up freshly to him the wisdom he had just picked up from his friend, the porter of the Stoic philosopher Crispinus, to the effect that most men lack freedom, including those who, like Horace himself, belonged to the gentry. We can well imagine how eagerly those slaves listened to the old arguments proving clearly that slavery had come into the world only through force, by war or man-hunts, and that no man was by nature born to be a slave.[66] That of course did not make the slightest difference to their real position but it could give them the elevating consciousness that they, too, were human beings, and not just nominally, but really men of equal worth, carrying within themselves as much as any king the capacity for *arete*, and that they were able to achieve the inner freedom that the ruler on his throne only too often lacked.

Among the intellectuals everyone might interpret the ideal of freedom according to his personal inclination or situation. Lucretius praised his master Epicurus because he had freed mankind from its heaviest burden, religion and superstitious fear of the gods and of death. Horace did not need a philosophy to help him overcome the fear of the terrors of the underworld. He too was grateful to Epicurus for showing him the way to be independent of everything that could disturb his comfortable enjoyment of life. But in his case the conception of freedom was coloured by his personal circumstances. For, although he was bound by a genuine friendship to Maecenas, it carried with it heavy social obligations, which the poet found the more burdensome because he valued above all the freedom to live one's own life, *sibi vivere*, and unresticted leisure, *otia liberrima*, which he would not surrender for all the treasures of Arabia.[67] That aroused his interest in another philosopher who was famous precisely because he had kept company with the most powerful men on earth and preserved his freedom. Aristippus became for him the model of a man who preserved his individual personality even while adapting himself externally to the most diverse situations, and who understood the art of "dominating things and not letting things dominate him".

The Stoics remained the real advocates of the ideal of freedom.[68] When the Peripatetic Aspasius developed the Aristotelian idea of the great-minded man, and the Christian Clement of Alexandria represented the complete Gnostic, these men unconsciously adopted features of the great Stoics, and the same applies to Cicero when he portrays Scipio as the ideal head of state, seeing and regulating all earthly things from the high viewpoint of philosophy and trying in his private life to raise himself above all that is worldly and low. When it is said of him that he had only one wish, to free his spirit from the prison of the flesh, the spirit that represents his true self, one cannot fail to recognise the influence of Plato and the first *Alcibiades* (cf. p. 101). On the whole however it is Stoic freedom that has made the deepest impression on that statesman.

There was for the Romans a close natural connection between *libertas* and manliness, and Ennius, in his play *Phoenix*, probably adapted freely from a scene of Euripides, had already argued that a man's morality was the basis not only of *virtus*, but also of real freedom: Freedom is to have a pure and constant heart, *ea libertas est, qui pectus purum et firmum gestitat* (fr. sc. 302). For Cato the Younger this became the dogma that was to guide him in life and in death (cf. p. 110).[69] The teaching of his school allowed him to choose suicide when he was convinced after an examination of his *logos* that a "natural" life was no longer possible for him. Others might survive the eclipse of political freedom in Rome but this was not possible for him. He died of his own free will, convinced that he "still was victorious over Caesar in those things that mattered most to him, morality and justice". In his last conversations he passionately championed the Stoic conception that only the good are free. That he had proved this himself and that even in death he remained free and unconquered – as the Academician Plutarch admiringly reported – was the unanimous verdict of the inhabitants of Utica whose well-being he had cared for until his last breath.[70]

By his act Cato became the martyr of the ideal of liberty and, following his example, many distinguished Romans of the Empire died as free men and even, like Seneca, raised compulsory suicide into genuinely free voluntary death.

Long before his end Seneca had asked himself the question, what is most important for men, and he considered above all else one thing: "To have the breath of life on one's lips. That is what makes a man free, not according to the law of the Quirites but according to the law of nature". When he adds: "A man is free when he has escaped enslavement to himself; the worst form of slavery is being enslaved to oneself", and elsewhere he recommends liberating the spirit from the chains of the flesh, valuing freedom more than gold or pleasure and mastering fate through the power of reason, then these are ideas we hear from others also. Personal experience taught him how hard it was especially for the all-powerful minister to preserve his freedom, and he was seriously pre-occupied with the problem whether the wealth and the life of luxury which went with his position were really compatible with his philosophy. But he felt as a Stoic justified in answering to jealous critics that wealth is not in itself evil, and that it even affords opportunities for moral action through social activity. The important thing is to protect one's freedom against it and not become tied to it, to "take it into one's house, but not into one's heart".[71] It is with reflections like these that the Christian preacher Clement later reassured the wealthy members of his congregation, who were troubled by the Lord's words that it is easier for a camel to go through the eye of a needle than for a rich man to enter the kingdom of heaven.

His personal circumstances also obliged Seneca to probe more thoroughly than his contemporaries did into other problems arising out of the issues of the age. The Romans too felt themselves πολιτικὰ ζῷα, beings made for life in the state community and, like the Greeks in the heyday of the *polis*, the Romans also took it for granted that the worth of the "good man", the *vir bonus* should manifest itself in his participation in the people's affairs, the *res publica*, and that it was his proper task to serve it. In the eyes of the Roman nobility the time remaining for one's private life after performance of one's political duties was *otium*[12], leisure time intended for rest and relaxation after these duties. During the Empire that situation changed, of course, as there was no longer any *libera res publica* and the influence that a private citizen might exercise on public life had vanished. Any one who now became a civil servant would often complain about the burden of office which left him no time for his private life; *otium* then became a profession chosen according to a man's personal abilities and inclination, and instead of the "practical" life, he chose the "theoretical" life of the scholar or any other way of life which pleased him as an individual. Nevertheless, the old feeling for the state was not

147

quite dead, and internal conflicts were inevitable, that is most clearly seen in the eventful life led by Seneca.[73] He was no doubt delighted when as Nero's favourite he was able to perform political duties beneficial to the whole Empire, and when he lost the Emperor's confidence it was not easy for him to ask leave to resign. But when he wrote a special treatise *De Otio*, in which he justified his action to himself and other people, he was able not only to console himself as a Stoic with the thought that he could now exert a literary influence on the whole cosmopolis; he could also argue: "Nature intended me to engage both in practical activity and in free theoretical work," *natura utrumque facere me voluit, et agere et contemplationi vacare* (5, 8). With the word *contemplatio* he renders the Greek term θεωρία. The word does not mean for him, as it did for Aristotle, a life devoted exclusively to scientific research, but "philosophy" as he pursued it, reflecting freely upon the whole of human life. The urge towards this was so powerful in him that he soon found that the enforced leisure was a liberation, enabling him to lead a really free life of his own.

One other thing now became clear to him which he had long felt vaguely; he recognised the real danger inherent in modern civilisation.[74] The noise of the great town, the pressure of official life, the pursuit of external success, the emptiness of the social round – all these threatened man with the loss of his best possession, his true self. As he had already lamented on more than one occasion, "No one is any longer his own master", *suus nemo est* (*De brev. vitae* 2, 4). Daily life made so many demands on people that there was no time left for the inner life. "Men need nothing so much as peace, not merely the break from work, when distraction is sought in the theatre or the circus, but peace in the heart, which makes reflection possible. What is necessary is not the flight into solitude but concentrated thought upon what is really essential, the dialogue with oneself, giving account of past actions and seeking the right road into the future. Only thus can man escape being swept along with the crowd. Only thus can he preserve his own outlook and himself be free and independent." He was already expressing views of this kind during the years when he was at the height of his political career. They now became the basic theme, recognisable in all his work. He keeps advising his young friend Lucilius who, as Governor of Sicily, was at the heart of practical life, "Withdraw into yourself, find leisure for your mind and yourself". At the head of the collection of letters addressed to him, Seneca wrote the motto: *Vindica te tibi!*

The impact made on receptive people in Nero's time by the idea of freedom is movingly apparent also in the fifth satire of Persius. This young man gives heart-felt thanks to his Stoic tutor Cornutus for having sheltered him during his critical and decisive years in the safety of Socratic philosophy and taught him the one thing that really mattered – liberty. He begins his own writings with the sentence: "*Libertate opus est*". That is fundamentally a thing that all men know. All do indeed strive "to live as they like". But their great mistake – we have heard Dio say something similar – lies in interpreting it as subjective desire instead of seeing clearly that all men are subject to the laws of nature. The real value of philosophy is therefore that it teaches us to desire the right things, the true good, which alone makes man free and brings him inner peace.

It is not really the slave obeying outer compulsion who lacks freedom but the fool who succumbs to "masters inside himself, in his own diseased liver". Unfree are the avaricious people, driven from bed early in the morning against their will through lust of gain, the pleasure-lovers enslaved to their desires, the lovers who cannot tear themselves away from their girls, the ambitious people who are reduced to having to curry favour with the common people. They are torn by conflicting desires and cannot find the longed-for peace of mind, not even by flinging themselves into the arms of the new Oriental religions. Only he who knows and does the right really lives "as he wills".

Among the paradoxes the Stoics liked to puzzle people with none attracted more attention or more bitter criticism than the dictum that only the wise man is free and all other men are slaves. But through the criticism there is always the realisation that the exaggeration of the ideal contained a kernel of truth. An ordinary person might smile on hearing what a Stoic like Persius had to say about the fool's lack of freedom. When Horace lets his slave Davus tell him that he is really no freer than his slave, it is not simply the comic element in the situation and the satire on the cheap wisdom of the moralist that amuses us. The point lies rather in Davus sketching a picture of his master that vacillates between extremes, praises to the skies the strict morality of the old Roman peasantry without dreaming of observing this code himself, but controlled by his whims and always, like a slave attempting to escape his master, evading his better self. When Horace becomes angry and drives this unwelcome preacher away, we are still meant to note with satisfaction how the poet feels the attack personally and enjoy the charming self-critical manner which recognises that there is a grain of truth in the reproach about his lack of liberty.

But even the positive portrayal of the "free" wise man could make the non-Stoic think. Cicero once amused himself by proving the validity of the Stoic paradoxes with such rhetorical skill that they seemed to fit into the actual life of Rome.[75] He was able to relate the notion of the free wise man to a specific historical case. When in the year 106 the orator L. Crassus, in an effort to win over the populace in a People's Assembly, made the appeal: "Do not allow us to serve any other than the whole community of yourselves, whom we can and we ought to serve", he was taken to task by the strict Stoic, Rutilius Rufus, who reprimanded him publicly for such unbecoming servility. Cicero seized upon that criticism in order to illustrate how the great lords of Rome through their ambitions and their noble passions made themselves into slaves. But he prefaced to this an account of the freedom of the wise man which might appeal even to the sober mentality of the Romans: "What then is freedom? The power to live as you will. But who does live as he likes except the man who follows the right course, who does his duty gladly, who has carefully planned and reflected upon his path in life, who obeys the laws not out of fear but respects them and conforms to them because he sees in this his true advantage, who neither does nor says, nor even thinks anything but by his own free will, the man whose every decision and act is determined from within, who values nothing above his own will and judgment, he before whom allegedly almighty Fortuna herself bows if, in the words of a wise poet, the fate of every man is determined by his own nature? The wise man is therefore the only man who does nothing against his will, nothing through pain or under compulsion".

Even Horace's Davus adopts a different tone when he comes to speak about the wise man (*Sat.*, II, 7, 83):

> Who then is free? The wise man who alone
> Commands himself and decides for himself,
> Fears neither prison, poverty nor death,
> Resists desire and does not care for fame,

The strong one whose foundation is himself
And like a smooth round sphere which will permit
Nothing which comes upon it to adhere,
He puts to shame even the wrath of Fate.

Philo of Alexandria, strongly attached as he was to the religion of his
fathers, made that ideal his own and sought, with the help of philosophy,
to modernise the old religion and make it attractive to the Greeks.[76] The
saying that only the good are free is for him a fundamental truth that is
valid also for the disciple of Moses. He must of course remember that
freedom includes submission to God's direction but that need not prevent
acceptance of the Stoic ideal, for Zeno himself had been inspired by the
Jewish Book of Laws. Thus Philo can conclude his work with the statement that the highest goal of human education is, in Zeno's phrase, "to
follow nature". And following his lead Bishop Ambrose made use of
the Stoic paradox to explain the Pauline conception of Christian freedom.

Freedom as a Principle to Live By

Among the great number of men who expressed a passion for freedom
during the Empire there is one so outstanding that he calls for special
consideration, since freedom was for him not a single good but the very
essence and principle of his existence.[77] It is the crippled Phrygian slave
Epictetus, who in Nero's reign was granted freedom by his master Epa-
phroditus, himself a former slave. Epictetus soon felt himself to be a
"new Socrates" with a divine mission to make known to men that
freedom is true manhood. Because of his independence he was banished
from Italy along with other philosophers under Domitian, and then
founded on the west coast of the Balkan peninsula a school where he
remained active until advanced old age as an apostle of freedom.

For Epictetus freedom is life's goal towards which nature leads man
from the moment of his birth. The basic urge of living beings is for him
not striving for pleasure, nor the preservation and development of the
self, but the urge to live "as it will", for that is in accordance with its
nature.[78] "Look at the little birds", he called out to his students in the
course of a lecture on freedom which we know from the notes of Arrian
"how desperately they try to escape when they are captured and kept in
a cage. Many of them will die from hunger rather than tolerate such an

existence. Those that do remain alive are miserable and pine away piti-fully and if they ever find the tiniest hole they are at once up and away, so great is their need for natural freedom, for an existence in which they are their own masters and unrestricted". "What is wrong with living in a cage?" "How can you ask? My nature is to fly wherever I will, to live under the open sky, to sing when I want to. You take all that away from me, and ask, "What is wrong with living in a cage?"". What for the animal is inborn instinct becomes for man conscious decision in life, which brings fulfilment of his nature and his proper purpose. For that reason nature has given him *synkatathesis*, so that he does not simply follow his ideas but "makes proper use of them". And no man can force him to agree that something false is true or something evil good. That is man's freedom which can be stolen from him by nobody – except him-self.[79]

It is a matter of daily experience that men forfeit their freedom through their own fault and make themselves slaves of external things. Epictetus, too, takes pleasure in portraying the foolish man's lack of freedom in the usual way. He describes the soldier, proud of his strength, who will do anything his girl requires, the feeble-hearted forever worrying about their daily bread, the society man who always has to make allowance for others and in particular the gentlemen of the old aristocracy who regard it as the finest thing on earth to be accepted after years of effort as "friends of the Emperor" and never again have an hour's peace, needing always to dance attendance on the master and eternally be in fear of incurring his displeasure. For then their punishment awaits them – "not a thrashing as a common slave would suffer, but, as is proper for a nobleman, death."

But the positive aspect is more real for him. Why do men throw away the highest good they possess? The answer of the old Stoics was this: "Ignorance, which fails to recognise that the only good for man is moral good and that, as compared with it, external things are valueless". Epictetus does not reject that distinction but from the point of view of freedom he can see a different one.

The problem of freedom of will does not exist for him, because for him it is obvious that men can freely decide and he does not need to ask whether *synkatathesis*, which gives them their ideas, is determined, since he takes it for granted that man is himself always responsible for the state of the *logos* on the basis of which he decides. There is therefore something which "remains within our power," ἐφ' ἡμῖν ἐστιν. Even so, however, it is certain that some things are withheld from our power (οὐκ ἐφ' ἡμῖν). That is the first thing man must recognise. It is certainly in accordance with the teaching of Epictetus when Arrian begins the little manual (*encheiridion*), in which he collects the main ideas from the masters' lectures, with these sentences: "Of all things that exist, some are within our power, others are not. Within our power are judgment, the urge to act, to desire, to avoid – in a word, everything that is our own doing; not within our power are the body, possessions, respect, honours – in a word, everything that is not our own doing. And whatever is in our power is by its nature free, not to be impeded, not to be confined. But what is not within our power is powerless, slave-like, restricted, subject to outside power. Note this – when you mistake for free what is slavish, and for your own what is alien, then will you meet obstacles and complain, lose your temper and curse gods and men. But if you take for your own what really is your own, and that which is not your own for what it is, then no one will compel you and no one will obstruct you; you will reproach no one and complain about no one. You will do nothing against your will; nobody will harm you and you will have no enemy, for nothing harmful can befall you".

In those sentences lies the whole secret of the influence of Epictetus. That two-fold division of reality, that *dihairesis*, man must use as his guide if he would live his life properly and be free and happy. That is the *prohairesis*[80], the general preliminary decision that he must make in order to deal properly with individual cases. For the recognition that external things do not lie within our power and that success does not depend on us does not mean that we ought to renounce action. Man is not made for doing nothing. Nor is he a wild beast that follows only its own desires; he is a good-natured, gentle, social creature impelled by his nature to fulfil his purpose in the human community. That, however, he is able to do only when he possesses freedom which is subject to no alien power and which is guaranteed to him only by a proper inner attitude, namely *dihairesis*. That also is the only thing that helps man to live the life he really wants to.[81] Whoever gives his heart to things which are not within his power will have to do much that he does not wish to and yet never have the certainty that he will reach his goal. He will not escape from toil and sorrow and, when failure inevitably comes, then will he grumble and weep and quarrel with gods and men and with himself. He forfeits that which he really desires, serenity and inner peace. Only he who confines his willing to what is within his grasp, only he whose sole aim is his own moral action, regardless whether it brings outward success or not, need fear no disillusion. Nobody can obstruct him. He can do what he wishes because he only wishes what he can do. And no blow of fate can trouble his peace of mind.[82] The loss of a close relative is to him the natural end of mortal man. Even less does he fear his own death, and with this all the fears disappear that terrify the foolish man who fears for his own life. If he is ill, he does not fear the end. For he cannot determine when the end shall be; only one thing he can and should determine, to bear suffering bravely. That is his moral duty, and that is also his will if his *logos* is healthy. In his bearing too he will be free and confident, even if the Emperor summons him to an audience or if he is threatened in court with the death penalty. He applies to himself the words of Socrates: "Anytus and Meletus can kill me, but they cannot harm me", and just as Socrates did not allow the threats of the Thirty Tyrants to move him to take part in their unjust acts, so he too will gently but firmly decline if his superior expects him to do anything contrary to his moral convictions.

Epictetus expressly repudiated the reproach that his attitude was incompatible with loyalty to the state. He commended to his audience fulfilment of their civic duties and, "the subordination of everybody to authority". He is also prepared if need be to sacrifice to the state life and property, even the life of his family. But there are limits even to the power of an Emperor. "My inner convictions are at my disposal alone, for by the will of Zeus they are the free property of man". No Emperor has any right to interfere with a man's inner self. We are reminded of the words of Jesus: "Render unto Caesar the things which are Caesar's and unto God the things which are God's". Similarly for Epictetus the commandment of the divine *logos* is not merely higher than any earthly monarch's will, but it is absolutely binding upon man. This claim Epictetus makes on behalf of individual men, but it is quite as much in the interests of the community, which cannot do without the inner freedom of moral personalities.

Everything depends upon these inner convictions, these *dogmata*. It is not things and persons as such that terrify us. It is not the child who fears the tyrant's guards and their swords, but the adult who at the sight of them mistakenly assumes that they can do him harm. Yet he too can defend himself against such error if he makes use of his natural ability to test the validity of all impressions. He must be fully prepared to distinguish the impressions themselves from the objects giving rise to them and must decide in any individual case, whether he himself is affected by it or not, and if he comes to the conclusion: "this is an empty impression and of no concern to me"[83], then that impression from outside has no power over him and he can, free and undeluded, listen to his inner voice and his *logos*.

For Epictetus the words "You do not concern me" are the magic formula which protects the inner life against all external attack. This "me" is for him a clear, meaningful concept. The Stoics had previously contrasted the *logos*, as the controlling part of the soul of man, with the body and the external. Not only did Epictetus sharpen the distinction through his teaching about what belongs to man's nature and what is foreign to it, but he also identified man's nature with the "true self", a conception which had long been familiar in Greek thought. That was for him the first lesson a young man should learn from the philosopher, he must become clear as to "what he himself is", $τί\ ἐστιν\ αὐτός$. Not without reason does the Delphic oracle advise us: "Man, know thyself". You are not just flesh and bone and muscle but that which makes use of these as its instruments. It is not nose and eyes which make man but his convictions, his spirit. In these lies man's nature, his self. So do not grumble, saying "I am ill". It is only your body that is ill, not you. Should a tyrant threaten you: "Am I not master of your body? I shall put you in chains", answer him calmly: "How does that concern me? You cannot put my *prohairesis* in chains." Diogenes was free not because he was born of free parents, but "because his self was free and offered no weak points to slavery". Socrates would not condescend to save his flesh because he knew he had something higher that was worth saving. It was that which grows and is preserved by righteousness, but withers and is destroyed by unrighteousness. That was his self and he saved it, not through ignominious flight but through his death. It is for that reason that he still exerts his influence on men today as he did throughout his lifetime.

The old idea of tragedy that there exists in man something which survives physical destruction is thus formulated as a philosophic teaching.

It is upon this self that man must concentrate, not in self-seeking isolation but in order to maintain freedom of action. What do other people's words matter to you? It is to yourself that you are responsible, with yourself that you have to come to terms. "To preserve what is one-self is a sacred duty." [85]

Epictetus had no definite word to express this "self", any more than had his predecessors. But what he means by the "self" which he so often mentions is shown by an expression of his which frequently recurs in his lectures. [86] Of Socrates he says it was not his body he wanted to save but the "reliable, moral man". He is always admonishing his listeners to do this and is even fonder still of dwelling upon the obverse of this. The old Stoa had sometimes said that he who goes against the law of reason surrenders his humanity (cf. p. 136). Epictetus kept hammering into his pupils: "Whoever acts immorally destroys the reliable and honourable human being within himself, the citizen, the man; and when any part of that is destroyed, the man himself is lost." Man's self is his moral personality.

His portrait of that self has ordinary human features. Yet it was not in vain that Panaetius stressed the importance of the individual human personality. Epictetus required of every individual that he give his life a definite shape ($\chi\alpha\rho\alpha\kappa\tau\tilde{\eta}\rho\alpha$) and perform faithfully the role alloted him by the ruler of the world. [87] Little as he wanted to set himself up as the ideal man, he was conscious, like Socrates, of having a quite personal mission to fulfil and of having been appointed by God as a leader and a teacher of men. Why he of all people? "Ask the bull what makes him go ahead of the herd and do battle with the lion."

"I am free" is the motif running like a shout of joy through all the discourses of Epictetus. But he feels that this consciousness of freedom must be complemented by another feeling. Man owes his freedom not to himself alone, nor is it merely his "nature"; it is a gift of God, who subjects all that happens in this world to the cosmic law and who has given only to man a share in that freedom which is his own. For that we must be even more grateful to him than for our physical existence. But from that we must also draw the consequences as regards our attitude to life. He can proudly declare: "No one has power over me, God has declared me free", but he goes on: "and I know his commandments." [88] The old Stoa had already recognised that the law of nature was the command of the universal God, the world *logos*. Epictetus on one occasion defines the reality of God as mind ($\nuo\tilde{\upsilon}\varsigma$), knowledge and the "upright *logos*". But he is the child of a new age whose religious sensibility has changed. God is for him the personality who accompanies him wherever he goes, who knows his innermost thoughts and calls him to account for all his deeds. But in the eyes of Epictetus that does not impair man's independence, because as a reasoning being he is free, like God himself. "You are yourself a part of God, you have within you a share of his being, and carry a god about with you!" [89] But that very fact ought to sharpen our sense of responsibility and warn us to do nothing that would be unworthy of that God.

God does not compel us. He himself created us for freedom. Man, however, because he is by nature akin to God, "wills everything that God wills". Others may feel proud of being known as "friends of the Emperor"; Epictetus can say: "I am free and a friend of God, whom I follow of my own inclination."

Epictetus avoided the word *heimarmene*. For him there is only the *pronoia* of the kindly father, who cares even for the individual and knows what is good for him better than he does himself.[90] Among his favourite utterances are the prayer in which Cleanthes joyfully vows to follow God unhesitatingly wherever he wants and the words of Socrates in prison: "If it pleases the gods, so let it be." Certainly much can happen to the individual which will seem to him evil. "But shall I, because I have a broken leg, criticise the cosmos which in its entirety bears such eloquent witness to God's providence." There is nothing more stupid than to quarrel with God and pointlessly embitter one's own existence. Only he who leads a life looking always up to God enjoys the peace of the soul that is far more precious than the much-praised peace of the Empire. "Should the vexations of daily life become unbearable, then God himself has opened the door leading to freedom, to those elements of the related cosmos from which you yourself came." Power to decide over one's own life is also a part of man's freedom.

Epictetus held that freedom without obligation does not exist.[91] "For me the law is all", he explained, even recalling that Diogenes had taken up the same position and for that very reason became truly free. Thus freedom can become the highest good. "Keep careful watch on your ideas. For it is no small matter you have to take care of, it is morality and trustworthiness, a life without passions, without pain, fear or exitement – in a word, freedom."

Man has to attain this with his own powers. But he can do so thanks to the God who gave him the *logos*. Hence Epictetus brings his high song of human freedom to its climax in a hymn of praise to the giver of all good things.

Epictetus' call to liberty made an immediate impact.[92] In the interior of Pisidia a rock inscription has been found celebrating the "divine" man who was born the son of a slave but came as a blessing to all mankind. Since that time his continued influence has been felt by heathens and Christians alike and still goes on helping many to inner freedom. But nobody derived from the discourses of Epictetus so much help for his own life as the man who in outward circumstances appeared the greatest contrast to the crippled slave, the Emperor Marcus Aurelius.[93]

Marcus Aurelius was the absolute monarch whom nobody could prevent from "living exactly as he liked". Yet in self-scrutiny he says to himself: "Be a free man". This was not a despairing prayer or a pious wish, but a serious, all-embracing ideal of behaviour which he sets himself. For this freedom is for him the highest good, but not a natural state or a gift, but a possession which a man wins by his own efforts and must earn afresh every day.

What does Marcus Aurelius understand by this freedom? He had to concern himself with the well-being of the many millions living inside his empire. That empire was however threatened by enemies within and without, and shaken by pestilence and natural catastrophe. Whether he would manage to fulfil his task was known only to God who had called him to that post. But there was one thing which he himself knew; he for his own part had to do everything that was within his power to that end. And no one could be allowed to hinder him, not even himself. For, just as with others, he was absolutely sincere with himself, and he did not conceal from himself the fact that dangers to his administrative duties could arise from within himself. Admittedly he was not subject to pleasure-seeking and selfish desires, and he was even able to overcome the longing for peace to relax from his official duties and so have time to follow his own inclinations.[94] But something else was more difficult to overcome. The first thing he requires of himself is this: "Say to yourself first thing in the morning – I shall be meeting a man who is pushing, ungrateful, impudent, cunning, unpleasant and lacking in social sense." For such is the day-to-day experience of the ruler. "Even the most decent people are difficult to bear." Well he knew that the very man who would cringe before him so dishonourably would slander him behind his back, and that many were only waiting for him to die so as at last "to get rid of the old schoolmaster". No wonder he was disgusted at times and asked himself whether there was any purpose in sacrificing himself in the service of such men. At such times it was philosophy that gave him the steadfastness of purpose and the strength to carry out his duties. And no one had more to tell him than Epictetus. From him he adopted the basic distinction: "Consider well what is within your power and what is not." Whether you succeed in what you do, whether you can alter the course of external events, does not depend on you. But there is within your power one thing which you can do and which you ought to do – do your duty and stick to the post to which God has called you. Be clear about this: it is not men themselves who annoy you but the subjective opinions you form about them, and these are within your power.[95] What other men report about you, whether they do as you say or not, whether they are evil and ungrateful, that "does not concern you". Remember that you yourself are not without blemish and the people who embitter you life are doing so unwittingly. Be patient with them, for your own sake too.[96] Because the annoyance, anger and passion which you allow to mount up inside you are worse evils than any that can come upon you from without. One thing alone must be your goal; unperturbed by outside influences, and even by your body and the lower urges of your own soul, do only that which your true self commands. For what is that self?[97] Your *logos*, your *daimon*, your spirit, that which is hidden inside you, one may call it "the man". To follow him is within your power. That is your freedom. Be a free man!

Then you can calmly contemplate earthly things. Then you have within you a stronghold impregnable by enemies outside or inside, the spirit free from passions.[98] Then you are like the rock over which the waves break, like the pure spring which turns aside everything alien and unclean. Then you have the freedom that is inseparably bound up with justice, nobility and morality. Then you have peace in your soul.

Man is entirely dependent upon himself. But there is one thing he must not forget. Marcus Aurelius did not feel so strongly as did Epictetus the religious need to envisage God as a person and as father. But the command: "Follow God" is for him too a binding law.[99] "Live with the gods!" That man does live with the gods who constantly shows that his soul is content with his lot and does everything which is required by the *daimon* which Zeus has given to each man as his supervisor and guide, a part of his own being. The *daimon* is the spirit and the reason of every man.

The other philosophers agreed with the Stoics that inner freedom was a necessary condition for morality and therefore for true humanity. During the Empire therefore men of the most diverse tendencies combined in a common front to combat that "semi-slavery", Stoic determinism; even if they conceded the validity of an indissoluble causal connection of events in nature, they tried the more passionately to show that one sphere remained outside of it, the *heimarmene*. The spirit is free and "virtue has no master" (cf. p. 132f.).[100]

This current of thought reached its climax in the neo-Platonist Plotinus who derived all being from the immaterial and who accepted the world of the senses only as a last emanation from it. It is to the immaterial sphere that the spirit of man belongs. Hence spontaneity is in his nature. In his nature he is incapable of suffering, since he has by nature *apatheia* and therewith absolute freedom. Man forfeits this, of course, if he allows himself to be dragged down into sensuality; but that too is a free decision of the *nous* for which he has full responsibility.[101]

We are reminded of Plato when we read in a later neo-Platonist: "The soul of man is free and unhindered in its activities but only in its existence outside the body. For, if it is ruled by the body and its passions, it loses that free existence and is not in a position to act as it will; it is enslaved and robbed of its own power of action."

CHAPTER V

RETROSPECT AND PROSPECT

GREEK AND CHRISTIAN FREEDOM

The Greeks of today still have as their national anthem the song written by Solomos in 1823 to greet "The freedom resurrected from the sacred bones of the Hellenes of long ago". The nature and destiny of the ancient Greeks can only be fully understood if we realise clearly the influence which the idea of freedom exercised not only on the political history but on the whole spiritual life of the people.

Some special impetus was certainly required before the urge to independence that lay in the Greek blood became the clear consciousness of freedom as man's most precious possession. But given that impetus it burst forward with all the greater power.

The decisive turn in Greek history was the battle for independence which they victoriously waged against the Persians. They did not coin the phrase "war of liberation"; but the feeling that it was a war of this kind did in fact inspire every fighting man and spur him on to make his utmost effort. One other thing always stood out with amazing clarity for them: this war was not just a matter of warding off a momentary danger; it was to preserve a possession which was inseparably bound up with the people's very being: the free state based upon law, the *polis*, which distinguished them from all barbarians. Political freedom, they suddenly felt, was the only form of existence in which Greeks could prosper. Awareness of this had its effects, however, far beyond the purely political sphere.

When the Germans revolted against the Napoleonic yoke in the "War of Liberation" then the "breath of freedom blew strongly throughout the world"; and Ernst Moritz Arndt could teach young people that freedom is "man's highest possession". But in peace time that ideal did not prove strong enough against the forces of reaction to bring about a revolution in internal policy or in spiritual life in general. An all round liberation of the spirit had indeed been effected by the Renaissance, but the humanist leaders of the movement had forgotten the political legacy of the ancients.

161

The Greeks were the "political" men, for whom the liberation of the fatherland and of the human spirit went hand in hand. Pride in the outstanding achievements they had realised as free men powerfully stimulated the release of all the latent powers of the people and led to a heightening of their vitality which operated in every aspect of their life.

To that freedom there were natural limits. For it was self-evident that even the democratic state required of its citizens obedience to the laws and the authorities. But the new idea proclaimed by Pericles was that in his Athens that obedience should rest not on force but on voluntary subordination to the whole community. Freedom cannot exist without obligations. But those obligations should be accepted willingly.

This seemed to be the ideal solution to the eternal problem of the proper relationship of the individual to the state. But the ideal could not stand up to reality. It was the tragedy of the Greek people that the very characteristic to which they owed their greatness when carried to excess became their undoing. Just as in the relations of the city-states with each other, the aversion to all restraint led to a separation which prevented the unification of the nation, similarly within the state the urge to freedom, once aroused, led to an individualism demanding the right of the individual "to live as he liked". In consequence liberty degenerated into license, resisting any obligation, regarding authority as compulsion, and thus undermining public order. The individual no longer felt himself a member of the whole, but a partner with equal rights, so that the state became an organisation men looked upon as a welfare institution without feeling towards it any of the old sense of duty. The consequence was the loss of national independence.

But Pericles' ideal of freedom was not confined to politics in the narrow sense of the word. He did not merely want to show the individual the role he had to play in the state, but to provide him with the opportunity to shape for himself a personal life in accordance with his own inclinations. So a new freedom was thus discovered, the freedom of the personality. But it was soon apparent that its realisation was a difficult matter. For if the individual is to decide how he is to live, one thing is indispensible – he must himself know what he wants, he must have a definite standpoint from which to survey his whole life and to base his future actions upon sound principles. But how was that to be achieved at a time when all traditional conceptions of social order were being questioned?

It was this crisis in spiritual life that roused Socrates to action, and that is why his main object was to convince men that they should not let themselves be ruled by subjective desires but must strive with all their might towards knowledge of objective good, which alone could be their guiding principle in action. For man by his nature really desires only this objective good, and the freedom he longs for can consist only in a man's directing his actions to that end and not being misled by external influences.

To questions about the nature of the good and whence it springs Socrates himself had really no conclusive answers. But one point keeps recurring in all his dialogues. Man is made for life in society and his most binding duty must be to fit himself into it through moral conduct. And "Only through his moral behaviour can he be free and powerful". Outwardly, of course, that meant restrictions on his liberty, but only in this way could he fulfil his human destiny. Modern man is accustomed to individualistic habits of thought and Sartre can create a figure like Orestes who must first "chase the flies away" and must free himself from all conventional ties before he can enter as a free man into self-imposed obligations. Socrates, the Greek, is aware that the individual owes his whole physical and spiritual existence to the community and that only in it can he live. He is therefore by his nature outwardly tied and inwardly committed to that community. He thus does not have absolute freedom but remains within an objective commitment from which he cannot free himself without forfeiting his own nature. But he can make that commitment a voluntary one if he accepts it himself by recognising moral good as his own real good and acting accordingly. The voluntary subordination to the whole which Pericles conceived as the ideal attitude of the citizen, is expressed most perfectly when Socrates, unjustly condemned, preferred to remain in prison rather than undermine the rule of law and the stability of the state. But what had been an intuitively felt attitude now became a clear decision made by a man on the basis of his knowledge of the real good. And if in the tragedy Antigone offers up her life for a great cause in obedience to a moral feeling, her action now gained a deeper significance in the recognition that it is not life that matters, but the good life, and that a man in freely sacrificing his physical existence is able to save the best part of himself, his moral personality.

In that way Socrates gave men the reliable standard they needed and pointed the way to inner freedom which acknowledges as its guiding principle only the true good. That freedom could be realised only if man remained conscious of its limits. Thus personal freedom presupposes obligation.

For the common people that was too high an ideal, and the democracy did not tolerate the man who preached the moral freedom of the individual. Some of Socrates' own disciples could not fully understand the master, since they did not share his deep feeling for the *polis*. They felt that the value of inner freedom consisted in its freeing individuals of their obligations and making them independent of things outside themselves. That this independence becomes possible, however, only if man is master of himself and if the intellect restrains the lower instincts of the soul which open the door to external influences on the inner life, Plato had first recognised; and from that recognition he had drawn the decisive conclusion. The freedom of men became the freedom of the intellect which sees the true goal and turns this knowledge into action, even despite inner resistance. The civic sense was still so lively in this descendent of the old Athenian aristocracy that he felt he had to make his discovery fruitful for the community too. There was no room in his ideal state for the subjective right to live as you please, but man learned instead to will what his own nature indicated and thus not merely the individual but the whole community attained that true freedom which elevates the "inner man" above physical things. Thus the limits of human freedom became at the same time more keenly felt. For the limiting power of the law of the community was made stricter and deeper by the conception of the actual state as a part of the divine order which determines physical events as well as spiritual things. For God, not man, is the measure of things. The religious obligation which Aeschylus had required both for the *polis* and for individual men, remained for the philosopher too the ultimate postulate.

In Plato it is still quite clear that the idea of inner freedom has the same spiritual roots as the political ideal and has developed in the course of continual conflict with it. In Hellenism this connection disappeared, but for that very reason the notion of inner freedom could be developed more purely. With the Stoa this became the basic characteristic of man, the basis of his morality and his whole spiritual being. The certainty that he possessed it was so strong that it could not really be shaken by the problem of whether or not a man's individual decisions are determined. Even the "thou shalt" of the universal spirit, which now governed moral conduct, did not impair the feeling of freedom, for it only asked what the individual *logos* itself naturally wanted. The law of reason in the *cosmopolis* expressed in that "thou shalt" certainly had a much stronger binding force than that of the *nomoi* of the small states. It was the power which none could oppose without surrendering his humanity and thus his self. But the citizen of that *cosmopolis* ought not to feel that obedience as compulsion but should, in clear consciousness of his true advantage, freely and gladly consent to what the *logos* of the universe required from him and ordained for him.

The urge to freedom thus remained at all times a basic factor in the Hellenic character. But with it was bound up a strong feeling for those obligations which man's nature lays upon him. Even when, in actual political life, freedom became lack of restraint and no longer recognised obligations, then the Greek sense of proportion, moderation and order immediately set up a resistance, and the best people had a clear and painful consciousness that such developments exceeded the proper human limitations and were a *hybris* that must lead to disaster. The feeling that man is subject to a higher order guided even the defenders of the "inner freedom"; even the supermen, who hoped to set themselves above human laws, let slip no occasion to appeal to the law of nature, according to which the strong have power over the weak.

The feeling that freedom and obligation belong together permeated the whole spiritual life of the Greeks. In Greek art, too, the chisel as well as the spoken word bears out Goethe's teaching, "Only the law can give us liberty". And the Greeks founded the sciences upon their belief in the independence of the scholar, whose mind forms its own judgment independently of tradition, together with objectivity, which requires him to respect the true facts and employ an exact method which is prescribed by the subject of his study.

That insight into its limits did not however disturb the conviction that man is born to freedom and that only through it can he fulfil his destiny. For a man is born to live reasonably within the community and to live a moral life and this is not possible without his freedom of decision and responsibility for his acts. In this case there must be within man the disposition to live morally but he must also have the capacity to put this

165

disposition into practice. This was necessary to satisfy the Greek view of the world, according to which each being had its own proper purpose in life, its *telos*, which it achieved by developing fully its natural dispositions.[1] The human goal is the moral life, which is not a duty imposed upon man from outside, but it is the "best state" to which he is inclined by nature, his *arete*, which his own being longs to attain and which by reason of his inborn intelligence he can attain.

The Greeks did not depart from that conviction despite the experience that men can use their intelligence in very different ways and that there are very many wicked men but few really good ones. They held firmly that every man has in him the capacity for good. Basically this is the only way to understand the fact that Pericles founded his democracy in the conviction that each of his citizens would, even without state compulsion and of his own free will, give his best in the service of the whole community. And this optimistic estimate of human nature, which we here see guiding the statesman, is expressed philosophically in Socrates' *dictum* that no man does wrong of his own volition, but only needs to be made aware of his own true interest and he will do what is really good. Plato was of course convinced as an aristocrat that, as in their nature as a whole, so also in their attitude to *arete*, people are very different; and through his psychological work he found an explanation to the effect that in the soul of some people it is the intellect, and in others the passionate *thymos* or else the *epithymetikon*, which is concerned with material things, that is dominant (cf. p. 94). Not every individual therefore will find his way to goodness without external help. But for that very reason Plato puts forward the political programme that at least within the state community the intellect must dominate and the government must be placed in the hands of men who have achieved spiritual freedom, so that their knowledge of the good may be combined with the power to perform it. Only thus can the good as a basic principle become dominant, at least in the community, and this will also make its impression upon the moral conduct of the individual citizen.

Painful experience gradually made Plato more aware how serious was the danger of wickedness for the masses if they did not have such guidance. In the *Theaetetus* he accepts unconditionally the view: "It is impossible to stamp out evil."[2] And when in his old age he wrote down the draft for the *Laws* he clearly knew that even the strongest government and the most painstaking education would not suffice to eliminate the wickedness of individuals. Even in that "second-best state" there would be anti-social elements, against whom society must protect itself, applying if need be the ultimate means, the death penalty. The burning question that thus arose for him was the metaphysical problem of where the evil in the universe and in mankind ultimately comes from[3]; he did not fear to draw the conclusion that to understand the world properly one must accept that, alongside of the good universal soul which brings perfection, there must be a second spiritual force working against it.[4] For his conception of the world that element could of course not be a radically evil principle hostile to God but only something negative, the imperfection that arises out of the fact that the eternal idea of the good cannot be perfectly realised in impermanent perceptible matter.

Much the same may be said about the human soul. Its real nature is the non-material spirit that yearns for the good, the true and the beautiful. But in its earthly existence it acquires the animal propensities that turn its striving towards material things. From this arises the conflict which can result in the defeat of the spirit, and that is the source of all human evil. We must not, however, speak of a radical evil, for the lower propensities are not in themselves something evil; they are part and parcel of man's existence as a creature on this earth, and are useful, indeed necessary, to his survival. They only lead to bad action when they exceed the proper limits and are allowed to overrule the intellect. But it is an "unhealthy" state of the soul in which the intellect lets itself be robbed of its natural leadership, surrenders its freedom, and makes itself the slave of desires and material things. The root of all evil is the false use made by man, through his misconception of the true good, of the freedom that is part of his nature.

How a man makes his decisions depends of course partly at least on the gifts he is born with. This raises the difficult problem of how far a man is responsible for his actions. We have already seen (cf. p. 126f.) that this was clearly recognised by Plato. Admittedly he broaches the subject only in mythical terms and he cannot solve it by rational means. His only certainty is that responsibility for the way of life a man adopts lies not with God but with the man himself. For responsibility only exists where the course of action is freely chosen. That freedom is essential to the idea of morality and thus to the proper understanding of human existence.

167

Man can choose evil but nature endows him with the capacity and the vocation for good.

The next people to accept with conviction this optimistic assessment of man's natural disposition and faith in his power to attain the goal of the moral life are the Stoics. Whereas they never tire of maintaining that, apart from the wise, practically all men are the victims of folly and vice and thus wretchedness, they nevertheless generally follow the teachings of Chrysippus, who energetically championed the view that man is ruined only by harmful influences coming from without but is naturally inclined to the good and also has the power in him to do good. In Chrysippus that contention is closely allied to his intellectualist psychology where the leading central organ in the soul of man was by its nature pure *logos*, while all instincts and desires followed from decisions of the intellect which contained an impulse to action (cf. p. 122f.). The doctrinaire way he developed this idea aroused opposition even in his own school. Panaetius already preferred to accept his own experience which showed him an independent instinct for life in the soul, and Posidonius, in a special monograph, rejected Chrysippus' view and agreed with Plato, who had rightly placed in the soul alongside the intellect two layers without intellect, the *thymos* and the *epithymetikon* (see p. 142).[5] Only thus could the origin of the vices be explained. For the evil influences coming from without could only affect the soul because the ground was already prepared for it there. "Just as for good, so for evil, we carry the seeds within ourselves."

That was a quite new conception of human nature. It was, however, a mistake to attribute to Posidonius the Greek discovery of original sin. Because for Posidonius, just as for Plato, irrational impulses were not things evil in themselves but necessary constituents of human nature and acceptable if kept within their proper limits, and evil appears only when man lets himself be dragged down by those animal urges to the level of the beast, instead of obeying only the godlike *daimon* dwelling in his breast. That this is the greatest calamity for man Posidonius passionately impressed upon his audience.[6] But he had also left no doubt that by its nature that *daimon* was able to keep itself free of the influence of the body, and consequently man was able to attain his life's goal. For the real self of man is precisely this *daimon*, this spirit that places him on the side of the divine which is destined to rule over what is earthly in this world. Posidonius even believed that the spirit of man can communicate directly with the universal God and the countless spirits freed of the body which exist in the universe, and can be helped by that spiritual communion to raise himself above the world of the senses. The deciding factor is that the *daimon* itself must remain strong enough to restrain the animal impulses. That it has the power to do so Posidonius did not doubt.[7]

On the road which he had thus pointed out, the Emperor Marcus Aurelius in turn advanced one step further. He well knew that according to the orthodox teaching of his school, it was superfluous for man to pray to the gods for help in striving to improve morally, since man must himself accomplish this by his own personal effort. His heart nevertheless urged him to offer that kind of prayer. "And why should the almighty gods not help us to perform what lies within our power?" – which might remind us of the old Greek saying: "When the man tries for himself the god helps too". (Aeschylus, *Persians*, 742). And for Marcus Aurelius the important thing is that the good is "within our power" and thus an act of free decision.

The Greeks did not close their eyes to the fact that man is capable of evil as well as of good. But this is inseparably linked with his highest good, his freedom of decision. Radical evil they did not know. They did know the significance of a man's spiritual inheritance for his moral conduct. But when Euripides' Electra complains that her mother Clytemnestra and her aunt Helen have by their actions brought disgrace on all the house of Atreus, Orestes answers her: "Be then better than the wicked since it is within your power" (*Orestes*, 251). That confidence in the individual's moral power was maintained by the Greeks and by the Romans in much later times when the religious feeling for the subordination to the will of God grew stronger. Seneca could subscribe to the motto "*Deo parere libertas est*" (*De vita beata*, 15, 7) and Epictetus not only agreed with him but emphasised the religious element by tending unmistakably to conceive of God as a personality to whom man owed obedience. Yet for both of them belief in freedom and in man's own power to fulfil his moral destiny remained the pillars of their philosophy.

That fact we must bear in mind if we would appreciate properly the relationship between that Greek freedom and the new conception of freedom proclaimed by Christianity. We must consider this briefly in conclusion. We may confine ourselves to St. Paul. For it is he who discovered the freedom of the Christian man and made of it glad tidings for the Jews and the Greeks. What we read about this freedom in the New Testament, as for example in the Gospel of St. John (8, 31–36) is unthinkable but for the influence of Paul. Jesus himself never mentioned it.

Just as Epictetus did, so Paul sings the high song of freedom, especially in his Epistles to the Galatians (4–5), and to the Romans (6–8)[8], and they agree even to the extent of the wording of the individual sentences.[9] No wonder then that it came to be thought that the Christian had been stimulated decisively by the Stoics. But in reality the new freedom had developed on quite different spiritual grounds.

Paul's own words leave us in no doubt as to how he arrived at the idea of freedom. The Damascus experience not only revealed to him that he whom he persecuted was the son of God but also effected a complete revolution in his whole way of life. The fanatical way he had at first attacked the followers of Christ arose from the feeling that they wanted to destroy the religion of their fathers, which was for him the obvious meaning of his existence. That religion was firmly anchored in the law in which God had revealed his will to men. Some of Paul's later utterances certainly allow us to surmise that he suffered early in his life under that law, because he was painfully conscious that despite all his efforts he was unable to fulfil its requirements and remained tainted with guilt and sin. That only spurred him on, however, to still greater efforts of will, until God's call to him personally awoke in him the recognition that his whole life up till that moment was a mistake. Many more years of reflection were needed before he saw clearly, and it was even longer before he dared to join the original disciples of the Lord as an apostle on an equal footing. But meanwhile he had developed a completely new attitude to the law, which was the focal point of his thought, like that of the other Jews.

The law still remained for him the essence of the inescapable demands that God made upon his creature, man. But 430 years before God formulated these demands through the medium of Moses he had spoken directly to Abraham and revealed to him that there was another way to justify oneself before God. That is faith. And now God has given his own son to be made flesh and die so as to satisfy the just requirement of the law for all men. Since that time God no longer demands the really unattainable fulfilment of all his commandments but faith in his mercy and in salvation through his son. Thus the moral law, freed of ritualistic accessories, still remains valid. But it is no longer to operate as slavish compulsion.[10] Christ brought to man a new law, the law of freedom, which fulfils God's will voluntarily. That freedom God could present to man because with the coming of Christ a new age began for mankind, a "new creation", in which the *pneuma* offers to the faithful quite a different kind of strength for the battle with sin and the snares of the flesh than was the case under the old law. For sin was intrinsically bound up with the law, since in its nature sin was nothing other than transgressing the law and so that law first brought full consciousness of sin to man. Both belong to the same situation in life and when a man guided by the Spirit can rise above obedience to the law, he attains mastery over sin, and in this new world the power of time and of death is broken. Such is the freedom which, through Jesus Christ, God has presented to mankind.

In proud awareness of that freedom, Paul wrote to the Corinthians (1 Cor., 6, 12) "all things are lawful unto me". But that does not indicate his approval of the libertinism which had become common among them. "For not all things are expedient". The new freedom does indeed mean being freed from all human regulations but not being freed of obligations to God's commandment and the responsibility to our fellow-men that he has laid upon us. Christian freedom is not something negative, the casting off of conventional fetters; instead it gives a most effective impulse to right conduct. It is realised in practical love of one's neighbour, *agape*, by which the redeemed serve one another (Gal., 5, 13).

To have raised the practical love of one's neighbour to a life-giving power for Christendom and for mankind was the wholly personal achievement of Jesus. It is quite insignificant for the history of mankind that a century later, Rabbi Akiba too taught in his school "Love thy neighbour as thyself". The Greek Stoics also believed in man's natural love for one another and required that they should help one another, but the urge to help others in trouble was undermined by the fact that their fundamental outlook taught them to take no notice of outward fortune. Even the term *agape*[11] was unknown to the Greeks. But the ways in which freedom worked out practically in thought and in action were the main points of contact with the Greek world and its ethics.

Are these so strong that we have to infer that they had any direct influence? That is a question that cannot be evaded since, as is generally recognised, Paul's idea of freedom cannot originate in Judaism.[12] We can certainly assume that Paul, born in Tarsus of a good Jewish family, and having presumably spoken Greek from childhood did not remain uninfluenced by heathen culture; and the years after being called Paul apparently did not spend only in quiet meditation but also in strenuous thinking. It would have been sheer narrowmindedness had he taken no notice of the Greek culture around him; such isolationism was quite impossible from the moment he felt himself called to bring the tidings of salvation to the Greeks. Paul was fundamentally different from the compromising Philo who in Alexandria was picking up as much of Greek philosophy as he could to modernise the religion of his fathers so as to win proselytes. Any variation on the Greek theme "only the wise man is free" would have been for him quite impossible. He was a strong, independent character who after his breach with the religion of the law had built up out of personal experience and feeling an impressively coherent theological system. That did not prevent the Greek idea of freedom which was preached on every street corner – not long afterwards Dio of Prusa gave lectures on this in Cilicia, see p. 144 – from making an impression on him. And when Paul expresses the not very obvious idea: "We praise God as the poor, yet making many rich, as having nothing yet possessing all things"[13], it is difficult to believe that its verbal correspondence to the famous teaching of the Stoa, certainly known to Philo, is mere accident. But precisely where the correspondence in subject matter is closest, as with the battle against the passions, the Stoic terms are not found. And one thing is particularly important for our theme: the philosophical problem of free will which is central in Greek ethics, is not taken up fundamentally either by Paul or elsewhere in the New Testament, not even where the distinction between man's real will and the lusts of the flesh is described (Romans, 7, 14–17). The formulation that something is "within our power" ($\dot{\epsilon}\varphi$' $\dot{\eta}\mu\tilde{\iota}\nu$ $\dot{\epsilon}\sigma\tau\iota\nu$) and that man has in his *logos* the gift of *synkatathesis* which enables him freely to assent to ideas or to reject them (cf. p. 124), does not occur.

We may certainly assume that Paul was influenced by Greek ideas about freedom, but in working out his own ideals he followed the path laid down by his personal religious feeling. Contact with the Stoics of his day might be all the easier for Paul since they too were able to reconcile consciousness of freedom with obedience to God. But this should not allow us to overlook the fact that even with the new religious attitude of Epictetus their view of God and man is completely different from Paul's.

Greek thought is dominated by the idea of *physis*. The specific nature of man as a reasoning being destines him for moral life in the community in which alone he can exist. In this he must find his "good" and his purpose in life. This moral life presupposes, however, his independence, his power of free, responsible decision. Freedom is essentially a part of human nature.

In his thoughts and feelings Paul does not set out from a "nature" that embraces God and man but from the relationship of man to the transcendental God who created him and demands unconditional obedience. For man good consists in doing God's will; disobedience is evil and sinful. History shows of course that since Adam's disobedience to God's command, mankind has been incapable of really doing good and has succombed to the power of forces hostile to God and to the sinful flesh. But then God himself brought about the great change. Through the sacrifice of his son and by his vicarious atonement he has broken the power of sin and has given man freedom. But that freedom is quite different from that of the Greeks. It is not the freedom of choice, which is planted in the nature of man, placing him throughout his life again and again before the choice between good and evil. It is a state of grace brought about by the death of the son of God, which liberates man from enslavement to the flesh, provided he has the proper faith in the divinity of Christ, and which gives him power to overcome sinful desires.

Greek freedom is the freedom of choice of the natural man; Pauline freedom is man's liberation by God from the power of sin, in other words, salvation.

That idea of salvation is quite foreign to the Greeks. They had mysteries which offered the initiated the prospect of a blessed life after death. But it never meant release from the guilt of sin. There were, too, religious sects who believed in the migration of souls and whose ideal was release from earthly entanglements, but this ideal was to be a human achievement. The idea of a saviour sent by God who could bring deliverance from guilt and sin, was quite strange to them, as strange, say, as Paul's idea that he can hear the groans of the whole created universe yearning for salvation (Romans, 8, 22). For Paul it is the idea of salvation that is new and extraordinary about his message to all men. For that reason he cannot have been inspired by any Greek thinker. But we must recall that in the oriental religions which were then spreading towards the west the longing for salvation was often the strongest motive.

How far Pauline theology was from the Greek way of thinking is clearly shown by the development of early Christianity on Greek soil. For a man like Clement of Alexandria, faith, *pistis*, which is the indispensible condition of the fullest perception of God, the *gnosis*, is in fact a spiritual attitude of man, which is only made possible through God's grace; but it is a decision man makes for himself because God has given him the power of free choice.[14] Stoic terms like τὸ ἐφ' ἡμῖν, τὸ αὐτεξούσιον are necessary parts of Clement's religious vocabulary, and he explicitly describes faith itself as a consent, as *synkatathesis*, a free decision, which though it means the surrender of the whole man to God, proceeds nevertheless from man's own will. Certainly a man needs the grace of God to make this decision and will pray to him for help.[15] But God gives help only to him who himself makes this effort. For Clement the significance of Christ lies not so much in his having once died in propitiatory sacrifice as in the educative influence exercised by him from the beginning of the world as the divine *logos* and consummated by his appearing in the flesh. As a living force, he brings to the faithful in whose hearts he dwells not only peace with God but also the "kingly freedom" that gives them control both over earthly things and over the lower instincts of the soul.

Most of the other Christian Greeks thought like Clement, and monks proudly adopted the Stoic freedom of *apatheia*. But faith in man's own moral strength dwindled more and more and along with the heavy feeling of sinfulness there grew up the need for redemption. It was of decisive importance that the doctrine of original sin was then spreading in the Roman church of the West; it reached its climax when Augustine successfully maintained against Pelagius that original sin was man's attempt, in his *hybris*, to be independent and rely on his own strength.[16] The consequence for all mankind of Adam's turning away from God is that the free will entrusted to him only leads to evil. Only through God's grace can he be redeemed and regain his original freedom to work for the good. That was the fundamental break with the Greek outlook on life.

Is the gulf thus created unbridgeable? That is a question that may be asked at the close of our enquiry. For it is of no mean importance when we must decide whether Christianity and humanism, the two pillars of our Western culture, support one another or remain irreconcilably opposed. Naturally, we cannot think of entering at this point on a thoroughgoing discussion of problems that have occupied mankind for thousands of years; we must be satisfied in drawing certain conclusions which follow from what has been said above upon the subject of this particular study.[17]

The decisive factor is our judgment of human nature. Whoever sees in man only the "radically evil" and assumes that because of original sin man has completely lost the capacity for good must be inclined to accept the incompatibility of Christianity with the Greek belief in man's own moral power. On the other hand, we must not forget that Augustine, although quite the most powerful personality of the early church, lived nearly five centuries after the birth of Christ, when the intellectual climate had completely changed and through his quarrel with Pelagius, in whom the Greek consciousness of man's power flared up once more, Augustine was forced to state in the most uncompromising terms his opposition to the Greek idea of freedom. Paul, whose line of thought he followed, was convinced that since Adam's disobedience mankind had fallen into the power of sin, but he did not discuss the philosophic problem of the freedom of the will, which for Augustine was of central importance, because of his conviction that thanks to Christ's redeeming grace the power of the lusts of the flesh was broken once and for all. Paul simply wanted to be the apostle of Jesus, and we cannot have any doubt as to how far the problems of Augustine were from the mind of Jesus if we study without prejudice the image of Jesus as it can be constructed from the oldest traditions. Not one word did Jesus speak about original sin, and he was equally unconcerned with the problem of free will. He is not a theologian or a philosopher. His intention is to help man in spiritual need and to make known to man God's grace, which looks only for faith and purity of heart and is ready to forgive sin if man repents and "changes his attitude" ($\mu\varepsilon\tau\alpha\nuoo\tilde{v}\sigma\iota\nu$). "Repent!" is therefore the constant and urgent call of Jesus, and this shows that he expects to find some response to his exhortations in men's own hearts. He calls those the blessed who listen to him and those wretched who resist him. He is thus taking into account men's own responsible decisions, and when he says that there is more joy in heaven for one sinner who repents than for ninety-nine of the upright who do not need to, he certainly does not mean that God finds joy in his own act of grace, but in the willingness awakened in the sinner's heart to do penance. When he tells his listeners: "No man can serve two masters; you cannot serve God and Mammon", he is confronting them, just as Epictetus did, and with similar words, with the great decision which every man must make by himself. He is fully aware of human weakness and sinfulness and he speaks in the parable of the weed sown by the enemy, but assumes at the same time that in the human heart the good seed also takes root and flourishes. He knows the power of evil and is aware that man is dependent upon God's grace and the forgiveness of sin; but men, to whom he turns in compassion, are not radically wicked.

"The call to repentance is the call to decide", writes Rudolf Bultmann in his book on Jesus; elsewhere Bultmann rightly draws a sharp distinction between the message of salvation brought by Jesus and the Greek ethic. The core of the efficacity of Jesus he sees in that call, confronting man with the question which is decisive for his whole existence, whether or not he means to lead his life as God wills. With the utmost emphasis he elaborates further: "The decision man makes is his free act for which he is fully responsible. For Jesus does not acknowledge hereditary evil and original sin. That which is bad in the world is a man's evil will and that is not a characteristic feature of human nature in general but the personal decisions of individuals."[18]

That is the conclusion reached by Bultmann on the grounds of his critical study of the gospel tradition and the importance of his opinion must be admitted even by those who cannot always accept his theological outlook.

The antithesis of Augustine on Greek soil is the Stoic Chrysippus who denies completely that man is naturally inclined to evil. We have seen, however, that that was an extreme attitude which met opposition within his own School (cf. p. 168). The Greeks were much too realistic to let optimistic illusions hide from them the dangers of evil. But they did not recognise fundamental evil in the life of men any more than in the cosmos. For them "evil" is the morally bad element which develops in the soul of man because under the influence of the lower instincts he chooses that which is bad, misunderstanding what is to his real advantage. It is the tragedy of man that freedom, which raises him above the level of the animals, can also drag him down to it again. But it is always taken for granted that he not only ought to strive to fulfil his proper destiny, a beneficent and moral life, but that he is able to achieve this end by his own efforts. And yet precisely among the Stoics, who were the loudest in their support of the teaching of man's moral power, we can hear a quiet undertone of another sort, which we must not ignore. When the Emperor Marcus Aurelius prays to God for support in his moral endeavour (cf. p. 169), he was doing it at a time when in general the old Greek confidence in man's own powers was beginning to dwindle. But the finest example of Stoic piety belongs to the earlier days of the school, and this we must now consider. It is the predecessor of Chrysippus as leader of the Stoics, the pure-blooded Greek Cleanthes, to whom we owe this. He wrote a hymn to Zeus which sprang from his own personal religious feeling but was intended for recitation at public festivals to express the feelings of the community. It begins with praise of the God of the universe, who as the bearer of universal reason decides and directs for the best everything that happens. But a reservation is needed: "Except by thy will, nothing happens on earth, or in the heavens above or in the waves of the sea", says Cleanthes impressively at the close of the first section, immediately adding, however, "except what wicked men do in their folly". With that he introduces a new part of the hymn, the main part which deals with mankind. First of all he describes in detail how by turning away from the divine *logos* men let themselves be led astray onto paths that lead to disaster. But that only prepares the way for a concluding prayer which is a climax to the whole hymn:

> But thou, Zeus, the giver of good, in the dark cloud
> Lord of the lightning, rescue us children of men
> Out of the darkness of folly, O Father, and give us
> Part of that wisdom and virtue with which you yourself rule the world.

A powerful inner emotion speaks in these lines and it is striking how instead of the proud stress on one's own moral strength that the rigid logic of the system might lead us to expect, the Stoic suddenly finds words for quite another feeling. Looking upon the divine majesty and perfection, he acknowledges the inadequacy and weakness of all human striving and he is moved to pray humbly for divine support. This does not affect the gravity and severity of the moral requirement that man must attain life's goal through his own efforts, and it never occurs to Cleanthes to take from man the responsibility for his actions. But he knows how difficult the general sinfulness makes it for the *logos* of the individual man to realise what his nature intends him for. And this brings to his lips the prayer that he may in his own striving receive help, which he receives from good men, also from the giver of all good. That prayer of the Stoic is far away still from the prayer of the Christian, who begs God for mercy and the forgiveness of sins; the idea of vicarious redemption is quite impossible for the Greeks. But the hymn at least shows us that on Greek soil too there were differences in the conception of human nature which could prepare the way for some rapprochement between Christians and Greeks. That rapprochement had in practice gone very far in the church before the time of Augustine.

Cleanthes does not have the feeling of utter dependence. He has the consciousness that by his nature and hence by God himself he was created for freedom and independent choice. But he knows too that the freedom is not subjective desire but has its limits in the world order into which man must fit as a member of the whole. Of all his sayings none had a more enduring effect than the short prayer where he vows to follow Zeus and fate unerringly wherever they may lead (cf. p. 134). The verses came via the booklet of Epictetus to Christian monks who found in the poems another way of expressing their prayer "thy will be done". Its adoption was possible only because, in spite of the fundamentally different religious outlook, they had something in common. That is first of all faith, which the Christians and the Stoics placed above mere obedience. But there was something else. Cleanthes expressly recorded in his verses the words of Euripides' Polyxena, who when faced with inevitable death before Troy adopts this death into her own will and thus raises it to a personal moral action (cf. p. 54ff.). That is an authentic Greek attitude. The Greek rebel against any external compulsion and detest servile obedience. But Pericles can expect from his citizens their highest qualities in the service of the state, provided that they are conscious that they are acting as free men. Does not Paul have something of that feeling when he rejoices that the time for obedience to the law has passed and that of the children of God has begun, who do God's will in freedom.

But the important thing is this: Paul's Christian freedom is in origin and nature wholly different from Greek freedom. But it can be no mere accident that in practical ethics they are so closely akin. And there is one thing that brings them together: it is the awareness that man can fulfil himself only if he frees himself from the shackles of the senses and material desires and earns the freedom of his real self, a freedom which seeks and finds a firm foundation in the obligation to a higher power.

NOTES

ABBREVIATIONS

Diog. Laert. Diogenes Laertius, *Vitae Philosophorum* (ed. Cobet), Parisiis 1862.
FGrHist. *Die Fragmente der Griechischen Historiker* (ed. Jacoby), Berlin 1923ff.
RE *Realenzyklopädie der klassischen Altertumswissenschaft* (ed. Pauly–Wissowa–Krolle–Ziegler).
SIG *Sylloge inscriptionum Graecarum* (ed. Dittenberger–Hiller–von Gärtringen), 3rd ed., 1915.
SVF *Stoicorum veterum fragmenta* (ed. J. ab Arnim), from 1903.
Vorsokr. Diels–Kranz, *Die Fragmente der Vorsokratiker*, 5th and 6th eds., 1934 and 1951.

The lyric fragments are quoted from the *Anthologia Lyrica* (ed.Diehl). The passages of Aristotle have the page numbers of the Berlin Academy edition, the *Dialogues* are according to the edition of Walzer (Firenze 1934).

For more detailed substantiation of the views expressed I have often had to refer to earlier works of my own. Their titles only are given in italics (e.g. *Die Stoa*).

The second volume of Alexander Rüstow's great work *Ortsbestimmung der Gegenwart* (Erlenbach-Zurich, 1952) is entitled *Weg der Freiheit*; it deals with the social-political concept of freedom but hardly touches on the problem of "inner freedom".

CHAPTER I

THE GREEK URGE TOWARDS INDEPENDENCE

(pp. 1–2)

1. Cf. my work, *Der hellenische Mensch*, Göttingen 1948, Ch. 1–3.
2. This is most impressively done in Heinrich Weinstock's book, written with much thought and feeling, *Die Tragödie des Humanismus*, Heidelberg 1953. A reaction against the humanism which saw in the Greeks only a blissful, care-free people, was undoubtedly needed. But to go further and transplant modern attitudes into the ancient world, making men like Aeschylus, Socrates and Plato representatives of a modern *Weltangst*, shows no less misunderstanding of what Greece really was (cf. the review of Weinstock's book by H. Drexler in *Südwestdeutsche Schulblätter*, 1953, 114).

CHAPTER II

THE DEVELOPMENT OF THE IDEA OF FREEDOM
IN THE ARCHAIC PERIOD
(pp. 3–9)

1. The best account of the material on slavery in antiquity is Westermann's article in the *Realenzyklopädie*, Suppl. VI, 894. It also gives the early literature on the subject.

2. Later *οἰκέται*. The word has a slightly different meaning in Gortyn, in Crete, where it signified peasant bondsmen. Busolt, *Griechische Staatskunde*, 286 etc.

3. Homer, *Il.*, VI, 324, etc.

4. *Il.*, III, 409 (scornfully) and *Od.*, IV, 12. It seemed so strange even to the early philologists, that in the second passage they took it for a proper name (cf. The Scholia). "The day of slavery", *δούλιον ἦμαρ* (*Il.*, VI, 463; *Od.*, XIV, 340; XVII, 323). *δουλοσύνη* (*Od.*, XXII, 423). The word *ἀνδράποδον* derives from military language, probably by analogy with *τετράποδα* "the four-footed ones", constructed to describe booty with "human" feet. Cf. Wackernagel, *Sprachliche Untersuchungen zu Homer*, 1916, 154f. who conjectures derivation from an Attic root and regards *Il.*, VII, 475 as an interpolation.

    Unfortunately, the etymology of *ἐλεύθερος* is uncertain. The starting point is unquestionably the fact that the place name *Ἐλεύθεραι* occurs in two widely separated places, one in Boeotia, the other in Crete, where its form *Ἐλεύθερναι* has a pre-Hellenic ending (Schwyzer, *Griechische Grammatik*, I, 491). This naturally suggests a pre-Hellenic origin. Dionysus' *Ἐλευθερεύς* is no argument in favour of an Indo-Germanic root, because the word here does not mean "the liberator" but "the one who has come from *Eleutherai*" (*Ἐλεύθερος* in Hesychius' Lexikon is a mistake). Attempts to equate this god with the Roman *Liber* are therefore properly refuted by Wilamowitz in *Glauben der Hellenen*, II, 334², and more recently by Heubeck, *Dtsche Litz.*, 1952, 401. This disposes of the main reason for associating *ἐλεύθερος* with the Latin *liber*. The main argument against this conjecture is the language of the epics, which clearly proves that *ἐλεύθερος* appeared late as a complement to *δοῦλος*. It would be a pity to give up the connection with the root *ἐλυθ-*, which was assumed even in antiquity. The etymology for *ἐλευθερία* given in *Etymol. Magnum*, 329, 44, as *παρὰ τὸ ἐλεύθειν ὅπου ἐρᾷ* or "to go where one will" is firmly based on a feeling for the language. The root *ἐλυθ-*, unlike the word *ἰέναι*, signifies going not merely as a physical act, but always as a motion directed towards a goal, and hence an act of will. Throughout the whole of antiquity, the commonest opposite to *ἐλευθερία* is to be bound up, which impedes free movement. A passage in Lucretius about the Epicurean defence of free will still defines this as the *potestas, per quam progredimur quo ducit quemque voluntas* (II, 257). Again Epictetus, IV, 1, 34, describes his freedom thus: "I go wherever I wish; I come from whence I wish." (*Πορεύομαι ὅπου θέλω, ἔρχομαι ὅθεν θέλω καὶ ὅπου θέλω*).

5. *Il.*, VI, 455, cf. XVI, 831; XX, 193. There is clearly a highly personal and slightly affected element in the expression. We admittedly often come across *μόρσιμον*, *δούλιον ἦμαρ* (the day of fate, the day of slavery) but then it always connotes a

specific day which brings about a change. Thus, in the *proem* to the *Odyssey*, I, 9, we read: "the god denied them the day of return" (ἀφείλετο νόστιμον ἦμαρ). Here, however, as Hesychius, the lexicographer has already pointed out, ἐλεύθερον ἦμαρ is not one specific day, but a circumlocution for the permanent state of freedom (ἐλεύθερον ἦμαρ· τὴν ἐλευθερίαν περιφραστικῶς). Perhaps the poet sensed in ἦμαρ the living quality of light. A sound instinct makes Herodotus, VIII, 77, quote a sentence about Zeus from the collection of oracles of Bacis: "he heralds in the day of freedom" (ἐλεύθερον Ἑλλάδος ἦμαρ... ἐπάγει); the later Megarian epigram attributed to Simonides (Simonides, fr., 96D) speaks less vividly of permitting the growth of the day of freedom: Ἑλλάδι... ἐλεύθερον ἆμαρ ἀέξειν.

6. *Od.*, XXIV, 252.
7. Solon, 24, particularly line 7: πρόσθεν δὲ δουλεύουσα, νυν ἐλευθέρα, also 3, 18; 8, 4; 10, 4 (δουλοσύνην).
8. Skolion, fr. 12, on the killers of the tyrants; ἰσονομους τ᾽ Ἀθήνας ἐποιησάτην. This term *isonomia* also appears in the account given by Herodotus (III, 142) of the events at Samos, which has a distinctly Attic flavour. An additional point is that evidence for the cult of Zeus Eleutherios does not appear until after the wars with Persia (on this see p. 11). Thus the altar in Samos could have received this name afterwards. So we should not regard Herodotus' account as certain.
9. Alcaeus 45, 10 (cf. 87, 1; 48, 11; 26, 4); Pindar, *Pyth.*, I, 61; II, 57 (also *Pyth.*, XII, 15, fr. 223). Theognis, 1212 and 538: οὐδέ ποτ᾽ ἐκ δούλης (φύεται) τέκνον ἐλευθέριον (derived from ἐλεύθερος to characterise the kind of being. On this see p. 47f.).
10. Cf. Critias, *Vorsokr.*, 88, fr. 44, who as an aristocrat is horrified by this.
11. Our collections quote as the oldest fragment of lyrical poetry two verses by Eumelus of Corinth, in which the word ἐλεύθερος appears, but these are a very special case. In his *Description of Greece*, IV, 33, 2 (cf. IV, 4, 1 and V, 19, 10) Pausanias wishes to show that from the very earliest times the Messenians had devoted themselves to the muses. To support this he quotes a passage from a processional chant to the Delian Apollo, which he claims Eumelus wrote for them and which was reputed to be his only undisputed work. The passage runs:

τῷ γὰρ Ἰθωμάτᾳ καταθύμιος ἔπλετο Μοῖσα
ἁ καθαρὰ⟨ν κίθαριν⟩ καὶ ἐλεύθερα σάμβαλ᾽ ἔχοισα.

There are some strange features here: two consecutive hexameters in a processional chant, the Corinthian poet using the Aeolian dialect and one further factual point. The words ἐλεύθερα σάμβαλ᾽ ἔχοισα ("with free sandals") *i.e.* free feet, can only be interpreted in the light of the free mixing vessel, the ἐλεύθερος κρητήρ, cf. *Il.*, VI, 528, as a symbol for the freedom of the country. That would fit admirably into the time of the second Messenian war, but Pausanias categorically states that the song goes back as far as a period prior to the battles with Sparta. This makes his intention clear: the chant is meant to show that prior to its subjection by Sparta Messenia possessed an advanced culture. The song probably came into being at a time when Epaminondas wanted once again to make Messenia Sparta's rival. Pausanias' source was one of the local tales which sprang up like mushrooms at that time.

CHAPTER III

THE CLASSICAL AGE
(pp. 10–105)

1. Herod., V, 49.
2. The Marathon epigrams have been widely discussed (Kirchner, *Imagines Inscriptionum Atticarum* no. 18, fig. 9; cf. F. Jacoby, 'Some Epigrams from the Persian War', *Hesperia* XIV, 157ff.) The substance of the first distich can be safely reconstructed from its conclusion in the second, which is certainly an addition, but according to Oliver of the same date. The first apparently sums up the achievement of the victors by saying they had prevented "all Hellas from seeing the day of slavery", *"Ελλάδα μὴ πᾶσαν δούλιον ἧμαρ ἰδεῖν"*. Despite Jacoby, *op. cit.*, p. 166, I cannot believe that as early as immediately after 490 the Athenians could have regarded their victory in this light (cf. note 4 below), and I am pleased to note that W. Peek in his latest study (*Studies presented to David Moore Robinson*, II, 304ff.) ascribes the epigrams to a period later than Salamis and contemporary with those on the Cimon Hermae. The epigram *Anth. Palat.*, VII, 257 (= Simonides fr. 119) which with its terseness fits the period admirably (even speaking of Persians instead of Medes was perfectly possible at that time; one has only to think of the tragedy of Aeschylus), merely says: "They warded off slavery for their fatherland." (*῎Ηρκεσαν ἀργαλέην πατρίδι δουλοσύνην*).
3. Jessen, *RE*, V, 2348; Ziegler, *Roschers Myth. Lex.* VI, 619.
4. Hiero thus need not have felt offended by mention of this, as Wilamowitz thinks (*Pindaros*, 305).
5. Cf. also Wilamowitz, *Sappho und Simonides*, 192ff. Simonides, fr. 95 is particularly instructive regarding the later spread of this idea. The model was perhaps the dedicatory epigram for Delphi (Simon., fr. 102) which refers only briefly to the warding off of slavery (*δουλοσύνης στυγερᾶς ῥυσάμενοι πόλιας*) and may well be genuine. On the dedication of Gelon and his brothers (Simon., 106) see Wilamowitz, 200. Of later origin too, is the Megarian epigram (Simon., fr. 96) with its unattractive expansion of *Il.*, VI, 455 (cf. Chapter I, note 5; also Simon., 122, from Tegea, 362 B.C.), "blooming in freedom" (*ἐλευθερία τεθαλυῖαν*) and the verses quoted by Demosthenes in *De Corona*, 289 *ὡς μὴ ζυγὸν αὐχένι θέντες δουλοσύνης στυγερᾶς ἀμφὶς ἔχωσιν ὕβριν*, cf. the epigram by Ceramicus (Geffcken, *Griech. Epigramm*, 151) which simply praises the dead for having wished to protect the holy soil of Hellas *ἱερὰν σῴζειν πειρώμενοι ῾Ελλάδα χώραν*. Timotheus begins his *Persians* ostentatiously: *Κλεινὸν ἐλευθερίας τεύχων μέγαν ῾Ελλάδι κόσμον*.
6. Fr. 109, 110; cf. *Isthm.*, VIII, 15, fr. 77; *Pyth.*, I, 72ff. (and my *Gestalten aus Hellas*, S. 94). In *Pyth.*, VIII, composed in 446 B.C. for an inhabitant of Aegina, he had to end with a fervent prayer to "dear mother Aegina" that she should preserve the island's freedom threatened by Athens.
7. More details in my book *Herodot, der erste Geschichtschreiber des Abendlandes* (Leipzig, 1937), particularly pp. 9–21 and 203ff.
8. The letter by Darius to the *δοῦλος*, Gadatas, *SIG³*, 22, together with the commentary. *δοῦλος* is the equivalent of *mana badaka* on the Behistan inscription. Mardonius is called *δοῦλος* in Herod., VIII, 102. The contrast makes Artemesia use

183

FREEDOM IN GREEK LIFE AND THOUGHT

the term "Master", ὦ δέσποτα. But she had started her speech with Βασιλεῦ, cf. Demaratus, VII, 102ff., and also the two Spartans, VII, 136, and the herald VIII, 114, ὦ βασιλεῦ Μήδων. In the royal council (VII, 9, 10) Artabanus addresses the king as ὦ βασιλεῦ, Mardonius ὦ δέσποτα (though he sometimes uses also ὦ βασιλεῦ).

9. Herod., VII, 5; 8, 3; VI, 44; 94 *et passim*. Cf. also Plato, *Laws*, III, 698b; *Menex.*, 239d ff.

10. Herod., VII, 140; Plut., *De malign. Herod.*, 34; Simon., 103; cf. my *Herodot.*, S. 205.

11. Cf. my book *Hippokrates* (Berlin, 1938), SS. 3–30, 81ff. The Greeks are specifically mentioned only in an incidental note to Ch. 16, p. 71, 3. This opinion of Asiatics is still operative in the low regard for the Persians shown by Isocrates, *Paneg.*, 150f.

12. Xenophon, *Hell.*, II, 2, 23; VI, 1, 31.

13. *Menex.*, 245a–246a. For more details, see Chapter III, note 94.

14. *SIG*³, 147, 10, 20; 148, 20 *et passim*. The model was the treaty with Chios (384/3 B.C.) 142, 20. In the fifth century, αὐτονομία was still used alone, *e.g.* Thuc., V, 18, 5. Among literary examples are Isocrates, *Paneg.*, 117, and *Plataicus*, 24, Ep., 8, 7. Among later negotiations, cf. for instance, Hegesippus (Demosth., VII) 30; 32, also Ps. Dem., XVII, 8. Demosthenes himself regarded ἐλευθερία and αὐτονομία as pre-requisites for the *eudaimonia* of the State (*De Corona*, 305). Cf. Hyperides' *Epitaphius*, 25.

15. For what follows cf. my article 'Staatsgedanke und Staatslehre der Griechen', *Wissenschaft und Bildung*, 183 (Leipzig, 1923).

16. *Nachr. Gött. Ges.*, 1919, 101ff.

17. στρατοπέδου πολιτεία (Plato, *Laws*, 666c; Isocrates, *Archid.*, 81; Plutarch, *Lycurg.*, 24).

18. Cf. the scholion quoted in Chapter 2, note 8, on the killers of the tyrants. ἰσονομίη Herod., III, 80; 142; V, 37; Thuc., IV, 78; III, 82, 3 (Hirzel, "Dike" in *Themis und Verwandtes*, 1907), 242ff., wrongly seeks to derive the word from νέμω and exclude the νόμος concept; for the contrary, cf. Euripides, *Suppl.*, 430ff). ἰσοκρατίη (as the opposite to tyranny) Herod., V, 92. ἰσηγορίη as "equal right to express an opinion" (Herod., V, 78). δημοκρατίη used by Herodotus only in VI, 43; IV, 137; VI, 131 (of Cleisthenes). In *Supp.*, 698, Aeschylus speaks of "the community of the people, which rules the State" τὸ δήμιον τὸ πτόλιν κρατύνει, but that is no proof that the term "democracy" was already in general use. In Euripides' *Cyclops* (119) Odysseus asks: "Does government lie in the hands of the Demos?" (ἦ δεδήμευται κράτος; cf. my *Staatsgedanken*, SS. 47 and 161, and now Vlastos, 'Equality in law, including political rights'. *Amer. Journ. of Philol.*, 1953, p. 337ff.

19. *Gestalten aus Hellas*, S. 176.

20. *Der hellenische Mensch*, S. 114. Pericles certainly not only spoke after the Samian war, but also, as Thucydides assumes, took the opportunity in 431 B.C. to work on morale in Athens and throughout Greece.

21. Herod., VI, 11–17.

22. Plutarch, *Cleom.*, 9.

23. ἤτοι κρίνομέν γε ἢ ἐνθυμούμεθα (Thuc., II, 40, 2).

24. *Gestalten aus Hellas*, S. 155.

25. Thuc., II, 37; Euripides, *Supp.*, 407; Thuc., II, 41, 1.

26. In my *Staatsgedanken* I did not do justice to the difference between the views of antiquity and of today.

184

27. "Arithmetical" and "geometrical" equality; Plato, *Repub.*, VIII, 558c; *Laws*, VI, 757b; Xenophon, *Cyrop.*, II, 2, 18; Isocrates, *Nicocles*, 14; *Areop.*, 21. Cf. my book *Aus Platos Werdezeit* (1913), 154, and *Staatsgedanke*, 134, 169. *Sophrosyne* became the descriptive term for the aristocratic "well ordered state". Thuc., VIII, 64, 5 σωφροσύνην λαβοῦσαι αἱ πόλεις of taking over the aristocratic constitution, cf. III, 82, 8; 62, 3 (τῷ σωφρονεστάτῳ – no need to alter – in speaking of the old aristocracy). A plea for σωφρονεῖν in political life is found as early as Aeschylus, *Eum.*, 519. *Akolasia*: Herod., III, 81 δήμου ἀκολάστου ὕβριν cf. Thuc., VI, 89, 5 *et passim*; *Ath. Pol.*, 1; 5; 9.
28. For Archelaus see *Hermes*, 1953, 418.
29. Plato, *Gorg.*, 484a, 485.
30. Xenophon, *Hellen.*, I, 7, 12.
31. Plato, *Repub.*, 562c–563c; Isocrates, *Areopag.*, 62; 20. On Demosthenes, see Jaeger, *Demosthenes* (Berlin, 1939) and Grundt, *Politik und Gesinnung bei Demosthenes* (Diss. Göttingen, 1939).
32. More details of Plato's direct reference to Thucydides on page 85.
33. Seneca, *Ep.*, 90; cf. my *Stoa*, I, 235; II, 120. Kleingünther, "Πρῶτος εὑρετής", *Philologus*, Suppl., XXVI (1935) 1. More on page 141.
34. *Ath. pol.*, 2, 8. Since this is preceded by an account of the advantages of overseas trade, and followed by one of the sacrifices and festivals in Athens, and both recur in Pericles' funeral speech (Thuc., II, 38), we can extend to the middle section Jaeger's conjecture that the author was reproducing Pericles' thoughts.
35. Lammermann, *Von der attischen Urbanität* (Diss. Göttingen, 1935).
36. *Der hellenische Mensch*, SS. 401ff.
37. Gorgias, *Helena*, 8.
38. See my book on Hippocrates, pp. 85ff., 91ff. Ps. Hippocrates, *Concerning places in the Body*, 2.
39. Cf. my *Herodot*, SS. 56ff., 196 *et passim*.
40. Ὄψις τῶν ἀδήλων τὰ φαινόμενα(Anaxagoras B 21a),cf. Diller, *Hermes*,LXVII (1932) 14ff.; Regenbogen, *Quellen und Studien zur Gesch. der Mathematik*, I (1930) 131ff.
41. See *Der hellenische Mensch*, SS. 250–253.
42. Aristophanes, *Frogs*, 1009 (also my article 'Die Anfänge der griechischen Poetik', *Nachr. Gött. Ges.*, 1920, 152ff.), 686 (*Acharn.*, 500); Thuc., I. 22.
43. Cf. *Acharn.*, 632, 504ff., 515, 516. That is precisely the legal position which the unknown author of the work on the *Constitution of the Athenians* (*Ath. Pol.*) presumes (2; 18) and which enables its date to be determined. The conclusion to be drawn from *Wasps*, 1284ff., is that even after the *Knights* there were again legal proceedings, in which Aristophanes played a somewhat lamentable part, but eventually came off lightly.
44. Diog. Laert., II, 40.
45. Cf. also St. Paul, Galatians, 3, 28.
46. *Ath. Pol.*, 1; 10; Pollux, III, 78.
47. Fr. 831, 511; *Hel.* 730ff. ; *Ion.* 854; fr. 495, 40ff. ; Soph. fr., 854. As γενναῖος (noble) the slave in Eur. *Hel.*, 729.
48. See my *Griechische Tragödie*², I, SS. 285f.
49. The word ἀνελεύθερος first found in Aesch. *Agam.*, 1494, then in Plato, Xenophon, Aristophanes (*Plut.* 591), etc. In Pherecrates, fr. 8 Dem., Naber's emendation to ἀνελεύθερον στόμα instead of σῶμα is to be accepted. ἐλευθέριος is used by Xenophon (e.g. *Symposium*, 8, 16), Plato in *Gorg.*, 485b (as opposite of δουλο-

πρεπές, Callicles!) and in the *Laws* (e.g. 823e). It is not otherwise used in Attic but is found in Democritus, B 282 and Theognis, 1211. (See Chapter I, note 9).

Xenophon, *Mem.*, III, 10, 5 τὸ μεγαλοπρεπές τε καὶ ἐλευθέριον καὶ τὸ ταπεινόν τε καὶ ἀνελεύθερον ("Pride and servility").

50. ζῆν ὡς βούλεταί τις as the safeguard of democracy in Aristot., *Pol.*, 1317b, 12 *et passim*; Plato, *Repub.*, 557b; Isocrates, *Panath.*, 131 *et passim*. For the purely ethical usage in the Hellenistic period, see p. 152ff. Cf. my *Staatsgedanken*, S. 160.

51. On Prometheus cf. my *Griech. Tragödie*[2], I, SS. 73, 81.

52. Euripides, fr. 142; *Phoen.*, 390ff.; *Supp.*, 864ff.; *Tragödie*, I, S. 283.

53. Iphigenia: *Tragödie*, I, SS. 460ff. τῷ τ'ὄχλῳ δουλεύομεν said by *Agamemnon* line 450, also 513ff., 1012. Cf. 443 (ἀνάγκη) with Aesch., *Agam.*, 205ff. For Achilles, *Iph.*, 924–931.

54. Consciousness of the self: *Der hellenische Mensch*, SS. 9ff.

55. For the following see not only my *Tragödie*, but also in particular Franz Egermann, *Vom attischen Menschenbild* (München, 1952), and for the concept of the self, Untersteiner, *Sofocle* (Firenze, 1935), pp. 537ff., and *La fisiologia del mito*, (Milano, 1946), pp. 286ff.

56. *Agam.*, 755 δίχα δ'ἄλλων μονόφρων εἰμί; *Tragödie*, I, S. 108.

57. Cicero, *De officiis*, I, 112, 113; cf. my *Antikes Führertum* (Leipzig, 1934), S. 70.

58. *Tragödie*, I, pp. 93ff.

59. *Ant.*, 821 ἀλλ'αὐτόνομος ζῶσα μόνη δὴ θνατῶν 'Αΐδαν καταβήσῃ, cf. 875 σὲ δ'αὐτόγνωτος ὤλεσ' ὀργά ("By choosing to be obstinate you brought yourself to ruin"). *Tragödie*, I, 193.

60. *Alcestis*, 962ff.

61. Johanna Schmitt, 'Freiwilliger Opfertod bei Euripides', *Religionsgesch. Versuch. u. Vorarbeiten*, XVII, 2. *Tragödie*, I, S. 429.

62. For the following section I must draw attention to the detailed treatment in my *Tragödie*.

63. Jaeger, *Paideia*, I, 364. My conception of Socrates is in *Gestalten aus Hellas*, S. 352.

64. Particularly in the *Gorgias*, 471–481.

65. I, 1, 16. Not until the end does he mention other questions about which Socrates thought man should have knowledge, if he truly wishes to be upright, καλὸς κἀγαθός, and not a slave-like, ἀνδραποδώδης, man. That is, however, Xenophon's own formulation. II, 1, 11, gives *Eleutheria* as the aim of life for Aristippus. On IV, 5, 3 and Xenophon's specific ideal of *Enkrateia*, see p. 82.

66. *Gestalten aus Hellas*, S. 358.

67. Erwin Rohde, *Psyche*, 9/10. Ausg. (Tübingen, 1925). *Der hellenische Mensch*, S. 15 *et passim*. The epigram from Potidaea, *Inscr. Graecae*, I, S. 442 = Geffcken, *Griech. Epigr.*, S. 87. Euripides, *Supp.*, 531ff., cf. 1140, fr. 839. For the terminology in tragedy, see Bernhard Meissner, *Mythisches und Rationales in der Psychologie der euripideischen Tragödie* (Diss. Göttingen, 1951).

68. For further details, *Der hellenische Mensch*, SS. 210ff.

69. Cf. Plato's *Protagoras*, 338bff., where it is obviously intended to be taken as a sophisticated trick of interpretation for Socrates to read his own convictions into Simonides' poem. More on p. 134.

70. *Tragödie*, I, SS. 272, 425. Polemics against Socrates: Snell, *Philologus* (1948), 125ff., and also Meissner (Chapter II, note 67), p. 126ff.

71. *Thymos* here is probably passionate anger, cf. Plutarch, *Coriolanus*, 22. ψυχῆς = "life" as rightly stated by Wilamowitz, *Glaube der Hellenen*, I, S. 370[1]. In ad-

dition to Hesiod., *Works and Days* 686, cf. epigram 87c in Geffcken's collection ψυχὰς ἀντίρροπα δέντες ("they threw their life into the scales"), and Anon. Iambl. (*Vorsokr.*, S. 89) 4: τῆς ψυχῆς ἀφειδής ("not sparing his life"), (referring to ἐγκρατής).
Later generations considered it as characteristic of the angry man that in his zeal to harm others he does not care for his own life.

72. As early as Aeschylus, *Seven against Thebes*, 750 κρατηθεὶς ἐκ φίλων ἀβουλιᾶν ("overpowered by the irrational urges of the beloved self"). As Pericles boasts in Thuc., II, 60, 5, he is above money, χρημάτων κρείσσων, so others were often described as "weaker than pleasure", ἥσσονες ἡδονῶν, or similarly. "To be slave to the belly", γαστρὶ δουλεύειν, Xenophon, *Mem.*, I, 6, 8. In *Phaedrus* 238e Plato speaks of the lover who is "overcome by desire and enslaved by pleasure", τῷ ὑπὸ ἐπιθυμίας ἀρχομένῳ δουλεύοντί τε ἡδονῇ. According to Xenophon, *Ages.*, 8, 8 it is "more honourable to make one's own soul impregnable to money and pleasure and fear than to build fortifications impregnable to the enemy", καλὸν μὲν δοκεῖ εἶναι, τείχη ἀνάλωτα κρᾶσθαι ὑπὸ πολεμίων· πολὺ μέντοι ἔγωγε κάλλιον κρίνω τὸ τὴν αὐτοῦ ψυχὴν ἀνάλωτον κατασκευάσαι καὶ ὑπὸ χρημάτων καὶ ὑπὸ ἡδονῶν καὶ ὑπὸ φόβων. More in Joel, *Der echte und der xenophonistische Sokrates* (1893, 1901), II, 607.

73. εἶναι ὁμολογεῖται (ἡ σωφροσύνη) τὸ κρατεῖν ἡδονῶν καὶ ἐπιθυμῶν. Weitlich, *Quae fuerit vocis σωφροσύνη vis ac natura etc.* (Diss. Göttingen, 1922, = *Jahrb. Phil. Fak. Gött.*, 1922).
Material on ἐγκρατής – ἀκρατής in Liddell and Scott. As early as Aeschylus, *Prom.*, 55 ἐγκρατεῖ σθένει. On the *kratos* of the victor Soph., *Oed. Tyr.*, 941 οὐ Πόλυβος ἐγκρατής ἔτι; cf. Herod., VIII, 49 χωρέων ἐγκρατέες. Often used of the body by doctors, also ἑωυτοῦ ἀκρατής Hipp. *Morb.*, II, 6, meaning "unconscious". Antiphon, V, 26, says of a drunkard that "he was not in control of himself": οὔτε γὰρ αὐτοῦ κρατεῖν ἴσως ἂν ἐδύνατο Plato, *Laws*, I, 645e ἥκιστα τότ' ἄν αὐτὸς αὐτοῦ γίγνοιτο ἐγκρατής.

74. Kramer, *Quid valeat ὁμόνοια in litteris Graecis*, (Diss. Göttingen, 1914). Democritus frequently contrasts the body, for which he used the remarkable term, the soul's "tent" σκῆνος (possibly a correction for σῆμα) with the soul, which he regards as the vehicle of *ethos*, *gnome*, etc. (57, 223 etc.), but he does not show any concern over the soul in the Socratic sense.

75. On Antiphon (*Vorsokr.*, S. 87) the best material is Bignone, *Studi sul pensiero antico* (Napoli, 1938), together with the important review by Regenbogen, *Gnomon* (1940) 97, and also Stenzel, *RE*, Suppl. IV, 33, and Untersteiner, *I Sofisti* (1949), 300ff. Bignone has pointed out the right path to understanding the papyrus, even though I do not believe that the first fragment is specially directed against Protagoras. The important fact in assessing Pap. 1797 is that the phrase in col. 2, 19: "Neither to do wrong, nor to suffer wrong oneself", μηδὲν ἀδικεῖν μηδὲ αὐτὸν ἀδικεῖσθαι, alludes to the social contract (Plato, *Repub.*, II, 359a), which is also indicated by the first papyrus (col. 1, 29) with ὁμολογηθέντα. It does not fit in well with this interest in the social contract, however, that the *nomos* regards it as just that the witness, who has suffered no wrong, should harm the person against whom he acts as witness (Pap. 1797, col. 1, 19ff).
The explanation for Plato's *Protagoras* making no mention of Antiphon is that the latter belonged to a younger generation. Xenophon (*Mem.*, I, 6) quotes him simply as typical of the money-making sophist; he has virtually no conception of

the man's personality. Antiphon's indebtedness to Democritus can be deduced from comparison of individual fragments, S. Luria, *Arch. Gesch. Phil. u. Soziol.*, XXXVIII, 209ff. Particularly important are Antiphon, B 51 and Democritus, 257.

76. Cf. also Anon. Iamblichi (*Vorsokr.*, S. 89), 7.

77. Scanty and unreliable as are our records of the teaching of Aristippus, which he most probably never developed into a formal "system", there is a clear picture of his personality, which persisted through the whole of antiquity; it is so well-rounded that it must be regarded as true to life. Among its various features is phronesis, and for the Hedonists this can only have had the same meaning as it did for Antiphon, who demands (B 58) that if mankind is to gain self-mastery and live life with a conscious purpose, it must resist the momentary attraction of pleasure (cf. p. 76). This, however, constitutes the basis of μετρητική expounded by Plato in *Prot.*, 357, and which Epicurus certainly did not derive from him. Consequently, I have already expressed the opinion in my book *Aus Platos Werdezeit* (1913), S. 108, that Plato reshaped some of the thoughts of the hedonist Aristippus for his own purposes. Cf. Stenzel, *RE*, XII, 144; *Der hellenische Mensch*, S. 214.

Concerning Diog. Laert., II, 86–92, Budde, *Quaestiones Laertionae* (Diss. Göttingen, *Jahrb. Phil. Fak. Gött.* 1920, 73).

78. Diog. Laert., II, 75 ἔχω, ἀλλ᾽ οὐκ ἔχομαι· ἐπεὶ τὸ κρατεῖν καὶ μὴ ἡττᾶσθαι ἡδονῶν ἄριστον, οὐ τὸ μὴ χρῆσθαι.

79. On this view in Xenophon, see p. 82.

80. Diog. Laert., VI, 11 αὐτάρκη δὲ τὴν ἀρετὴν πρὸς εὐδαιμονίαν, μηδενὸς προσδεομένην ὅτι μὴ Σωκρατικῆς ἰσχύος.

81. μανείην μᾶλλον ἢ ἡσθείην, Diog. Laert., VI, 3, Clem. Al. *Strom.*, II, 121 and 107.

82. Diog. Laert., VI, 2; I, 15. The chapter 'Diogenes der Hund und Krates der Kyniker' in Ed. Schwartz' book *Charakterköpfe aus der Antike* has the great merit of having clearly determined the true factual position. – ἀγωγή: Hippobotus in Diog. Laert., I, 19.

83. τῦφος, Diog. Laert., VI, 26; 83 (Monimus, cf. *Sext. Math.*, VIII, 5), 85 (Crates). The punishment of Prometheus, Dio *Pr. Or.*, 27–29.

84. παραχαράξαι τὸ νόμισμα. A literal interpretation gave rise to the legend that he was a counterfeiter. (Diog. Laert., VI, 20, cf. 64).

85. Euripides, *Hyps.*, 757 δεινὸν (wrongly emended by Stob. to αἰσχρὸν) γὰρ οὐδὲν τῶν ἀναγκαίων βροτοῖς "nothing should terrify us which is a necessity of nature", has nothing to do with this sentence.

86. μαινόμενος Σωκράτης, Diog. Laert., VI, 54; Aelian. *Var. hist.*, XIV, 33.

87. Crates, Diog. Laert., VI, 85–93. Diels, *Poet. philos. fragmenta*, 207. Stenzel in *RE.*; Hipparchia, Diog. Laert., VI, 96; Stilpon, *ibid.*, II, 113–120; Menedemus, *ibid.*, II, 125–144; Bion, *ibid.*, IV, 46–58; Onesicritus, *FGrHist.* II, 134; Cercidas, Wilamowitz, *Kleine Schriften*, II, 128. Gerhard in *RE*.

88. Diog. Laert., IV, 46; Stobaeus, II, p. 218. The text has been wrongly altered by Bergk. Bion specifically refers to Hesiod's poem about the ages of the world, and in his first group he has in mind the men of the Golden Age, who had no need to learn anything, since everything came to them; they lived ἄτερ πόνων (without care and labour), *Works and Days*, 113.

89. Xenophon, *Hell.*, IV, 1, 35; *Anab.*, I, 7, 3 (cf. *Anab.*, III, 2, 13; *Hell.*, IV, 4, 6); *Mem.* III, 5; *Constitution of the Lacedaimonians*, 8. On Aristippus, *Mem.*, II, 1, 8, 11; on Antisthenes, *Symposium*, 4, 34ff.

90. *Mem.*, IV, 5, presupposes the *Oekonomicus* passage or similar discussions.
91. Dümmler and Joel, *Der echte und der xenophontische Sokrates* (Berlin, 1893, 1901) have admittedly discredited their correct suppositions by heavy exaggeration. Cf. also H. Maier, *Sokrates* (1913) 62, who wrongly ascribes dislike of Antisthenes to Xenophon.
92. ὑπὸ τῶν διὰ τοῦ σώματος ἡδονῶν, *Mem.*, IV, 5, 3, 11, τῶν περὶ τὸ σῶμα ἡδονῶν *Hell.*, VI, 1, 16 (cf. IV, 8, 22). In addition *Mem.*, 1, 2, 23 and *Hiero*, 1, 4f. (where unexpectedly purely psychic pleasures also crop up). Further material in Joel, II, 578, 609ff., *Aus Platos Werdezeit*, S. 157².
93. Alongside ὁ ἀκρατής, ὁ ἐγκρατής. Although Araspes, *Cyrop.*, VI, 1, 41, says that he has two souls in his breast, a good one and a bad one, that naturally has nothing to do with psychology.
94. *Menexenus*, 244e–246a, particularly 245a. Athens could not bring itself officially to support the Great King αἰσχυνομένη τά τρόπαια τα τε Μαραθῶνι καὶ Σαλαμῖνι καὶ Πλαταιαῖς, but it did allow the Athenians to enter his service as volunteers, and thus "as is generally recognised, saved him", ὁμολογουμένως ἔσωσε and 246a ἀγαθοὶ δὲ καὶ οἱ βασιλέα ἐλευθερώσαντες. More details in *Aus Platos Werdezeit*, SS. 289ff. The decisive words are usually overlooked by those who do not share my opinion, and also by Wilamowitz, *Platon*, II, 126ff. His view is that Plato seriously competed with the orators and genuinely wished to make his peace with Athenian politics. Although in 238d Plato says that for the πλῆθος of the Athenians there was only one ὅρος for the filling of official posts: ὁ δόξας σοφὸς ἢ ἀγαθὸς εἶναι κρατεῖ καὶ ἄρχει, for Wilamowitz that constitutes express approval. But in *Repub.*, VIII, 558b, Plato most vigorously derides democracy, because it is so generous in filling official posts and demands no special training from candidates for them, although it is only in the most exceptional cases possible to be an ἀνὴρ ἀγαθός without it, only asks whether he is εὔνους τῷ πλήθει. When he wrote *Menexenus*, Plato surely already had the same views about such things as the selection of officials by lot. If, therefore, his words in this work were intended to express specific approval, then he not only belonged to the worst κόλακες τοῦ δήμου, who "sought to earn public approval by flattery" (Wilamowitz, *Platon*, II, 141), but he was also making himself simply ridiculous, because the contradiction with his own real opinions was obvious to everybody. At a distance of two thousand years, the mixture of satire and seriousness in *Menexenus* causes us great difficulties. But Plato could be sure that the Athenians of his day would immediately distinguish between them. It is very possible that he was using satire to project the picture of his ideal Athens (Harder, *Neue Jahrb.*, 1934, 500), but that ideal was extremely remote from the contemporary democracy.
95. Detailed reasons in *Aus Platos Werdezeit*, SS. 247–256; cf. in particular Thuc., II, 41, 1 μετὰ χαρίτων... εὐτραπέλως with Plato, *Repub.*, VIII, 563a εὐτραπελίας καὶ χαριεντισμοῦ. I am still of this opinion despite its rejection by Wilamowitz, *Platon*, II, 127, and Schwartz, *Das Geschichtswerk des Thukydides*, S. 152¹.
96. *Aus Platos Werdezeit*, SS. 253–255.
97. 701d ὅπως ἡ νομοθετουμένη πόλις ἐλευθέρα τὲ ἔσται καὶ φίλη ἑαυτῇ καὶ νοῦν ἔξει repeated word for word from 693b-d and 694b.
98. Further details in my *Staatsgedanken*, SS. 97–106; particularly *Laws*, 756e, 757, 768b
99. *Staatsgedanken*, SS. 100ff.
100. Slaves: *Laws*, 776b–778a; 868; 872c (does not deal with one's own slaves); *Repub.*, 469c.

101. The word ἐλεύθερος, when not used of purely political freedom, always sounds elevated, e.g. *Laws*, 808a αἰσχρὸν καὶ οὐκ ἐλεύθερον, 741e ἦθος ἐλεύθερον. For ἐλευθέριος, cf. 823e: Fowling is οὐ σφόδρα ἐλευθέριος ("not exactly in keeping with the manner of a free man"); cf. even Callicles, *Gorg.*, 485cd.

102. The view expressed about this section in my book *Aus Platos Werdezeit*, SS. 100ff., has been partially modified here.

103. *Aus Platos Werdezeit*, S. 106, is incorrect.

104. In particular 503ff., 506e. The influence of Pythagoras seems certain. *Aus Platos Werdezeit*, SS. 152ff.

105. Pp. 64–69. Reference to *Protagoras* (354 B.C.) particularly in 68de; cf. also 81e–84b.

106. 65a ὁ μηδὲν φροντίζων τῶν ἡδονῶν αἵ διὰ τοῦ σώματός εἰσιν; 82c τῶν κατὰ τὸ σῶμα ἐπιθυμιῶν; 83d ὥσπερ ἧλον ἔχουσα; 65d on αἰσθήσεις: τῶν διὰ τοῦ σώματος. Cf. Chapter III, note 92 on Xenophon.

107. 430e Κόσμος πού τις ἡ σωφροσύνη ἐστὶ καὶ ἡδονῶν τινων καὶ ἐπιθυμιῶν ἐγκράτεια, ὥς φασι, κρείττω δὴ αὑτοῦ λέγοντες οὐκ οἶδ᾽ ὅντινα τρόπον.

108. It is in itself certainly conceivable that when Plato wrote *Phaedo* he had already conceived the three-fold division of the soul, and that it was only his concentration on the subject which induced him to keep silence about it (Wilamowitz, *Platon*, I, 339). Yet he must even then have foreseen the objection that a σύνθετον, any being composed of parts, could not be immortal (*Repub.*, 611b). It might therefore be expected that Plato would have robbed the argument of some of its force at least by some passing reference. Just how necessary a reference of this kind was can be seen from the passage in the *Republic*, which expressly describes the proof of the *Phaedo* as incomplete and therefore argues that the immortality of the soul can be maintained even with the new psychology. In *Phaedo*, 94d, Plato uses the passage from Homer, "he struck his breast and upbraided his heart with words" (στῆθος δὲ πλήξας κραδίην ἠνίπαπε μύθῳ *Od.*, XX, 17), to prove the opposition of body and soul. When he uses the same passage again in *Repub.*, 441b to demonstrate the distinction between intellect and *thymos*, his intention is clearly to correct the earlier work. Cf. *Aus Platos Werdezeit*, SS. 233f. The conjecture expressed there that Plato may first have conceived the three-fold division of the State is perhaps an oversimplification. Many lines of thought may have come together here. Among them was the problem of self-mastery.

109. *Repub.*, 580d–588a.

110. The *Laws* begin with the proof that education for military valour is inadequate, because it may lead to dangerous opposing factions both within the Republic and within the individual. The Cretan taking part in the dialogue immediately expresses the view founded on his experience of life: τὸ νικᾶν αὐτὸν αὑτὸν πασῶν νικῶν πρώτη τε καὶ ἀρίστη, τὸ δὲ ἡττᾶσθαι αὐτὸν ὑφ᾽ ἑαυτοῦ πάντων αἴσχιστόν τε ἅμα καὶ κάκιστον. The Athenian confirms that: εἷς ἕκαστος ἥμων ὁ μὲν κρείττων αὑτοῦ, ὁ δὲ ἥττων ἐστί, and rounds it off by adding that it applies also to the community, household, village and republic (627a). Even there mastery over oneself consists in one's better part dominating one's worse. That provides the law-maker with his objective. He should not educate one-sidedly for valour, but must always bear the whole of *arete* in mind, particularly *sophrosyne*, which can keep in check the lusts and desires of the individual soul. This is the only way to ensure harmony and inner peace for the citizens, which is the sole guarantee for freedom and stability, and more important than victory over external enemies

(632d). Self-mastery is the ascendancy of spirit over the lower impulses (645b). Only in this way is the best life possible (662d, 664b). Cf. also 645e (in excitement man is "least of all master of himself", ἥκιστα αὐτὸς αὑτοῦ ἐγκρατής) and 710a, where the vulgar *(δημώδης) σωφροσύνη* mentioned in the *Phaedo* again appears. Plato's own definition 415a: ἐλεύθερον τὸ ἄρχον αὑτοῦ ("freedom is self-mastery").

111. *Laws*, 951c–952d; *Staatsgedanken*, S. 106.
112. *Staatsgedanken*, 113; cf. also Isocrates, *Panath.*, 119: "In ancient times monarchy prevailed among the γένη (elsewhere usually ἔθνη) τῶν βαρβάρων as in the *poleis* of the Greeks".
113. *Pol.*, 1279a, 21; *Eth. Nic.*, 1134a, 27; *Pol.*, 127, 5a, 22.
114. *Pol.*, IV, 4–6, particularly 1291b, 34; 1317a, 40ff.
115. *Pol.*, IV, 11; cf. 1309b, 18ff., on Solon II, 12 and 1296a, 37; *Staatsgedanken*, S. 126.
116. 1261a, 23. *Staatsgedanken*, S. 112; *Eth. Nic.*, X, 10, particularly 1180a, 24–29; *Met.* Λ, 1075a, 19.
117. 1252b, 8.
118. *Eleutheriotes*: *Eth. Eud.*, III, 4; *Eth. Nic.*, IV, 1–3. The word ἐλευθέριος also in a wide sense applied to education, style of life, etc. In 488b, 16, lions are contrasted as ἐλευθέρια ζῷα with ἀνελεύθερα, such as snakes. *Megalopsychia*: *Eth. Eud.*, III, 5; *Eth. Nic.*, IV, 7–8. Jaeger, *Antike*, VII, 97.
119. *Eth. Nic.*, VII, 1–11; *Magn. Mor.*, II, 4–6, and *Eth. Eud.*, 1231b, 2; Kapp, *Das Verhältnis der eudemischen und der nikomachischen Ethik* (Freiburg, 1912), S. 23⁴⁰. On Socrates *Eth. Nic.*, 1145b, 25; *Magn. Mor.*, 1200b, 25 and also *Eth. Eud.*, 1230a, 7; 1246b, 35; 1240a, 14. In *Eth. Nic.* 1145b, 11 ἐγκρατής = ἐμμενετικὸς τῷ λογισμῷ; 1168b, 34 καὶ ἐγκρατὴς δὲ καὶ ἀκρατὴς λέγεται τῷ κρατεῖν τὸν νοῦν ἢ μὴ; 1128b, 34 οὐκ ἔστιν δὲ οὐδ᾽ ἡ ἐγκράτεια ἀρετή, ἀλλά τις μικτή.
120. The *Eudemian Ethics* has no parallel to this passage or to 1177b, 19. In the formulation of the concept of the self, *Eth. Eud.*, 1245a, 30; *Eth. Nic.*, 1166a, 32, seem to indicate that the old designation of a friend as one's second self ἄλλος αὐτός, played some part. Cf. also Jaeger, *Aristoteles*, S. 256.
121. The authenticity of the first *Alcibiades* has not been proved even by Friedländer, *Der Große Alkibiades*, I (Bonn, 1921) and II (Bonn, 1923) and his work on Plato. We should not allow ourselves to be dazzled by some truly beautiful themes, such as the comparison between the spirit's and the eye's perception (132). That even this was taken from elsewhere is the only conclusion to be drawn from the section's obscurities, which Schleiermacher has already attacked. The sense of the comparison is this: "Just as the eye, in order to see itself, must look into another eye, and precisely into that part of the eye, where its ἀρετή, the ὄψις, is manifest, and the pupil, the κόρη, immediately reflects the physical self of the observer, so it must be with the soul. If it wishes to know its own being, it must gaze into the soul of another – a specific human being such as Socrates is out of the question – and precisely into its best part, where its *arete* stands revealed". This comparison is consistently developed until 133b ἡ ψυχῆς ἀρετή. But what are we to make of the next phrase καὶ εἰς ἄλλο ᾧ τοῦτο τυγχάνει ὅμοιον ὄν? Here even Friedländer notes (*Alkibiades*, Teil, II, 15) that "these words, which extend and round off, go beyond the strict argument". What really happens is that the analogy with the eye suddenly stops, and the words simply introduce a new theme, the divinity of the soul's "best" part. But Socrates, instead of portraying its special qualities, as might be expected, and deducing the divinity from them, goes on to say: "Can you

now name anything more divine in the soul than that part where knowledge and thought have their abode?" He thus immediately assumes this divinity to be an acknowledged fact, and goes on to conclude that the nature of the human self should be deduced from the nature of that divinity. The conclusion is in line with Plato's meaning. In fact, in the passage of the *Republic* discussed (589e), he says that the *logistikon* is the "divinest thing" in the soul. But the conclusion there reached comes after a long study. In *Alcibiades*, it is simply assumed, and the conclusion is reached by a *petitio principii*. It is only superficially linked with the comparison between the soul and the eye. The divinity of the soul is so obvious to the author and his readers that he does not consider it necessary to go into details and truly to exploit it as his major theme. Here, as elsewhere, he has superficially linked various different subjects together.

The lack of internal relationship was felt already by the interpolator, who added the passage not found in our manuscripts ἄρ' οὖν-ναί (133c), (Jachmann, 'Der Platontext', *NGG*, 1941, Fachgr., I, 4, 308). Even though he places a "purer and clearer" image in the divine above the image in the pupil, this only establishes an outward correspondence. That the image in the pupil mirrors itself in the divine is not stated and is certainly not meant. A visual image, such as we have at the start, is not thus produced. In saying οὕτω καὶ ὁ θεὸς τοῦ ἐν τῇ ἡμετέρᾳ ψυχῇ βελτίστου καθαρώτερόν τε καὶ λαμπρότερον τυγχάνει ὄν, the interpolator was obviously prompted by 134d εἰς τὸ θεῖον καὶ λαμπρόν; but there, as is clearly shown by 134e εἰς τὸ ἄθεον καὶ σκοτεινόν, he had in mind the cave comparison in the *Republic* (518a σκότος and φῶς also ὑπὸ λαμπροτέρου, cf. 520c, 516e).

The self, which the author of the dialogue has in mind, is primarily the individual soul (cf. the passage from Plato's *Laws*, 959a, quoted in the next note). That one must climb from this αὐτὸ ἕκαστον to αὐτὸ τὸ αὐτό and to the αὐτό of the human soul as such (and that to achieve this an accurate study of the nature of the soul is necessary), he hints in 130d, but in 133c he does not return to this decisive point.

It is typical of the writer's style that in 130d–132d he brings in not only trivialities but also echoes of Plato (δημεραστής in 132a recalls *Gorg.*, 481d, 513b; for the following sections, cf. *Republic*, 492), with the result that in 132b he has to sum up what has gone before in order to be able to proceed.

Bluck clearly shows in *Classical Quarterly*, 1953, 46, that the tone and the subject matter of the dialogue agree with other pseudo-Platonic writings, but also with Aristotle's *juvenilia*. He dates it at 343/342 B.C.

122. 959a τὸ παρεχόμενον ἡμῶν ἕκαστον τοῦτ' εἶναι μηδὲν ἀλλ' ἢ τὴν ψυχήν.

123. In this passage, Cicero speaks only of *animus*, but in *S. Scip.* 26, he uses the word *mens* and means more accurately νοῦς. I have perhaps wrongly assumed that Cicero was following Posidonius in my commentary on the *Tusc.*; nevertheless cf. Plutarch, *De facie*, 944f. On continued effects upon later writers see Gronau, *Poseidonios und die jüdisch-christliche Genesisexegese* (Leipzig, 1913), SS. 283, 282[1]. Also Heinemann, *Poseidonios metaphysische Schriften*, I, Breslau, 1921), S. 62; Harder, Über Ciceros *Somnium Scipionis*', *Schr. Königsb. Ges.*, VI, 3 (1929) 126.

124. The first *Alcibiades* concludes with the finding that *arete* resides in the being of a free man, evil in that of a slave. The words ἐλευθεροπρεπής and δουλοπρεπής are not found in the genuine Plato.

125. *Antid.*, 304, cf. 290 (αὐτοῦ πρότερον ἢ τῶν αὐτοῦ ποιήσασθαι τὴν ἐπιμέλειαν); *Euag.*, 41.
126. *Antid.*, 258ff., particularly 271; *Panath.* 9.
127. In particular *Panath.*, 97ff.
128. *Areop.*, 16; 20ff.; *Panath.*, 131ff. Derivation from Theseus, *Hel.* 35, and – with the cautious ὡς λέγεται – *Panath.*, 129.
129. *Areop.*, 43 τοὺς ἐλευθέρως τεθραμμένους καὶ μεγαλοφρονεῖν εἰθισμένους. *Paneg.*, 49 τοὺς εὐθὺς ἐξ ἀρχῆς ἐλευθέρως τεθραμμένους. Cf. also the passages from Xenophon (Chapter 3, note 49) and Aeschines, *Against Ctesiphon*, 154 ἄνθρωπος Ἕλλην καὶ παιδευθεὶς ἐλευθέρως (Cobet's alteration to ἐλευθερίως is unnecessary; ἐλεύθερος had long since taken over the functions of ἐλευθέριος, cf. Plato, *Laws*, 919e; *Menex.*, 245e, etc.).
130. *Panath.*, 131; *Areop.*, 20 (where the reading should be πάντα ποιεῖν not ταῦτα π.); *Peace*, 102; 103; *Antid.*, 164.

The unknown schoolmaster, who, following the tradition of Isocrates' *paideia*, seeks to give young Demonicus advice (ὑποθῆκαι) on life, draws attention in the old way to *enkrateia* and brands it as shameful "to be the slave of desires". He does not use the word ἐλευθερία.

CHAPTER IV

THE HELLENISTIC AGE

(pp. 106–160)

1. *Inscriptions from Priene*, 19. Philo, *Quod omnis probus liber*, 139.
2. On the following see Klösel, *Libertas* (Diss. Breslau, 1935); Fritz Schulz, *Prinzipien des römischen Rechts* (München, 1934), SS. 95ff.
3. R. Stark, *Res publica* (Diss. Göttingen, 1937).
4. Val. Max., II, 9, 5; Klösel, S. 13; Münzer, *RE*, V, 1862.
5. On Plato see Chapter III, note 97; on Panaetius my *Stoa*, I, 205. Cicero, *De re publica*, e.g. I, 69.
6. Seneca, *De constantia sapientis*, 2, 2; *De providentia*, 2, 9 etc. Cf. my book *Stoa und Stoiker* (Zürich, 1950), S. 352.
7. *Monumentum Ancyranum*, 1. On the following Klösel, SS. 58ff.
8. *Stoa*, I, S. 234f.
9. Aristides, 213, 214 with clear allusion to Thuc., II, 65.
10. *SIG³*, 814.
11. *Praecepta reipublicae gerendae* 32; V. Flaminini, 11. *Gestalten aus Hellas*, SS. 690, 694.
12. Westermann, *RE*, Suppl. VI, 927ff.
13. Polybius, XXX, 5; Livy, XLV, 34. Posidonius, *FGrHist.*, 87, fr. 117, 38. *Gestalten aus Hellas*, SS. 615, 619.
14. *SVF*, III, 352 and (Chrysippus), 351; Epictetus, I, 13, 3.
15. Stobaeus, *flor.* 62 A.D. (Περὶ δεσποτῶν καὶ δούλων) in connection with an old tradition, followed also by Papyrus no. 28 from the second century A.D. in Schubart, *Griechische literarische Papyri* (Berlin, 1950). Cf. Alfonsi, *Aegyptus* (1953) 310 and on the tradition of the anthologies as a whole Peretti, *Teognide* (Pisa, 1953), pp. 119ff.; Philemon, fr. 22 (Stob., 62, 21).

16. This is called to mind by Seneca, *Ep.*, 47, 14.
17. Florentinus, *Inst.*, I, 2, 2 *iure naturali ab initio omnes homines liberi nascebantur.* Tryphonius, *Dig.*, XII, 6, 64 *libertas naturali jure continetur, dominatio ex gentium iure introducta est.* Florentinus, *Dig.*, I, 5, 4; *Inst.*, I, 3, 2; Klösel, S. 21.
18. Philo, *Quod omnis probus liber*, 79; St. Paul, I *Corinthians*, 12, 13 and *Ephesians*, 6, 5.
19. More about the *polis* in *Staatsgedanken*, SS. 4ff.
20. Plutarch, *Moral.*, 69c.
21. *Artes liberales* probably first in Cicero, *De invent.*, I, 35; cf. *Ep.*, IV, 4, 4 *a prima aetate me omnis ars et doctrina liberalis et maxime philosophia delectavit.* More in *Thesaurus linguae latinae*, II, 662. In *Ep.* 88, 23 Seneca gives as the Greek equivalent for *liberalis* ἐγκύκλιος (ἐγκύκλιος παιδεία in *Quintil.*, I, 10, 1, etc.). But he had certainly come across the word ἐλεύθερος in Posidonius' distinction of the four *technai* (not teaching subjects!), where it is applied to the highest category, which, as Seneca says (23, cf. 21) are *solae liberales, immo, ut dicam verius, liberae*. According to Cicero, the division into *artificia liberalia* and *sordida* goes back as far as Panaetius (*De off.*, I, 150). This would account for its transference to teaching subjects. On the relationship between Seneca and Posidonius, see Reinhardt, *Poseidonios*, 49.
22. Epicur., fr. 199; *Gnomol. Vat.*, 77 "The fairest fruit of self-sufficiency is freedom" τῆς αὐταρκείας καρπὸς μέγιστος ἐλευθερία. The ἀταραξία τῆς ψυχῆς and ἀπονία τοῦ σώματος (fr. 2) refer only to the factual position, the absence of spiritual and bodily disturbances, not the inner state, which lifts itself above them. Epicurus does not use the term ἐλευθερία in this connection. This characteristic also does not appear in the description of the wise man.
23. For the following cf. the detailed treatment in *Stoa*, I, SS. 55, 88ff. *Synkatathesis*: Zeno, fr. 61 *adsensionem animorum, quam esse vult in nobis positam et voluntariam.* *SVF*, II, 115; 981 (τὸ ἐφ' ἡμῖν = "what lies in our power" depends upon approval by the *logos*). II, 91 (approval of the movement called forth by the idea in the soul lies in the power of him who does or does not allow it to affect him). 979, 992 and particularly Chrysippus' *Opinions*, II, 974, which will be further discussed in the next chapter. *Stoa*, I, 55.
24. More detailed treatment of the following in my article 'Zenon und Chrysipp', *Nachr. Gött. Ges.*, 1938, Fachgr. I; NF. II, 9; *Stoa* I, SS. 90ff., 141ff. together with notes. Pathos as ἄλογος καὶ παρὰ φύσιν κίνησις ψυχῆς and as πλεονάζουσα ὁρμή Zeno (*SVF*, I), fr. 205ff.; cf. the passages given in Arnim's Index IV, 109.
25. *Stoa*, I, SS. 141ff.
26. On the problem of free will, *Stoa*, I, SS. 101ff. As one example of the modern attitude towards the will, see Max Planck, *Vom Wesen der Willensfreiheit* (Leipzig, 1936), S. 19 (translated): "A man's will leads the way for his intellect. It does indeed allow itself to be influenced by the intellect, but never wholly dominated by it".
27. Impulsive desire is often expressed by ἐθέλειν, but this word more and more takes on the meaning of readiness to do something at another's request. (*Der hellenische Mensch*, S. 210).
28. *Liberum arbitrium* as a term for "free will" probably occurs first in Tertullian, *De anima*, 21: *liberam arbitrii potestatem, quod αὐτεξούσιον dicitur.* The term is derived from legal-political language (*Thesaurus linguae latinae*, II, 413). *Arbitrium* by itself is found as early as Lucretius, II, 281. Among the Greeks, Pindar,

Pyth., 8, 76: τὰ δ' οὐκ ἐπ' ἀνδράσι κεῖται ("that does not lie in the power of men"). Positively ἐφ' ἡμῖν, *e.g.* in Herodotus, VIII, 29; by Aristotle's time, it was a firmly entrenched philosophical term.

29. *Der hellenische Mensch*, SS. 13–15.
30. Plutarch, *Coriolanus*, 32.
31. According to Maschke's book *Die Willenslehre im griechischen Recht* (Berlin, 1926) the concept of ἑκών also urgently needs special investigation (Simonides, fr. 4; Wilamowitz, *Sappho und Simonides*, S. 159; Gundert, *Festschr. für Regenbogen*, 1952, SS. 71ff.). On Euripides Bern. Meissner, *op. cit.* in Chapter III, note 67. Kreter: *Suppl. Eur.*, 23, 10: ἔστι δ' οὐχ ἑκούσιον κακόν (*Hipp.*, 373–489; *Tro.*, 914–1032, particularly 987–990).
32. *Repub.*, X, 614b ff., particularly 617: οὐχ ὑμᾶς δαίμων λήξεται, ἀλλ' ὑμεῖς δαίμονα αἱρήσεσθε...ἀρετὴ δὲ ἀδέσποτον...αἰτία ἑλομένου, θεὸς ἀναίτιος and 618b–619b. Stenzel, *Platon der Erzieher* (Leipzig, 1928), SS. 179ff.
33. Aristotle: *Eth. Eud.*, II, 6–11; *Eth. Nic.*, III, 1–7, particularly 1111a, 22 and III, 7. The word ἐπαινετόν ("praiseworthy") as early as *Eth. Eud.*, 1248b, 20, and later used, often terminologically with ψεκτόν, cf. Bonitz' *Index*, S. 264, and immediately taken over by the Stoics. On this whole subject, cf. Rich. Loening, *Die Zurechnungslehre des Aristoteles* (Jena, 1903), particularly SS. 273–318, and also Carlo Diano, *Giornale critico della Filosofia italiana*, 1942, p. 1ff.; *Der hellenische Mensch*, S. 235.
34. On the following, cf. *SVF*, II, 974–1007, and *Stoa*, I, 101–106.
35. On the Stoic teaching about causes, cf. 'Grundfragen der stoischen Philosophie', *Abh. Gött. Ak.*, Ph.-hist. Kl., 3. Folge, XXVI, 104ff.; *Stoa*, II, 60. On doctors, *Stoa*, II, 61. Particularly important is Galen's statement *De causis procatarcticis* (*Corpus Medic. Graec.*, Suppl. II), 174 that as early as the time of Chrysippus, Erasistratus, who wrote a Monograph Περὶ αἰτιῶν, gave a causal sequence starting from the external reason for the disease right down to the ultimate "cause" of the pathological change.
36. *SVF*, II, 974; 1000.
37. *Stoa*, I, 106; II, 61; *SVF*, II, 998–1005. According to 998 (Diogenianus) the whole of the second book in Chrysippus' work on *heimarmene* was devoted to proving that his teaching did not abolish moral responsibility and make praise and blame meaningless.
38. Carneades in Cicero, *De fato*, 39. Epicurus, *Ep.*, III, 133; 134 (he speaks of φυσικοί probably because Zeno had dealt with the problem in his work on the human *physis*; however, there is no need on account of Oenomaus in *SVF*, II, 978, to think of Democritus, who admittedly accepts a necessity imposed by natural laws, which Epicurus rejects, but he never made *heimarmene* the master of the human will). Περὶ εἱμαρμένης in Usener, S. 99. The fragments from Περὶ φύσεως (unfortunately not dated) are now in Diano, *Epicuri Ethica* (Firenze, 1946) fr. 22, pp. 24ff. and 126ff.
39. That is also admitted by Diano, who took great pains over explaining it, both in his commentary and in his earlier work in *Giornale critico* (cf. Chapter IV, note 33).
40. However, Lucretius, II, 251ff. certainly follows Epicurus himself when he relates this arbitrary movement to the "deviation", παρέγκλισις, *declinatio*, of atoms, which brings it about that their vertical fall through endless space deviates "a tiny little bit" (particularly lines 259, 292). Originally, this *parenklisis* hypothesis

had merely a physical meaning, in order to explain the collision of various atoms and the build-up of atom complexes. It was not easy to transfer the deviation from the vertical to the free movement of the atoms of the soul. I therefore firmly maintain my view explained in detail in *Stoa*, II, S. 59, that Epicurus' transfer of *parenklisis* to the soul's atoms came later, and he then gave it a different meaning.

41. He is probably meant in Cicero *De fato*, 40; *Stoa*, II, S. 90, cf. I, S. 174. For Carneades' main source, Cicero *De fato*, see *Stoa*, I, S. 177; II, S. 89. Oenomaus, *SVF*, II, 978. Details of the development of the conflict can be found in my *Stoa*; cf. the lists there under the headings "Free Will", ("Willensfreiheit"), "ἐφ' ἡμῖν" and "*heimarmene*".

42. Clem. Al., *Strom.*, IV, 124, 2 (*Stoa*, II, S. 201). Origen, *Stoa*, II, S. 205; Augustine, *Stoa*, I, SS. 459–461.

43. Max Planck (see Chapter IV, note 26) does not do justice to subjective consciousness of free will, when as an observing natural scientist, he explains this as pure self-deception by man, who at the moment of decision, does not see all the causal relationships, and consequently regards the problem of freewill as an apparent problem only. At a later stage, when man weighs up the causal relationships, he cannot avoid feeling that he made his decision freely.

44. *Stoa*, I, S. 107.

45. *Stoa*, I, S. 106.

46. *SVF*, II, 975; I, 527. Cleanthes' ὡς ἔψομαί γ' ἄοκνος· ἢν δὲ γε μὴ θέλω, κακὸς γενόμενος οὐδὲν ἧττον ἔψομαι is a direct reference to the words of Polyxena in Euripides' *Hecuba*, 346; "I shall follow because necessity requires it, and because I long for death. If I do not will it, I shall appear a cowardly woman, hanging on to life", ὡς ἔψομαι γε τοῦ τ' ἀναγκαίου χάριν θανεῖν τε χρήζουσ'· εἰ δὲ μὴ βουλήσομαι, κακὴ φανοῦμαι καὶ φιλόψυχος γυνή.

The feeling of "total collapse" (Nebel, *Griech. Ursprung*, I, 351) was never felt by a Stoic.

47. By extension of meaning, the *polis* can also be the state in general and men be described as φύσει πολιτικὰ ζῷα. Thus Chrysippus, *SVF*, III, 314.

48. *Cosmopolis*; *Stoa*, I, SS. 133, 137. For what follows, *SVF*, III, 308ff.

49. Cicero, *De re publ.*, III, 33; *Stoa und Stoiker*, S. 137.

50. *Stoa*, I, S. 134.

51. *Stoa*, I, SS. 134ff.

52. *SVF*, III, 340ff.

53. On the definition of the aim of life as ὁμολογουμένος ζῆν (from Cleanthes' time onwards also ὁμολογουμένως τῇ φύσει ζῆν) see *Stoa*, I, S. 116. Ortega y Gasset, *Das Wesen geschichtlicher Krisen* (Stuttgart, 1951), SS. 60ff., also insists on "man's living in accordance with himself", but he does not know the Stoic ideal, and does not fully emphasise accordance with the *logos*.

54. *SVF*, III, 593ff.; *Stoa und Stoiker*, SS. 167ff.

55. Zeno, fr. 218.

56. ἂν μή τι κωλύῃ (*SVF*, III, 697). Zeno, fr. 271.

57. Panaetius and Posidonius: *Stoa*, I, SS. 191–238.

58. Cicero, *De off.*, I, 69ff.

59. Cicero, *De off.*, I, 101f.; 85 and 66–73. Detailed treatment in my book *Antikes Führertum. Cicero de officiis und das Lebensideal des Panaitios*, (Leipzig, 1934).

60. The *telos* of man: τὸ ζῆν θεωροῦντα τὴν τῶν ὅλων ἀλήθειαν καὶ τάξιν καὶ συγκατασκευά ζοντα αὐτὴν κατὰ τὸ δυνατόν (Clem. Al. *Strom.*, II, 129).

61. Seneca, *Ep.*, 121; Nemesius, Ch. 2, pp. 121, 122. Cf. my article 'Tierische und menschliche Intelligenz bei Poseidonios', *Hermes* LXXVI (1941) 1. *Stoa*, I, S. 227. See page 124.

62. Cf. my dissertation, *De Posidonii libris Περὶ παθῶν* (*Fleck Jahrb.*, XXIV, 1898) particularly 625 τὸ δὴ τῶν παθῶν αἴτιον... καὶ τοῦ κακοδαίμονος βίου τὸ μὴ κατὰ πᾶν ἕπεσθαι τῷ ἐν αὐτοῖς δαίμονι συγγενεῖ τε ὄντι καὶ τὴν ὁμοίαν φύσιν ἔχοντι τῷ τὸν ὅλον κόσμον διοικοῦντι, τῷ δὲ χείρονι καὶ ζῳώδει συνεκκλίνοντας φέρεσθαι.

63. Reinhardt, *Kosmos und Sympathie* (München, 1926), SS. 308ff., 353ff., and also *Stoa*, II, S. 116.

64. Plut. *De facie*, 944f. αὐτὸς γὰρ ἕκαστος ἡμῶν οὐ θυμός ἐστιν οὐδὲ φόβος οὐδ' ἐπιθυμία, καθάπερ οὐδὲ σάρκες οὐδ' ὑγρότητες, ἀλλ' ᾧ διανοούμεθα καὶ φρονοῦμεν.

65. Dio, *Or.*, XIV, XV, LXXX; particularly XIV, 1; 13; 3; 5; 8; 18 and LXXX. It may be correct that, as conjectured particularly by Joel, *Der echte und der xenophontische Sokrates*, II, SS. 565ff., Dio had read the writing of Antisthenes, *Περὶ ἐλευθερίας καὶ δουλείας*. But Dio is no mere imitator, and his approach to problems is determined by Aristotle's teaching on "men who are slaves by nature".

66. Particularly Dio, XV, 24–26. Similar ideas in Philo, *Quod omnis probus liber*, 32ff.

67. Horace, *Ep.*, I, 18, 107 and I, 7, 36, also, on Aristippus, *Ep.*, I, 17, 13–24 (in 23 *decuit* =ἔπρεπε, *color*, the colour of the chameleon) and I, 1, 19 where *et mihi res* naturally refers to the famous ἔχω, οὐκ ἔχομαι (note 78 above). On the whole subject cf. Hans Drexler, *Horaz, Lebenswirklichkeit und ethische Theorie*, unfortunately published only on micro-film, Vandenhoeck und Ruprecht, Göttingen, 1953.

68. *Stoa*, I, S. 157; Cicero *De re publ.*, I, 26–29; VI, 15, 26 (Cf. Chapter 3, note 123).

69. Cato's suicide: Plutarch, *Cato*, 67–69. Further material *Stoa und Stoiker*, S. 353.

70. Seneca, *Nat. Qu.*, III, pr. 16 (*Stoa und Stoiker*, S. 357); *Ep.*, 65, 20ff.; 104, 34; 51, 9; 37, 3 (more in *Stoa*, II, S. 157). *De vita beata*, 21; cf. *Nachr. Gött. Akad.*, 1941, 71.

71. *Quis dives salvetur* (τίς ὁ σῳζόμενος πλούσιος), *Stoa*, I, S. 421; II, S. 202.

72. The transformation of the Roman conception of *otium* has recently been well elucidated by Grilli, *Il problema della vita contemplativa nel mondo Greco-Romano* (Milano, 1953), pp. 192ff. Any Christian monastic undertones of "contemplative meditation" must be rigorously excluded from Seneca's *vita contemplativa*. His meaning is also absolutely different from Aristotle's purely scientific θεωρία.

73. On Seneca, see, besides Grilli, my paper 'Philosophie und Erlebnis in Senecas Dialogen', *Nachr. Gött. Akad.*, phil.-hist. Kl., 1941, 55.

74. Particularly *Ep.*, 7, 8; 53, 9 (*vaca bonae menti!*); 68, 6; 56, 1–5, also *Nat. Qu.*, IV, pr. 20; *De otio*, 1, 1. More in *Stoa*, I, S. 318; II, S. 158. *Vindica te tibi!* (*Ep.*, 1, 1).

75. *Par.* V, 33ff.; on Crassus, 41 and also *De or.*, I, 225–227.

76. Philo, *Quod omnis probus liber*, particularly 20, 57.

77. Epictetus: *Stoa*, I, S. 327; *Gestalten aus Hellas*, S. 645.

78. The speech on freedom begins there with the generally accepted definition: "The free man is he who lives as he wishes", ἐλεύθερός ἐστιν ὁ ζῶν, ὡς βούλεται and is intended to explain this. *Synkatathesis*, III, 22, 42 etc.

79. IV, 1, 6ff., particularly 46ff.

80. *Prohairesis*: *Stoa*, I, S. 332. οὐκ ἄπρακτον τὸ ζῷον (I, 10, 7).

81. *Ench.*, 1, 2 and 8.

82. IV, 7, particularly 30–35; I, 25, 7ff. Anytus and Meletus: *Ench.*, 53 etc.
83. *Ench.*, 1, 5, and throughout.
84. IV, 7, 32; 5, 20. Γνῶθι σαυτόν I, 18, 17, fr. 1; *Ench.*, 9 etc.; III, 1, 46; IV, 7, 18. Diogenes and Socrates: IV, 1, 152–169 (152: ὅτι αὐτὸς ἦν to be understood following IV, 7, 32, not with the addition of a predicative ἐλεύθερος).
85. IV, 6, 6; II, 16, 28.
86. IV, 1, 161; II, 10, 14–23; I, 28, 21. Cf. Schenkl's *Index sub* ἀπόλλυμι. The word means "to lose through one's own fault".
87. *Ench.*, 33, 1; III, 1, 22 etc.; II, 8, 24.
88. IV, 7, 17; II, 8, 2.
89. II, 8, 9–14; IV, 1, 89; IV, 3, 9.
90. *Ench.*, at the end. I, 12, 24; II, 16, 46; III, 13, 12. III, 13, 14 (as so often τὴν θύραν ἤνοιξεν).
91. IV, 1, 158; IV, 3, 7; I, 16.
92. Schenkl, p. XVIII.
93. Marcus Aurelius: *Stoa*, I, S. 341. Greek and German by Theiler (Zürich, 1951). ἐλεύθερος ἔσο IV, 3, 9.
94. II, 1, 1; V, 10, 4; XI, 14; X, 36.
95. XII, 23 ("Everything is subjective opinion, ὑπόληψις, and that is within your power"), 25, etc.
96. V, 33, 6 where he makes his own the advice given by Epictetus ἀνέχου καὶ ἀπέχου. "endure and renounce" (Fr. 10, IV, 8, 20).
97. IV, 3, 9; VIII, 40, 2; XII, 3, 1; X, 38, 1.
98. VIII, 48 (cf. Epictetus, IV, 1, 86); IV, 49; VIII, 51; II, 5, etc.
99. V, 27.
100. Plotinus and freedom *Stoa*, II, S. 191 (ἀδέσποτος ἀρετή, II, 3, 9).
101. Ps. Plutarch: *Parsne an facultas animi sit vita passiva (Mor.*, VI, 3), chap. 5.

CHAPTER V

RETROSPECT AND PROSPECT

(pp. 161–179)

1. *Der hellenische Mensch*, S. 90.
2. Theaetetus, 176a. The sentence is valid not for the Heavenly Kingdom, but only for the mortal *physis*, in which evil constitutes the necessary antithesis to good.
3. *Laws*, 896ff. Wilamowitz, *Platon*, II, 314–322.
4. As early as in *Timaeus*, he had shown that full understanding of the world of the senses involved consideration not only of the "best" but also the "necessary" cause concerned with the materialisation and individualisation of the eternal Ideas. This is clearly his starting point in the *Laws*, 896d: but here Plato expressly states that since all movements, good as well as evil, have their origin in a principle of the soul, one must therefore postulate not only the soul which does good but also another soul capable of producing the opposite (τῆς τε εὐεργέτιδος – sc. ψυχῆς – καὶ τῆς τἀναντία δυναμένης ἐξεργάζεσθαι). The second is responsible for the imperfection of the world of *phainomena*; it is also ultimately the cause of the moral evil which men do through ignorance of the true good.

The question of the cause of evil can be discussed here only insofar as it is important for the subject of freedom. The great difficulties the problem created for Plato has recently been underlined in the penetrating paper by Cherniss, 'The sources of evil according to Plato', *Proc. Amer. Philos. Soc.* 98 (1954) 23ff.

5. Posidonius in Galen *Ὅτι ταῖς τοῦ σώματος κράσεσιν κτλ.* p. 78, 8 M. *καὶ γὰρ οὖν καὶ τῆς κακίας ἐν ἡμῖν αὐτοῖς σπέρμα, Stoa*, I, S. 225. Against the interpretation of radical evil by Nebel, *Hermes*, 1939, 34, also Reinhardt *RE*, XXII, 751.
6. *Stoa*, I, SS. 229ff.; II, SS. 116f.
7. IX, 40. *Stoa*, I, S. 347.
8. Cf. in particular Bultmann, *Theologie des Neuen Testaments* (Tübingen, 1948), SS. 326–348 with its references to older literature (one important article is Schliers' *ἐλευθερία* in *Kittels Theologisches Wörterbuch*).
9. Joh. Weiss, *Die christliche Freiheit nach der Verkündigung des Apostels Paulus* (Göttingen, 1902). He, however, does not mistake the difference in the basic approach.
10. James, 1, 25; 2, 12 (influenced by Paul).
11. *Agape*: *Stoa*, I, 406. Aldo Ceresa-Castaldo, *Aegyptus*, XXXI, 1951, 269ff. shows that common speech in Egypt also used *ἀγάπη* outside Christianity, but his reliable proofs only date from as late as the 3rd century A.D. He also deals with the use of language in the Septuagint.
12. Cf. my article "Paulus und die Stoa", *Zeitschr. neutest. Wiss.* XLII, 1949, 69ff., particularly 80.
13. 2 *Cor.*, 6, 10, cf. *SVF*, III, 590ff., 596.
14. Cf. my paper 'Klemens v. Alexandreia und sein hellenisches Christentum', *Nachr. Gött. Akad.*, phil.-hist. Kl., Fachgruppe V, 5 (p. 103), particularly pp. 145, 150. Also *Stoa*, I, S. 417; II, S. 201; *Gestalten aus Hellas*, S. 706. Synkatathesis: *Strom.*, II, 54, 6 etc.
15. *Strom.*, VII, 46; *Nachr. Gött. Akad.*, 172 and 148ff.
16. Augustine; *Stoa*, I, S. 480. Harnack, *Dogmengeschichte*, III, 166ff. (Criticism of Augustine, 216ff.). More recently on the question of original sin, cf. Stange, *Zeitschr. system. Theologie* XVIII, 263ff.
17. This comes out most clearly in Weinstock (p. 189 above). He regards it as a dogma that "the impelling consideration in Christian teaching on man is original sin" (cf. p. 197). Whether Jesus upholds this, he does not ask. He himself firmly believes that Christianity and Greek culture do not exclude each other, but he fails to prove this by his statement that the earlier Greeks possessed within themselves that true humanism which feels the pressure of evil and therefore has no reliance on its own moral strength. I trust I have shown here, as in my book *Tragödie* that this and also his cosmic terror means introducing something utterly foreign into Hellenism.
18. Bultmann, *Jesus* (Tübingen, 1951), particularly SS. 31, 43–46 (44 (translation); "For Jesus man's nature consists in will, in the free act"); S. 130 ("Man's true nature lies in the full freedom of his deciding"); S. 83 (Responsibility). No theory of original sin and no original evil in Jesus; SS. 45, 176, 165, 117 etc. cf. also Bultmann's *Urchristentum* 1949, 99ff.

Bultmann rightly shows that Jesus preached no systematic ethics but the mere call for obedience to God would hardly have sufficed to tell a man in a concrete situation what God wanted of him. The Sermon on the Mount clearly shows that Jesus wished to express by some outstanding examples what true obedience to

God consists in, and there can be no doubt that it was only a collection of sayings which Jesus repeatedly preached.

Far more effective than individual admonitions was undoubtedly the example which Jesus set by his whole life. It is therefore to be regretted that Bultmann's book strictly limits itself to Jesus' teaching and to the "word", and consciously disregards his "personality". But can such a distinction really be made. The evangelists provide us with few certain facts about Jesus' personality. Yet there can be no doubt that it was from the personality that came the tremendous effect exercised by his message both on his contemporaries and on later generations. Finally, the fact remains, despite all the tendency of modern theology, that Christianity began not with Paul, but with Jesus. Paul himself says so in 1 Cor., 1, 12, though there he is speaking not of Jesus but of Christ. Our subject does not warrant any detailed discussion of the problem of "removing myths".

"Catholic theology is convinced that man is by no means simply damned by his nature", Kuss, *Münch. theol. Zeitschr.*, 1954, 82.

INDEX OF PROPER NAMES

Aeschylus 2, 11–13, 15–17, 30f, 37, 39f,
    47–52, 55–58, 68, 75, 95, 125, 134, 164
Agathon 40, 68
Akiba 171
Alcidamas 146
Alexander 20, 80, 96, 97
Ambrose 151
Anaxagoras 45
Anonymous, Constitution of the
    Athenians 33, 103
Anouilh, J. 53
Antiphon 32, 69–72, 89
Antisthenes 71, 73f, 82, 116, 118
Archelaus 32
Arcesilaus 132
Archilochus 9, 51
Arndt, E. M. 161
Aristides 111
Aristippus 71–74, 81, 89f, 116, 120, 145
Aristophanes 37f, 43f, 55
Aristotle 3, 15, 34, 46, 96–103, 105f, 112f,
    115, 118, 127f, 137, 148
Aspasius 146
Augustine 133, 174–176, 178

Bion 80
Bultmann, R. 176

Callimachus 115
Carneades 91, 132
Cercidas 80
Chrysippus 113, 122f, 129–133, 135, 140,
    143, 168, 176f
Cicero 52, 102, 107, 110, 140, 146, 150
Cleanthes 134, 177f
Clement of Alexandria 132, 146f, 174
Cornutus 149
Crassus 150
Crates 78f, 81, 118, 136
Crispinus 145
Cynics 75, 78–80, 145

Democritus 35, 42f, 68–70, 72, 90, 119
Demosthenes 20, 33
Diogenes 75–81, 118, 155, 157
Dio 144f, 149, 172

Ennius 146
Epictetus 63f, 113, 151–159, 169f, 173,
    176, 178
Epicurus 35, 72, 114–116, 118–120, 131f,
    135, 137, 139, 144f
Erasmus 124, 143
Euripides 23, 26, 37, 39, 47–50, 53–55, 58,
    65, 67, 89, 99, 106, 125f, 134, 146, 169

Frederick the Great 139

Goethe, J. W. 165
Gorgias 136

Hekataeus 40
Heraclitus 40, 48, 56, 67, 135
Herodotus 8, 9, 13, 14, 16f, 23, 39, 41
Hesiod 5, 35, 51
Hippias 36
Hippocrates 17, 39f
Homer 2–5, 47, 65, 77, 101
Horace 72, 145, 149f
Humboldt, W. von 28

Isocrates 20, 29, 33, 98, 103–105, 116, 118

Jesus 154, 171, 175f

Leucippus 42
Lucilius 114, 148
Lucretius 132, 145
Luther 124

Marcus Aurelius 139, 158f, 169, 177
Marx, K. 29
Menander 116

Menedemus 79

Neo-Platonists 102

Oenomaus 132
Onesicritus 80
Origen 132
Orphics 65

Panaetius 52, 109f, 122, 140–143, 156, 168
Parmenides 40, 42
Paul 115, 170–173, 175, 178
Pericles 18, 24–38, 42, 44f 48f, 51, 56, 58,
    62, 64, 68, 84, 88, 103, 105, 111, 135,
    162f, 166, 178
Pelagius 174f
Persius 149
Peripatetics 132, 143
Pindar 12, 22
Philemon 113, 116
Philo 151, 172
Plato 34, 43f, 64, 96–99, 101–104, 109,
    116, 118f, 122, 142f, 160, 164, 166–168
    Alcibiades 101
    Crito 61, 90
    Gorgias 29, 91–93, 134
    Laws 43, 86–88, 95f, 107, 166
    Menexenos 19
    Phaedo 92f
    Phaedrus 95
    Protagoras 89f, 92f
    Republic 33, 36, 74, 83f, 93–95, 126f
Plotinus 160

Plutarch 21, 26, 111f, 125, 146
Polybius 107–109
Polycletus 39f
Posidonius 35, 112, 122f, 141–143, 168f
Protagoras 36, 43, 59, 68
Pythagorians 65

Rutelius Rufus 150

Sartre, J.-P. 163
Scipio 107, 109, 140, 146
Seneca 114, 144, 146–148, 169
Socrates 43, 45, 59, 61–67, 71–83, 88,
    90–93, 99, 102–105, 121, 144, 155–157,
    163
Solomos 161
Solon 6–8, 35, 98
Sophists 38, 43f, 60
Sophocles 31, 37, 39, 42, 47, 52f, 57
Stilpon 79, 118
Stoa 79, 115, 122f, 133f, 136, 143f, 156, 164

Themistocles 22, 27
Theognis 8
Thrasymachus 36
Thucydides 21, 23f, 26f, 31, 37, 39, 41, 44,
    58, 83, 95, 111, 130

Xenophon 19, 33, 64, 71, 73, 81–83

Zeno 113, 118–124, 128f, 131–133, 135–
    137, 139, 143, 151
Zeus Eleutherios 8, 11f, 46, 111